T0372010

RESOURCE EFFICIENCY, SUSTAINABILITY, AND GLOBALIZATION

Exploring India-European
Union Cooperation

RESOURCE EFFICIENCY, SUSTAINABILITY, AND GLOBALIZATION

Exploring India-European Union Cooperation

Edited by
Manoranjan Mishra, PhD
Manoj Kumar Dash, PhD
Dinoj Kumar Upadhyay, PhD
Raj Kishor Kampa, PhD

APPLE
ACADEMIC
PRESS

First edition published 2022

Apple Academic Press Inc.
1265 Goldenrod Circle, NE,
Palm Bay, FL 32905 USA

4164 Lakeshore Road, Burlington,
ON, L7L 1A4 Canada

CRC Press
6000 Broken Sound Parkway NW,
Suite 300, Boca Raton, FL 33487-2742 USA

2 Park Square, Milton Park,
Abingdon, Oxon, OX14 4RN UK

© 2022 Apple Academic Press, Inc.

Apple Academic Press exclusively co-publishes with CRC Press, an imprint of Taylor & Francis Group, LLC

Reasonable efforts have been made to publish reliable data and information, but the authors, editors, and publisher cannot assume responsibility for the validity of all materials or the consequences of their use. The authors, editors, and publishers have attempted to trace the copyright holders of all material reproduced in this publication and apologize to copyright holders if permission to publish in this form has not been obtained. If any copyright material has not been acknowledged, please write and let us know so we may rectify in any future reprint.

Except as permitted under U.S. Copyright Law, no part of this book may be reprinted, reproduced, transmitted, or utilized in any form by any electronic, mechanical, or other means, now known or hereafter invented, including photocopying, microfilming, and recording, or in any information storage or retrieval system, without written permission from the publishers.

For permission to photocopy or use material electronically from this work, access www.copyright.com or contact the Copyright Clearance Center, Inc. (CCC), 222 Rosewood Drive, Danvers, MA 01923, 978-750-8400. For works that are not available on CCC please contact mpkbookspermissions@tandf.co.uk

Trademark notice: Product or corporate names may be trademarks or registered trademarks and are used only for identification and explanation without intent to infringe.

Library and Archives Canada Cataloguing in Publication

Title: Resource efficiency, sustainability, and globalization : exploring India-European Union cooperation / edited by Manoranjan Mishra, PhD, Manoj Kumar Dash, PhD, Dinoj Kumar Upadhyay, PhD, Raj Kishor Kampa, PhD.
Names: Mishra, Manoranjan, editor. | Dash, Manoj Kumar, editor. | Upadhyay, Dinoj K., editor. | Kampa, Raj Kishor, editor.
Description: First edition. | Includes bibliographical references and index.
Identifiers: Canadiana (print) 20210239425 | Canadiana (ebook) 20210239662 | ISBN 9781771889599 (hardcover) | ISBN 978-1-77463-882-8 (softcover) | ISBN 9781003130833 (ebook)
Subjects: LCSH: Sustainable development—India. | LCSH: Natural resources—India—Management. | LCSH: Globalization—India. | LCSH: India—Foreign economic relations—European Union countries. | LCSH: European Union countries—Foreign economic relations—India.
Classification: LCC HC440.E5 R47 2022 | DDC 338.954—dc23

Library of Congress Cataloging-in-Publication Data

Names: Mishra, Manoranjan, editor. | Dash, Manoj Kumar, editor. | Upadhyay, Dinoj K., editor. | Kampa, Raj Kishor, editor.
Title: Resource efficiency, sustainability, and globalization : exploring India-European Union cooperation / edited by Manoranjan Mishra, Manoj Kumar Dash, Dinoj Kumar Upadhyay, Raj Kishor Kampa.
Description: Palm Bay, FL : Apple Academic Press, [2022] | Includes bibliographical references and index. | Summary: "Resource Efficiency, Sustainability, and Globalization: Exploring India-European Union Cooperation takes a unique approach to exploring the efficient management of resources in the era of resource depletion due to climate changes and business expansion, in conjunction with considering the multiple dimensions of India-European Union cooperation. The EU is a major trade partner with India, and economic linkages continue to deepen. India and the EU have increased their political interactions and are crucial partners in promoting sustainable development. Recent trends in India-EU relations show that New Delhi and Brussels are keen to expand their partnership in multiple areas, including sustainable development and natural resources management. This volume analyzes regional and global trends in the process of globalization and sustainable development, particularly in the context of natural resource management and resource efficiency. It offers a variety of perspectives through useful and current information in this field, providing a concise and holistic understanding of the issues and challenges faced when exploiting natural resources for sustainable and efficient resource utilization. Some chapters highlight the concept of sustainable development in agriculture; micro-, small, and medium-sized enterprises (MSMEs); artisanal businesses; living standards of slum people; microfinance; and more. Key features: Discusses current trends in processes of globalization and sustainable delevelopment Considers the economics of natural resource availability Looks at sustainable consumption and resource management from the perspectives of India and the EU Explores the prospects and challenges for India-EU cooperation This volume will be a pragmatic resource for business managers, administrators, academics, researchers, and students who need to understand the importance of resource efficiency and sustainable development in a globalizing era from both theoretical and practical perspectives in order to harness the true potential of sustainable resource utilization"-- Provided by publisher.
Identifiers: LCCN 2021026730 (print) | LCCN 2021026731 (ebook) | ISBN 9781771889599 (hardback) | ISBN 9781774638828 (paperback) | ISBN 9781003130833 (ebook)
Subjects: LCSH: Natural resources--India--Management. | Natural resources--European Union countries--Management. | Sustainable development--India. | Sustainable development--European Union countries. | India--Foreign economic relations--European Union countries. | European Union countries--Foreign economic relations--India.
Classification: LCC HC85 .R4724 2022 (print) | LCC HC85 (ebook) | DDC 333.7--dc23
LC record available at https://lccn.loc.gov/2021026730
LC ebook record available at https://lccn.loc.gov/2021026731

ISBN: 978-1-77188-959-9 (hbk)
ISBN: 978-1-77463-882-8 (pbk)
ISBN: 978-1-00313-083-3 (ebk)

About the Editors

Dr. Manoranjan Mishra

Manoranjan Mishra, PhD, is an Associate Professor and Head in the Department of Natural Resource Management and Geoinformatics at the Khallikote University, Berhampur, Odisha, India, where he has been a faculty member since 2018. He completed his PhD from Jawaharlal Nehru University, New Delhi, India. His research interest lies in areas such as natural resource management, climate change modeling, resource efficiency mapping, coastal zone management, and sustainability analysis. He has handled more than 10 international projects and several consulting projects and has three ongoing research projects. Dr. Mishra is the author or co-author of more than 25 papers published in refereed journals, several book chapters, and more than 50 conference/workshop contributions as an invited speaker. He has organized international conference and workshops for academic and professional in geoinformatics.

Dr. Manoj Kumar Dash

Manoj Kumar Dash, PhD, has published more than 72 research papers in various national and international journals. He is also the author of seven research books, including *Social and Sustainability Marketing: A Casebook for Reaching Your Socially Responsible Consumers through Marketing Science* (published by Routledge, Taylor & Francis); *Applying Predictive Analytics in Service Sector, Intelligent Techniques and Modeling Applications in Marketing Analytics, and Fuzzy Optimization and Multi-Criteria Decision Making in Digital Marketing* (published in IGI Global USA); *Applied Demand Analysis and Think New-Think Better: A Case Study of Entrepreneurship* (published by Serial Publication India); as well as two textbooks: *Managerial Economics* (published by Global Professional Publishing, United Kingdom) and five edited books. He was a visiting faculty at the Indian Institute of Management Indore, an adjunct faculty at Lancaster University (United Kingdom), visiting professor at the

Indian Institute of Science and Education Research, visiting professor at IMI Kolkatta, and visiting professor at the Symbiosis Institute of Operation Management (Nashik, India) and GD Goenka World Institute (Gurgaon, India). He has conducted 32 Faculty Development Programs sponsored by All India Council for Technical Education (AICTE), Ministry of Human Resource Development (MHRD), and Indian Institute of Information Technology and Management, Gwalior (India)on data analytics, data visualization, multivariate analysis, econometrics, research methodology, multi-criteria optimization, multivariate analysis in marketing, SPSS software, etc. He has delivered a lectures as a resource person and keynote speaker in 91 programs organized by reputed institutes in India and abroad, i.e., the Indian Institute of Management Lucknow, IIM Rohtak, Ho Chi Minh City University of Technology and Education, Vietnam, etc. He was chair member of the International Conference of Arts and Science held at Harvard University, Boston (USA) and chair member of the World Finance Conference held in Cyprus. A total of five research scholars were awarded their PhD degrees under his able guidance, and five research scholars are currently pursuing their PhDs under his direction. Out of seven funded projects he is working on, three projects were completed to date. He has visited two countries (USA and Cyprus) to present papers at international conferences. He can be reached by email at manojdash@gmail.com.

Dr. Dinoj Kumar Upadhyay

Dinoj Kumar Upadhyay, PhD, is a Research Fellow at the Indian Council of World Affairs, Sapru House, New Delhi, India. He received his PhD in International Relations from the Center for European Studies, School of International Studies, Jawaharlal Nehru University, India. His major research areas include Europe, Afghanistan, and Indian foreign policy.

Dr. Raj Kishor Kampa

Raj Kishor Kampa, PhD, is a multi-faceted professional with 14 years of experience in library and information science as well as editing and content writing. Dr. Kampa is an Assistant Professor in the Department of Library and Information Science, Khallikote University, Berhampur, Odisha, India. He graduated from Sambalpur University, Odisha, with a major in English literature. He obtained a master's degree in English literature as well as in Library and Information Science from Sambalpur University, Odisha. He earned his PhD degree from the University of Rajasthan, Jaipur, India. Prior to joining Khallikote University, he was associated with O P Jindal Global University, Sonipat; Jaipuria Institute of Management, Jaipur; Indian Institute of Dalit Studies, New Delhi; and Indian Institute of Technology, Kharagpur.

Contents

Contributors

Tamoghna Acharyya
Xavier School of Sustainability, Xavier University Bhubaneswa, Odisha.
E-mail: acharyyat@xsos.edu.in

Prerna Agarwal
Urmul Seemant Samiti, Bikaner, Rajasthan. E-mail: prerna@urmul.org

Rajashree Banerjee
Xavier School of Sustainability, Xavier University, Bhubaneswar, Odisha, India.
E-mail: us18017@xustudent.edu.in

Agni Kumar Behera
Assistant Professor, Department of Mass Communication and Media Technology,
Khallikote University, Berhampur, Odisha, India

Hemanta Kumar Biswal
Department of Library and Information Science, Khallikote University, Berhampur 760001, Odisha,
India. E-mail: hemantab@gmail.com

Biswajit Prasad Chhatoi
Assistant Professor, Department of Economics and Management, Khallikote University, Berhampur.
E-mail: chhatoiprasad@gmail.com

Manoj Kumar Dash
Indian Institute of Information Technology and Management Gwalior (India).
E-mail: manojctp@gmail.com

Ishita Gupta
Xavier School of Sustainability, Xavier University Bhubaneswa, Odisha.
E-mail: US18012@xustudent.edu.in

S. S. Kalamkar
Agro-Economic Research Centre, Sardar Patel University, Vallabh Vidyanagar, India

Raj Kishor Kampa
Department of Library and Information Science, Khallikote University, Berhampur 760001, Odisha,
India

Kalpana Kapadia
Agro-Economic Research Centre, Sardar Patel University, Vallabh Vidyanagar, India

D. M. Mahapatra
PG Dept. of Commerce, FM Autonomous College, Balasore, Odisha.
E-mail: durgagreaternoida@gmail.com

Pallabi Mishra
Assistant Professor, Department of Business Administration, Utkal University.
E-mail: pallabi.iitkgp@gmail.com

Arunita Padhi
PhD Research Scholar, Department of Business Administration, Utkal University, Bhubaneswar.
E-mail: arunnita@gmail.com

Alaka Panda
Research Scholar, Utkal University, Bhubaneswar,Odisha, E-mail: panda.alaka05@gmail.com

Bandita Kumari Panda
Department of Mass Communication and Media Technology, Khallikote University, Berhampur,
India. E-mail: bandita.p@gmail.com

Neha Pandey
Assistant Professor, Department of Mass Communication and Media Technology,
Khallikote University, Berhampur, Odisha, India

Sangram Charan Panigrahi
Assistant Professor, Dept of Economics, Fakir Mohan Autonomous College, Balasore, 756001,
Odisha, India. E-mail: spsangramjrf@gmail.com

Anita Pareek
Research Scholar, School of Commerce & Management, Ravenshaw University, Cuttack
E-mail: anitapareek005@gmail.com

Raj Kishore Patra
Assistant Professor, Department of Mass Communication and Media Technology, Khallikote
University, Berhampur, Odisha, India. E-mail: rkpatra_media@yahoo.co.in

Soumendra Kumar Patra
Department of Business Administration, Ravenshaw University, Cuttack-753003, Odisha.
E-mail: soumendra.patra@gmail.com

Pradip Kumar Pradhan
G. M. Jr. College, Sambalpur, Odisha, India. E-mail: kumarpradip80@gmail.com

Prasanta Pradhan
Faculty G. M. Jr. College, Sambalpur, Odisha, India-768004. E-mail: pacificpradhan@gmail.com

B. Anjan Kumar Prusty
Department of Natural Resources Management and Geo-informatics, Khallikote University,
GMax Building on NH 16, Konisi, Berhampur 761008, India.
E-mail: bakprusty@khallikoteuniversity.ac.in; anjaneia@gmail.com

P. Rekha
Department of Media Sciences, Anna University, Chennai, India

Jyotshna Sahoo
Department of Library and Information Science, Khallikote University, Berhampur 760001, Odisha,
India

Sharada Prasad Sahoo
Assistant Professor, Dept. of Economics and Management, Khallikote University, Berhampur.
E-mail: spsahoo@khallkoteniversity.ac.in

Sanjay Kumar Satapathy
Dean, School of Commerce & Management, Ravenshaw University, Cuttack.

E-mail: sanjayasatapathy2020@gmail.com

Mrutyunjay Sethy
Department of Library and Information Science, Khallikote University, Berhampur 760001, Odisha, India

Leena P. Singh
PhD Research Scholar, P. G. Department of Business Management, Fakir Mohan University, Balasore. E-mail: leenapsingh@gmail.com

Desul Sudasana
Department of Library and Information Science, Khallikote University, Berhampur 760001, Odisha, India

Mrutyunjay Swain
Department of Economics and Management, Khallikote University, Berhampur, Odisha, India. E-mail: mrutyunjay77@gmail.com

Sanket Kumar Tripathy
Xavier School of Sustainability, Xavier University Bhubaneswar, Bhubaneswar, Odisha, India. E-mail: us18010@xustudent.edu.in

Abbreviations

APL	above the poverty line
BITA	Broad-based Trade and Investment Agreement
BPL	below poverty line
BRI	Belt and Road Initiative's
BTAI	Bilateral Trade and Investment Agreement
CAGR	compound annual growth rate
CBRN	chemical, biological, radiological, and nuclear
CIPET	Central Institute of Plastic and Engineering Technology
CPEC	China–Pakistan Economic Corridor
CR	community radio
DOSE	dopamine, oxytocin, serotonin, and endorphins
EF	environmental flow
EFA	environmental flow assessment
EIA	environmental impact assessment
ES	ecosystem services
ESI	economic status index
EU	European Union
FCs	field channels
FDI	Foreign Direct Investment
FTA	Free Trade Agreement
GDP	gross domestic product
GFCF	Gross Fixed Capital Formation
GHG	greenhouse gas
GWRDC	Gujarat Water Resources Development Corporation
HLTG	High-Level Trade Group
HVDS	voltage distribution system
IHDS	Indian Household Development Survey
IMF	International Monetary Fund
IWRM	integrated water resource management
LPG	liquefied petroleum gas
MIS	micro-irrigation system
MSDs	musculoskeletal disorders
NIMZ	National Investment and Manufacturing Zones

NMP	National Manufacturing Policy
NRIs	Non-Resident Indians
PCPIR	Petroleum, Chemicals and Petrochemicals Investment Region
PINS	pressurized irrigation network system
PRC	People Republic of China
RAM	resource assessment and management
SD	sustainable development
SEZs	Special Economic Zones
SJR	Scimago Journal Rank
SSI	social status index
SSNNL	Sardar Sarovar Narmada Nigam Limited
SSP	Sardar Sarovar Narmada Project
TUA	tubewell users association
UGPL	underground pipeline system
VSA	village service area
WOS	Web of Science
WUAs	water user associations

Preface

The Earth system is witnessing unprecedented population pressure, climate change, invasive species, overutilization of natural resources, pollution, and so on, which have potential to alter entire ecosystems. Industrialization and postindustrialization societies have been using natural resources much more rapidly than they are being regenerated. The concept of resource efficiency is itself rooted in the paradigm of neoclassical economics-efficient utilization of resources; economic scarcity of resources measured in costs; substitution of scarce resources with alternate technology alternatives.

Amid deepening debate over the multiple narratives, the focus is on maximizing economic output with a given resource input-increasing resource productivity, alternatively on minimizing resource input with a given economic output with a decreasing resource intensity, or sometimes both.

The United Nations Environment Programme (UNEP) promotes the normative goal of minimization of natural capital depletion and byproducts of pollution associated with resource use. Work on ecological modernization grew out of the belief that the decoupling of economic growth from environmental destruction may become an emerging feature of certain advanced industrial economies. Technological innovation was supposed to achieve "dematerialization of economic growth," for example, an increase in resource efficiency by a factor of four could result in the doubling of GDP with only half of the original resource input. Concepts of resource efficiency, dematerialization, or decoupling used currently in the political debate originate in this school. The concept of eco-efficiency, coined by the World Business Council for sustainable development, is for the entire humanity. It is defined as delivery of competitively priced goods and services that satisfy human needs and bring quality of life while progressively reducing environmental impacts of goods and resource intensity throughout the entire life cycle to a level at least in line with the Earth's estimated carrying capacity.

However, the concept of "circular economy," currently being successfully implemented in China, is based on the acknowledgment that the economy is embedded in a planetary bio-geophysical system and depends on both in terms for securing the necessary raw materials and absorbing or processing waste. Thus, out of 17 sustainable development goals, 12 goals deal with efficient use of natural resources. The sustainable economy is characterized by a much reduced use of renewable and nonrenewable inputs and closed-loop reuse and recycling of material outputs, thus drastically reducing or eliminating waste. Industrial process clusters or chain of industries level aims to achieve full resource circulation in the local production system through reuse and recycling of resources. The resources flow into among industries and concrete systems, requiring development of municipal or regional byproduct assortment, storage, processing, and distribution systems. Combined efforts in the least of three levels produce a robust economic impetus for investment into new ventures and job creation. Thus, India and European Union have to pursue various strategies of efficient resource use and stewardship with target of keeping negative social consequences within planetary boundary. This is possible when both regions participate in knowledge and technology transfers promoting resource use efficiency and stewardship.

Global environmental and social impact of resource use is difficult to measure. It is particularly difficult to measure long-term impact as well as take into account substitution effects. Therefore, it requires a proper academic debate whether resource efficiency will make economies or ecosystems more resilient or how trade with underdeveloped countries will be affected if developed countries become more resource efficient.

Now, the original debate on limits to growth and resource scarcity, these issues are back on the global agenda of European countries and institutions. At the political level, there is an increasing recognition that economies are fundamentally dependent on the capacity of the environment to support and generate preconditions for human and societal development. In light of skyrocketing commodity prices, economies can no longer ignore resource scarcities and affordability. The inefficient resource use at a time of growing demand is leading to increasing environmental pressure and substantial costs, and also to an increasing resource scarcity that will face Europe and other parts of the world over the next years and decades. There is additionally a broad acknowledgment that heretofore environmental policy, despite current technological improvement and bound environmental policy instruments, has been only scratching on the surface of finding solutions and providing frameworks for absolute decoupling of resource usage from economic process. Recent policy initiatives show a conceptual progress in bridging product and waste strategies and integrating policies related to individual life-cycle stages of resource use. There are recently adopted ideas, tools, and policy initiatives (e.g., eco-efficiency, industrial ecology, life-cycle management, integrated product policy, extended producer responsibility, circular economy, property materials management, low-carbon economy, or the 3Rs "reduce, reuse, recycle") have an identical final objective of decoupling economic process and development from resource use and its connected environmental impacts—and to try to therefore in ways in which enhance well-being for this and future generations.

Withal, they additionally share variety of challenges. India and the European Union share a comprehensive strategic partnership. The EU is a major trade partner, and economic linkages are further deepening. India has been pursuing economic reforms; consequently business climate has improved. India and the EU have increased their political interactions, which would positively contribute to the strategic partnership. India and the EU are crucial partners in promoting sustainable development. As protectionist and isolationist tendencies are rising, the West and far-right parties have enlarged their electoral base; they have to recalibrate their strategy and policies to take the globalization process forward. Recent trends in India-EU relations show that New Delhi and Brussels are keen to expand their partnership in multiple areas, including sustainable development and natural resources management.

This book was motivated be the desire that people have to manage resources efficiently in the era of resource depletion due to climate changes and business expansions. The primary objective of the book is to enhance understanding of the regions and politics surrounding them. It will analyze regional and global trends in process of globalization and sustainable development, particularly in the context of natural resource management and resource efficiency. Finally, it will explore multiple dimensions of India-EU cooperation.

The current holistic understanding of resource efficiency in the era of globalization is explored in the various chapters of the edited book, which is needed for business practitioners and researchers alike. This book aims to fill that gap and offers a variety of perspectives through useful and current information in this field. This book provides a concise and holistic understanding of the issues and challenges that can be encountered when exploiting natural resources for sustainable and efficient resource utilization. Some chapters highlight the concept of sustainable development in sectors like agriculture, MSMEs, among artisans, living standards of slum people, microfinance, etc.

We hope this book will be a very pragmatic resource for business managers, administrators, academics, researchers, and students who need to understand the importance of resource efficiency, sustainable development in a globalizing era form both theoretical and practical perspective, in order to harness the true potential of sustainable resource utilization.

CHAPTER 1

Prospects and Challenges for India–EU Cooperation

PRASANTA PRADHAN

G. M. Jr. College, Sambalpur, Odisha 768004, India

E-mail: pacificpradhan@gmail.com

ABSTRACT

In the current multi-polar world, the world politics is influenced by multiple players and stake holders. With the end of the US hegemony, other players such as India and China have a major role to play in the new geopolitics of the world. With the present growing status of India, economic as well as military, a meaningful collaboration and cooperation, between India and the European Union (EU) will do wonder. Inspire of the diminished role of the EU as a global economic power, still it is one of the most dominated political power as they are the major stake holders in the International financial organization like the IMF and World Bank. France and England, which are part of the EU, are permanent members of the UN Security Council and are influencing the international politics. Apart from being global players, the EU and India share common values of democracy, rule of law, equality, liberty, human rights, and so on. Both India and the EU need each other. India needs the EU for strengthening its sociopolitical and economic condition in the world order and the EU also needs India considering its huge market as well as abundant cheap human resource. The EU can use India as an alternative to the PRC (People Republic of China) on whom they are at present depending a lot. Besides the above, there are numerous other fields such as environment, sustainable development, human rights, international trade, international peace and security, on which collaboration and cooperation are required between the EU and India.

1.1   INTRODUCTION

India and the European Union (EU) are two major power centers in the contemporary world. India enjoys the record of being the fastest-growing economy. In comparison to it, the EU has retained its political status as a major political power in the world, though economically it has failed to do so. In most of the research papers on the subject matters, it has been observed that only economic, trade, or financial expects of Indo–EU relations have been discussed. But besides that, the social, political, and cultural relations between the Indo–EU matters a lot for strengthening their relationships. It is true that in the present century, economy has replaced the military power to decide the influence of a nation in the international power politics. But the sociocultural and political relations cannot be ignored. It helps in building international relations among the nations.

It is said that 19th century was the century of Europe; 20th century was dominated by Americans. Professor Masahiro Kawai has prophetically asserted that "the 21st century is becoming the Asian Century".[1] In his article Seven Perspectives on Asia & 21st Century Globalization, Jean-Pierre Lehmann writes that "Asia was peripheral to globalization in the 19th century and still subjected to the West during much of the 20th, Asia has now moved to global center stage."[2] Chandran Nair says that "All the talk in the West is about an Asian century. This sentiment is essentially rooted in the belief (and/or the fear) that Asia will become the engine of global economic growth and that its two largest countries, China, and India, will come to dominate the world in more ways than one."[3] Indeed, the present Century belongs to the Asians. India, China, and Japan will play a very crucial role in the contemporary multipolar world. In 2005, Indian Prime Minister Manmohan Singh asserted that "the 21st century will be an Indian century." Singh expressed hope that "The world will once again look at us with regard and respect, not just for the economic progress we make but for the democratic values we cherish and uphold and the principles of pluralism and inclusiveness we have come to represent which is India's

[1]Kawai, M. (2017) Will the 21st Century Be an Asian Century? A Global Prospective, ERINA Discussion Paper No.1702e, https://ideas.repec.org/p/eri/dpaper/1702.html

[2]Lehmann, J-P. (2015) Seven Perspective on Asia & amp; 21st Century Globalization, *Forbes*, https://www.forbes.com/sites/jplehmann/2015/03/05/seven-perspectives-on-asia-21st-century-globalization/#4b4139e27744

[3]Nair, C. (2012) Is the 21st Century the Asia Century? *The Globalist*, https://www.theglobalist.com/is-the-21st-century-the-asia-century/

heritage as a centuries old culture and civilization."[4] According to a study commissioned by Asian Development Bank, Asia 2050: Realizing the Asian Century, Asian countries will keep growing and eventually account for more than half of global GDP by 2050."[5] China, India, and Japan will play a very important role in the world of the 21st century. According to the Focus Economics, "among the top ten largest economy in 2019 China, India, and Japan stand in 2nd, 3rd, and 6th position, respectively."[6] From the above, it is obvious that India is a major player in the present century but the role of the EU cannot be ignored.

The EU is still a major politico-economic power to be recognized with. "It is the largest trade block in the world. It is the world's biggest exporter of manufactured goods and services, and the biggest import market for over 100 countries."[7] The European Union is the world's leading donor of humanitarian aids supporting 120 million people each year.[8] With the organization like the NATO and the EU, the European Union is politically influencing the world affairs. Its population is next to China and India only. It means it has huge population working for the growth of Europe. With the above facts, it is clear that the EU is a major player in the present world. The EU will continue to be important politically and a trading bloc says former ambassador of India to Brussels D P Srivastava.[9] Both India and the EU share a common value of democracy, rule of law, equality, liberty, human rights, and so on. So both can work together to avail the opportunities given by the world and overcome the challenges. The world of the 21st century is more inter-depended and inter-connected than ever in the history of the human civilization. The rapid means of communication and the development in Science and Technology has turned the world into a global village. India and the EU are not exceptions to this development. India and the EU have many common issues and challenges which they can fight jointly. But the relations between the two have not grown as rapid as it should be. Though both are among the oldest civilizations histori-cally connected with each other, politically followed the same principles

[4]https://yaleglobal.yale.edu/content/can-asia-step-21st-century-leadership
[5]Kawai, M. (2017) Will the 21st Century be an Asian Century? A Global Prospective, ERINA Discussion Paper No.1702e, https://ideas.repec.org/p/eri/dpaper/1702.html
[6]Focus-economics.com/blog/the-largest-economies-in-the-world
[7]Europa.eu/European-union/about-eu/eu-in-brief_en#the-eu-in-the-world
[8]Europa.eu/European-union/about-eu/eu-in-brief_en#the-eu-in-the-world
[9]Srivastava, D. P. (June 2019) Europe's Future and India's Relations with the Union, Livemint, livemin.com/opinion/online-views/

of modern democracy, economically growing very fast and having a long sociocultural relation, yet the speed of relations between the two is very slow. The global world has global issues where India–EU both can contribute. The study will assess the relations of India–EU in these fields.

The objective of the study is to find out the prospects and challenges in India–EU relations not only in the field of economy, but also in the areas of socio-economic, political, and religious, etc. Again, the study has revealed whether in the present world the relations between India and the EU have advanced, devalued, or deteriorated. The study has found out the relations of India and the EU whether it is just rhetoric or has really strengthened over the years.

International relation is a complex topic and it always creates interest among the researchers to go for new findings. The India–EU study is a very interesting research topic which decides the relations between the two in present circumstances looking into the historical developments. The study will help in further research on the relations between the EU and India. It will help the scholars, researchers, and academicians to find out the ways and means to smooth the ties between the two thereby finding out new challenges and their solutions in new world order which is ever changing. The study is limited to find out the scope and challenges in social, political, economic, and cultural relations between India and the EU and its implications in their bilateral relations in particular and international politics in general. This study is limited to the India–EU Annual Summit and its implications on both. It also includes the interests of India and the EU in Asia and especially in South Asia region.

1.2   REVIEW OF LITERATURES

Though resources on the EU–India relations are very few in numbers and extensive research has not been carried out but the relations on the past up to the present time between the two is very interesting and challenging for the scholars. The following review of literature reflected the different challenges and possibilities between Indo–EU relations in the era of modern world which has close relations with the history. In different field, different scholars have done extensive research but the research on social, political, economic, and cultural together no research work has been carried out. It is in this aspect that the scholar has tried to find out the relations of the EU and India relations in the above-mentioned fields. The author has observed that the social, political, and cultural relations play a very important role in deciding economic relations. This research article will help the scholars to have intensive study on the topic.

As the research is historical, the author has observed that the relations between India and the EU in historical prospective. The following literary works have discussed in a historical way. In this book (Mukherjee, 2018), the author has discussed the Indo–EU relations in great details. It deals with the relations of India with the European Union from different perspectives in details from historical point of view to the development in the modern era. But it lacks the social and cultural aspects of the relationship. This literary work (Winand, Vicziany and Datara, 2015) discusses the relation of India and the EU from 1950 to the present day and has tried to find out its role in the present geopolitics scenario of the emerging world order. In another research work, the author (Qingjian, 2002) has analyzed the EU's relations with the developing countries in general and in particular it has discussed the India–EU relations since the end of the Cold war.

In this edited book (Wolf et al., 2014), the authors have discussed at large the developments in South Asia with a detail analysis in Chapters 5 and 6 on Indo–EU relations which is basically on the new economic developments between the two. In Chapter 5, Anneleen Vandeplas has discussed at large about the need of Free Trade Agreement (FTA) between India and the EU and in Chapter 6 Manika Premsingh writes about the EU–India Broad-based Trade and Investment Agreement (BITA). The article (Jain, 2014) reflects the importance of the multipolar world and the importance of the EU and India strategic partnership and the challenges it faces. In this book (Basham, 2004), the author has discussed the history of ancient India which reflects the social, political, economic, and religious development of India and India with the world. It speaks about the India's relations with the world. This book has been very useful to find out Indians relations with the West. This book (Tharoor, 2016) reflects the historical exploitation of India by the West. In this book, the author has described how a golden bird, that is, India has been turned into a barren land. It speaks about the India's relations with the West especially with the UK.

India's foreign policy has played a vital role in deciding India's relation with the West. In this context, the following literatures have helped to understand the foreign policy of India. From Neheruvian foreign policy to the present day policy, the foreign policy of India is both in continuity and change. From look West to the look East, the Indian policy always protected its national interests. The following research papers have helped in understanding the Indo–EU's relation through the eyes of India's foreign policy. In this article, the author (Jaffrrelot, 2006) has analyzed the increasing role of India in international sphere economically, techno-logically, and militarily which has caught the eyes of the different global players. India's foreign policy plays a great role in deciding India's rela-tions with the globe besides the EU. The literature (Dutt, 2011) reveals India's foreign policy with the world as a whole which has decided Indian position in global politics. This literary work (Malhotra, 2003) is a book on international relations which does focus on different theories of inter-national relations which guides India's relations with other countries of the world. In his selected speech of Nehru (Nehru, 1961), India's foreign relations are reflected. It reveals that how Indian foreign policy has been shaped by Nehru which decided India's relations with the West. In fact, the early foreign policy of India is also called as Nehruvian foreign policy.

The country which is economically powerful influences the nations of the world. It is clearly visible in Indo-EU relations in the present scenario of the world politics. It has been analyzed in different perspectives by different authors from economic and trade relations to the strategic part-nership at length. Again both India and EU have been failed to sign Free Trade Agreement and its impact on Indo–EU relation is one of the most debatale topics for the authors. The authors in this literature (Casarini et al. 2017) have discussed the India–EU's maritime security, cyber security, and defense cooperation in recent years. It speaks about the recent devel-opments in the above-mentioned fields. In this article (Solana, 2018), the author has discussed the EU relations in current perspectives which helps to know the India–EU relations in the present context. In this research article (Baroowa, 2007), a greater relation between India and the EU is essential due to the emergence of both as a global player which will be called as a strategic partnership. In this literary work (Kavalski, 2015), the author reflects the EU–India strategic relationship whether it is strategic or not. In another article (Baroowa, 2007), the author has reflected the Indo–EU relations in the present world scenario at the same time pointing out the neglected fields which need to be taken care. The research paper (Chaisse and Chakraborty, 2014) reflects the diverse fields of trade rela-tions between India and the EU. In this book (Kurian, 2001), the author has discussed about the Indo–EU economic relations with reflecting on the issues of challenges faced by both and finding out the possibilities to grow simultaneously. This literary work (Sharma, 2016) is a book which speaks about the ten rules of change in the post-crisis world where nations have been rise and fall. It thinks economic as a practical art and how population plays a very important role in it which has helped the author to justify the point that India is a young nation having lots of prospects for EU–India co-operation.

India and the EU not only have economic, trade, or commercial tie, but also have great sociocultural and political relations which is as old as their own civilizations. In fact, in almost all countries of the EU the non-resident Indians are living and playing a very vital role in strengthening the social, political, and cultural relations besides the economic tie. In this paper, emphasis has been given to these gray areas of research between the EU and India with the economic development.

1.3 DATA SOURCE AND METHODOLOGY

The method used here is historical analytical to examine a problem or to understand a phenomena. Historical research is more suitable for understanding phenomena. In this case, we are trying to understand the relationship or future possible relationship between India and the EU. The present study is exploratory in nature. As basically, we are exploring and evaluating the existing status of India and the EU in the contemporary world order. It is analytical too as the present study analyzing the existing world order vis-à-vis past, present, and future role of India and the EU.

In this type of research, data are collected and interpreted from different sources like library, books, journals, net, etc. to have a comparative analysis. Historical research is one in which sources of history like documents, texts, books; manuscripts, historical remains, etc. are used to carry out research study. It helps in understanding the terms and supports the study by studying the growth in a particular time period of history. Thus, comparative analysis has been carried out to observe the relations between the two in historical as well as in the present context and conclusion can be drawn. The objective of this kind of study is to learn from the history and use it in present to find out the solution for the future.

1.4   INDIA–EU RELATIONS IN A HISTORICAL PROSPECTIVE

Neither globalization is new to India nor have the relations of India with the other countries started just in the modern era. For India, globalization is as old as the nation India is. It is a gift of its ancient culture and traditions. The Indian concept of "Vasudhaiva Kutumbakam" means the whole world is one family speaks about the global vision of India which is as old as the Indian civilization. The India–European relation is also not a new development of the modern era. Its root is historical and very old. From the very ancient period both have exchanged their relations mainly trade. "In the early centuries of the Christian era maritime trade became more vigorous, especially with the West, where the Roman Empire demanded the luxuries of the East in great quantities. With the fall of the Roman Empire, the trade with the West declined somewhat, though it was maintained by the Arabs and improved gradually with the rising material standards of medieval Europe."[10] India and the West had a numbers of trade relations in ancient time. Not only that but "there was a great deal sociocultural between India and the West. Contacts between India and the West are testified in language. Even a few Hebrew words are believed by some of the Indian origin-notably koph, "monkey" (Skt. Kapi) and tuki, "peacock," (Tamil togi)."[11] A. L. Basham writes "this religious objection to sea travel was a measure of the growing fear of and distaste of the sea, which in some degree existed in all times."

Alexander invaded India in 326 BC and with these Indo–Greek relations were established. Culturally, the Gandhara art is a good example of the impact of the Greek artistic tradition on Indian art. The Greek influence on Indian astronomy is remarkable, and the Greek influence on Indian coins is to be remembered. In conclusion, it can be said that though India was not only fully influenced by the culture of Greece due to the invasion of Alexander's invasion, but also the impact of Greek on Indian culture of later times is of considerable importance. In Gupta's period, this relation was considerably increased.

After the Vasco da Gama's discovery of passage to India in 1948, many European countries entered to Indian Territory and later on occupied it. Britain, Portuguese, Italy, France, Dutch, Denmark, etc. established their colonies in India. However, Britain occupied the majority of Indian

---

[10]Basham, A. L. (2004) *The Wonder That was India*, London, Pan Macmillan ltd., p. 228.
[11]Basham, A. L., *The Wonder that was India*; Pan Macmillan Ltd.: London, 2004; p. 232.

Territory, and France and Portuguese controlled Pondicherry and Goa, respectively. This gave a new direction to Indian relation with the West in modern history. Both Indians and the West exchanged their relations in all most all fields of sociocultural and politico-economic.

1.5 INDIA–EU RELATIONS IN MODERN ERA

The Republic of India got independence in the year 1947 and was greatly influenced by the philosophy of the West and especially the EU nations. Both enjoy very good relationships in almost all fields of life. These can be classified in to Social, Political, Economic, and Cultural. In The social relationship, multi-lingual, secular, and diversities in the society are the common pattern in both. The political relationship is decided by the common system of governance like democracy, rule of law, human rights, bill of rights, liberty, equality. In the field of economy capitalism, global-ization, privatization, liberalization, and free-trade play a very important role in the growth of their economy. In the field of cultural life both respect the composite culture of each other and believe in the diversities which are promoted by the cultural exchange and people to people contract. It means the influence of the political systems of the European Union in modern Indian constitutional system can be observed clearly. They have many things common which build a natural alliance in the politics of the world. Thus, India and the EU relation is not a new development rather it is a gift of the history, a gift of the civilization, a gift of the modern socio-economic, and political circumstances. Thus, the above can be described as follows:

1.6 SOCIAL RELATIONS BETWEEN INDIA AND EU

India is a land of diversities which consists of 29 States and 8 Union Territories. It has a geographical area of 32,87,263 sq km making it as the seventh largest country in the world. It is the second largest country in the world having a population of 1,210,193,422 as on March 2011.[12] All most all nine great religious people live in this holy land. It is diverse in religion, caste, culture, language, tradition, custom, etc. India is the place

---

[12]India.gov.i/india-glance/profile

for all the five major racial types of people such as Australoid, Mongoloid, Europoid, Caucasian, and Nergroid. It is the birth place of Hinduism, Jainism, Buddhism, and Sikhism. Besides these, the country enjoys the sharing place for Islam, Christianity, Zoroastrianism, and Judaism. It has 22 constitutional languages and Hindi is the official language.[13] But English is also used as a language for the official purposes. The government of India has recognized six languages as classical language such as Kannada, Malayalam, Odia, Sanskrit, Tamil, and Telugu. As per 2011 Census, there are 99 non-schedule languages and 270 numbers of languages are spoken in mother tongue by 10,000 or more people.[14] Again India is divided into four main castes as Brahman, Kshatriya, Vaisya, and Sudra with a numbers of sub-castes. This diversity puts India into a high place in the world. India believes in "Sarva Dharma Sambhaba" mean all religions can live together and the present famous saying of Modi Government "Sav ka sat Sava ka Vikas" means all will support for the developments of all reflects the age old sociocultural traditions of Indian civilization. It speaks about the secular and liberal ideology of India which is a gift of the Indian society. The Preamble of India declares India as a Sovereign, Socialist, Secular, Democratic, Republic with an aim to provide its citizens Justice, Liberty, Equality, and Fraternity which reflects the assimilations of above facts.[15]

The European Union is also a political and economic union consisting of 28 states of Europe. It covers an area of 4,475,757 sq. km and an estimated population of 513.5 million.[16] It has 23 official languages and English is the most widely spoken language. Besides these, more than 60 indigenous regional and minority languages and many non-indigenous languages are spoken by migrant communities.[17] The EU also believes in multilingualism, secularism, and liberalism. The present day EU is based on the principle of democratic values, liberal principles, and secular ideas. The creation of European Union itself is the best example of it. The EU believes in open society which is based on liberty, equality and rule of

---

[13]Schedule 8 of the Indian Constitution speaks about language listed in the Constitution and article 343 refers to the official language.
[14]Census of India 2011, Paper-1 of 2018, Language India, States and Union Territories, pp. 4–5, censusindia.gov.in/2011Census/C-16_25062018
[15]Preamble of India which begins with "We the people of India and ends in adopt, enact and give to ourselves this Constitution."
[16]Eurostat-population on January 2019, ec.europa.eu/eurostat/documents/2995521
[17]European and their Languages –Report-June, 2012. ec.europa.eu/public_opinion/arcieves/ebs/ebs_386

law. [18] The preamble of the treaty on EU reflects that the EU is based on the values of human rights, democracy, equality, and the rule of law which is based on the cultural, religious, and humanist inheritance of Europe.[19]

From the above facts, it is crystal clear that both the EU and India share many common values which provide them enough scope to grow together. First and foremost both are among the oldest civilizations believed in democratic values. They work for the protection of human rights, equality, and liberty and follow the rule of law. Diversity is fact in India as well as the EU. Thus, the multilingual, multicultural, and secular principles are the base of India as well as the EU.

1.7   POLITICAL RELATIONS BETWEEN INDIA AND EU

The Preamble of India declares India a sovereign, socialist, secular democratic, republic with an aim to provide its citizen's justice, liberty, equality, and fraternity.[20] The Indian democracy is based on the principles of Rule of Law, Human Rights, Fundamental Rights, etc. India is governed by the basic laws of the land which protects the fundamental rights of the people. The human rights are given utmost respect and importance in the secular land of India. The Federal Republic of India is divided into 29 States and 8 Union Territories. The parliamentary democracy of India headed by the President as the head of the state and the Prime Minister as the head of the government. The separation of power with checks and balances helps India to build of a vibrant democracy where the independence of judiciary protects the rights of the people and provides justice to them.

The EU also believes in democratic values in its political governance. It is a Union of 28 countries who have joined hands to form the European Council and the European Parliament. This international governmental organization is a de facto federal set up of 28 sovereign states. It does not interfere in the foreign policy, defense policy, or the majority of direct taxation policy. The Preamble of the EU says that "Conscious of its spiritual and moral heritage, the Union is founded on the indivisible, universal values of human dignity, freedom, equality, and solidarity; it is based on the principles of democracy and the rule of law. It places the individual at

18   Europe.eu/European-union/about-eu/eu-in-brief_en
19   The Preamble on treaty of the EU, eur-lex.europa.eu/legal-content/EN/TXT
20   Preamble of India

the heart of its activities, by establishing the citizenship of the Union and by creating an area of freedom, security and justice."[21]

The Constitution of Indian is which governs the nation has been influenced greatly by the philosophy of the West and particularly European countries. The parliamentary democracy of India is the best examples of it. In fact both share the common system governance and democratic values in running their political structures. So, there is lots of scope for both to work for democratic values in international politics.

India–EU Summit: India's relations with the Europe are nothing new as discussed earlier. In 1962, India was the first Asian country to recognize the European Community. Since then to the present European Union this relations have grown multidimensionally. The European Community has evolved from a community to a Union having its own currency and a common market. With this the relations between both have been institutionalized for having a smooth going in the name of Annual Summit. Since 2000 the EU and India are participating in Annual Summits and till now 14 Summits have been organized which are discussed below.

From the Annexture-1, it can be observed that the India–EU Summit is an excellent forum to discuss all issues and challenges between the two. In fact, from the First Summit in Lisbon June 28, 2000, up to the last Summit of October 6th, 2017 in New Delhi many issues have been discussed and deliberated. It covers almost all areas of relationships between the two. It covers the challenges and issues between the two from Sociopolitical to the Economic. Both have join hands in the fields of Science and Technology, Clean Energy, Sustainable Development, Water Problems, Education, Health, Customs, Research and Innovation, High Level Trade Group (HLTG), India's participation in Galileo satellite and International Thermonuclear Experimental Reactor Project etc.

Not only the issues of bilateral importance have been discussed but of international issues and challenges were also discussed and deliberated. Issues like Climate Change, Sustainable Development Goal, support to Paris Convention, Counter International Terrorism, UN Reforms, Nuclear Proliferation, Migration and Refugee Crisis, Problem of Asia in general and Afghanistan in particular, etc. have been discussed. Details of the Summits are as follows. From the data given below it is clear that both the EU and India have discussed almost all fields of issues and

[21]https://fra.europa.eu/en/charterpedia/article/0-preamble retrieved on 09.07.2019.

challenges which are of both bilateral as well as international in nature. Most of these issues seem to be tigers on paper having no direct result on the ground.

On Terrorism: India and the EU met in Brussels on 12th of November 2018 to discuss on terrorism as a global threat. It was the annual meeting of both on Counter Terrorism and Political Dialogue. The discussion was focused on the threat of terrorism in Europe, South Asia, and the Middle East. India and the EU agreed to find ways to enhance bilateral cooperation, for example, in the field of countering violent extremism and radicalization and chemical, biological, radiological and nuclear (CBRN) threats. They declared their full support to the United Nation, the Global Counter Terrorism Forum and other multilateral forums to combat terrorism which has turned into a global headache.

On Cyber Dialogue: The fifth European Union – India Cyber Dialogue took place in Brussels on 12 December 2018. They deliberated on the issues like cyber policies and international cyberspace issues, such as applicability of international law, norms of responsible State behavior, and confidence building measures, as well as capacity building, cyber-crime and respective data protection regimes. India and the EU agreed to share their views on recent developments and identify the potential areas for increasing their co-operations to strengthen relationships. On 10th of December 2018, the EU has adopted the new EU Strategy on India where cyber security has been declared as a joint priority. The regular EU–India Cyber Dialogue is held within the framework of the political and security cooperation.

EU Strategy Paper to Strengthen Ties with India: In this particular paper of "EU Strategy Paper to Strengthen ties with India" which was revealed on November 21 2018 by the European Union ambassador to India Tomasz Kozlowski reflects that "the EU has considered the following points as a serious agenda of discussion which includes a broader Strategic Partnership Agreement, intensify on Afghanistan and Central Asia, strengthen technical cooperation on fighting terrorism. Besides these, other areas of interests are to develop military-to-military relations, consider deploying an EU military advisor in the EU Delegation in New Delhi and vice versa, consider negotiation of a broader Strategic Partnership Agreement, intensify dialogue on Afghanistan, and Central Asia, strengthen technical cooperation on fighting terrorism, countering radicalization, violent extremism, and terrorist financing."[22] According to the Ambassador of EU to India EU gives top priority to India in strengthening the bilateral relations.

From the above paper, it can be observed that the EU–India relations have always been guided by the Economics strategy or say trade relations. But the gear has been shifted to include other issues to strengthen the relations in recent years especially after 2016. The India–EU Annual Summits are back on track after a 4 year gap and that too it is not only focusing on trade, but also on political, security, and strategic issues, broadening from trade and culture which had long been the defining characteristic of EU–India relations.

1.8   INDIA–EU'S ECONOMY RELATIONS

The Indo–EU trade relation is not the development of the modern era rather it is historical. Indians were very good sailors and they were trading with the West from the very ancient period of the history. India's trade relation with the Roman Empire in the early centuries of the Christian era especially for the luxuries of the East is a fact. Indian spices, jewels, perfumes, fine textiles and Indian iron were in high demand by the West besides live animals and birds. In returns, India exports gold. Again, it was the Greek who used gold coin in India first. The sailors were using the Indian Ocean from the Red Sea as a direct route for trade.[23]

The challenges of the newly independent India were many more. The economy was totally collapsed. Shashi Tharoor has rightly revealed that "after the collapse of the Mughal Empire, India's share of world GDP was 23% but when the British left India it was just above 3%."[24] Unemployment, underdevelopment, illiteracy, ignorance, population explosion, communalism, the challenges after partition, etc. were posing threat in the process of nation building and these were also a great threat to the unity and integrity of the nation. Still the share of India in the world trade is very poor. It is recognition of the strength in economic exchange between India and the EU the potential growing forward, that India and the EU have

---

[22]The Indian Express,22 Nov 2018
[23] Basham A. L., *The Wonder That was India*, Pan Macmillan Ltd.: London, 2004; pp. 228–232.
[24]Shashi, T. (2016) *An Era of Darkness*, Rupa Publication, New Delhi, India, p. 4.

decided to take the bilateral economic relationship to the next level.[25] It is just 2.4% of the world trade just after the Brazil among BRIC nations but the EU has a share of 16.75 of the world trade which is a huge share. India is one of the largest trading partners of the EU but India has to increase its share in the world trade.[26] The EU is also one of our major sources of foreign direct investment, with countries like the UK, Germany France, Belgium, Italy, and the Netherlands accounting for a large proportion of the investment.[27]

The EU is India's largest trading partner with a steady growth in volume and diversity since 1993. EU's top ten exporting partners are USA, China, Switzerland, Russia, Turkey, Japan, Norway, South Korea, UAE, and India. India is in the tenth position in the exporting list where there is always scope to increase the export to EU. India stands at ninth rank in Import of goods from the EU which is 2.4% share of total EU's imports whereas in case of Export it is 10th in the Rank.[28] There are always chances of improving the trade relations between the EU and India in both export and import of goods. The Trade relations between the two can be smoother if the FTA can be signed between the two. The EU–India relationship was mainly a trade bloc and that too without an FTA. The BITA which was a free trade agreement between the two was signed since 2007 but unable to go for a FTA after seven rounds of talk. If both are able to sign the FTA, the market of both will be open to all as well as both will be benefited out of it. The major argument which is given in favor of FTA is efficiency which ends the imposition of Tariffs and allows the players to trade freely. This allows the market to have the best products for the consumers. Anneleen Vandeplas writes "Strong complementarities between the economies of the EU and India implying that many Indian export products are not produced in the EU and vice versa. It widens the scope for mutual benefits from an FTA".[29]

---

[25]Wolf, S. O. et al. *The Merits of Regional Cooperation*, Springer International Publishing: Switzerland,2014; p. 55.
[26]http://europa.eu/rapid/press-release_STAT-12-80_en.doc retrieved on 25.06.2019.
[27]Eurostat News release 31 May 2012, http://europa.eu
[28]European Commission Director General for Trade, https://trade.ec.europa.eu
[29]Wolf, S. O. et al. *The Merits of Regional Cooperation*, Springer International Publishing: Switzerland, 2014; p. 45.

1.9   CULTURAL RELATIONS BETWEEN INDIA AND EU

Both India and the EU share the culture of the oldest civilization in the world. So, they love to protect and preserve the cultural heritage. EU Ambassador to India Tomasz Kozlowski observed that preservation of cultural heritage is a promising sector and in the list of priority between India–EU relations. In the Conference on "EU–India Partnership for Cultural Heritage Conservation" he told about the two cultural-based development projects in Gujarat's Ahmadabad and West Bengal that served as examples for India–EU partnership in realm of culture.[30] People to people contact are one of the best methods to enhance cultural relations between the two. The paper an EU strategy on India observes that more people to people exchanges utilizing diversities will enhance the cultural ties between the EU–India relations.[31]

Again, it has been observed that the Indians can be seen almost all countries of the European Union. Especially due to the colonization of India by Britain, France, Italy, Portugal, etc., the Indians can be seen in these countries as its citizens influencing the European countries in policy making. It speaks a volume about the interaction of the population both the EU and India in almost all fields of life. They are the Non-Residential Indians (NRIs) living in European countries as citizens having the right to vote. With this, they not only elect their leaders, but also take part in the decision-making process. In this way, they influenced the policy and sometime play a very crucial role in framing the policy toward the Indian Republic which strengthens the relations of India with the European Union. In UK, the presence of Indians is more than all other European countries and Bulgaria it is the lowest one.[32] However, the presence of Indians in almost all countries of the European Union proves that there is larger scope for both to strengthen their relations in almost all fields. Their role cannot be ignored in strengthening the relations.

Looking into the above facts, both India and the EU have tried engaging themselves in different forum. The Track II forum for discussion policy analysts is one such step. It is organized between the EU Institute for Security Studies and the Indian Council of World Affairs. The three joint declarations on education and culture cover the areas of education

---

[30]Business Standard, 4 Dec 2018, Business-standard.com/article/news
[31]Eeas.europa.eu/delegations/india/4010
[32]Non-Resident Indians online since 1997, www.nriol.com

and training, multilingualism, and culture is the frame work for Indo–EU cooperation. Organizing of cultural fest like the Europalia–India festival which was attended by President Pranab Mukherjee and King Philippe of Belgium strengthens their cultural relations. This kind of cultural initiatives must be held regularly to enhance cultural ties between the two.

1.10 CHALLENGES

India and the EU have a numbers of great challenges ahead. Bhaswati Mukherjee writes "A nation's foreign policy is strongly influenced by the imperatives of its strategic environment, its perception of its own neighborhood and the perception of its own status in the international community. On the basis of the above, India has sought to engage and build bridges with the European Union and the Commission."[33] There are many challenges before India and the EU which need joint efforts to deal with. Among them most prominent challenges are the growing assertive attitude of China, the Indian Ocean trade route and interest of both in the regions, the Free Trade Agreement and bilateral relations of India with the nations of the European countries and not with the EU. Both need to solve the problems for their comprehensive growth in almost all fields. Those are discussed as follows.

1.10.1 CHINA

Europe and India not only have similar concerns, but can also see the direct impact of BRI in their extended neighborhoods in Eurasia and the Indian Ocean.[34] China is a communist country and it is clear from its foreign policy that it is more assertive in nature than allowing its neighbors or partners to share. It always plays to the role of a big brother and never allows others to grow. It has boundaries issues with all its neighbors including India. After USA, China is the second country having trade relations with the EU in both Import and Export. But it is a fact that it is not a country which is to be believed. Its increasing presence in Europe

[33]Mukherjee, B. (Feb,2015, Feb) India and the European Union: Future Perspectives, www.mea.gov. in retrieved on 10.01.19.
[34]Garima, M. Rediscovery of Europe: New Avenues for the Europe-India Partnership, Observer Research Foundation, Aug 09, 2019.orfonline.org/expert-speak/

and South Asia is a serious threat to both India and the European Union which is creating not only economic concern but political and security problems also. The EU has to rebalance the diplomatic relations between China and India. The Indians are of the believe that though China has no good records of keeping fundamental rights, human rights, and rule of law in true sense but is given more importance than India whose foundation is rest on above values.[35] But it has been observed that Chinese influence in European countries has become a concerned for the EU. With the Belt and Road Initiative China has entered to Europe and 38 Chinese cities are now connected to 34 European cities via trade and transport links. It has become a concern for the EU. On the other hand, India has always opposed the one belt one road project of China in this region. India has opposed the project called China–Pakistan Economic Corridor (CPEC) as it goes through the Pakistan Occupied Kashmir. Thus, China is a concern for both the EU and India.

1.10.2 INDIAN OCEAN

Indian Ocean is a region which has a geostrategic and geopolitical importance. It is one of the world's largest trade route. According to Garima Mohan, "More than 35% of all European exports and around 20% of all German exports go to Asian markets with a majority (approx. 90%) transiting through this route. Similarly 80% of India's oil requirements and 95% of its trade pass through this route of Indian Ocean."[36] After the end of the Cold War and the decreasing influence of the US in the Indian Ocean has created a vacuum which needs to be filled up. Both the Asian powers India and China want to fill the gap. China has a more aggressive policy and wanted to repeat the tactics used in South China Sea which is not supported by the Indian Ocean Rim Region. The presence of China in this region is a great threat to the interest of both India and the EU. China is increasing its presence in this region and posing threat to others. Its role and assertiveness in the South China Sea are the open secret. China's Belt and Road Initiative's (BRI) massive economic investments along

[35]Jaffrrelot, C. (2006) *India and the European Union*, Sciences Po, 2006.sciencespo.archieves-ouvertes.fr retrieved on 10.01.12019.
[36]Garima, M. (2018, Aug) Politics over Trade: A Revival of the EU- India Partnership, GPPi, gppi.net retrieved on 20.01.19.

the Indian Ocean have raised concerns of debt traps, increasing Chinese political influence in domestic politics, and regional stability. It is a great challenge to both which needs immediate solutions.

1.10.3   FREE TRADE AGREEMENT

India is EU's one of the top ten trading partners and the largest numbers of FDI comes to India from the European Union. In terms of Import India stands in ninth rank and in Export it is ninth. But the Free Trade Agreement between the two is yet to be signed. It is officially known as the Bilateral Trade and Investment Agreement (BTAI). Even after 16 rounds of deliberation and discussion, both have not reached to a final agreement on FTA. On March 1, 2009 Kozlowski said EU is ready for an Asymmetrical agreement but has its political compulsion too. He further said without lowering the tariff on car and car parts the FTA cannot be signed as it is a political issue and is to be passed by the EU Parliament.[37] Both are not happy with each other in dealing with the trade matters. While the EU wants more tariff reduction on automobile sectors, wines and spirits and not happy with the offer given by India, India wants more access for its professionals and recognition as a data secure country. Thus FTA has become a myth in India–EU relations.

1.10.4   BILATERAL RELATIONS WITH THE EU'S COUNTRIES

The bilateral relations of India with the European countries are growing in almost all fields of trade, commerce, business, and political, social and other aspects. Whereas with UK, Germany and Italy, India has the largest trade relations than the other EU nations, France is trying to increase its share in India. It is clear from the visit of the French President Emmanuel Macron's visit to India in March 2018 and its declaration that "Choose France," rather than "Choose Europe." Both India and France signed 20 Contracts related to the industrial, renewable energy, mobility, and sustainable development sectors amounting to a total value of around 13 billion Euros were presented, accounting for 200

---

[37]The hindubusinessline.com/economy/india

million Euros of investment in India.[38] Again in August 2019 in a press conference both declared for delivery of Rafale combat aircraft in time, construction of six nuclear reactors in Jaitapur, Space Surveillance for a joint maritime domain awareness mission in the Indo–Pacific region, and roadmap on cyber security and digital technology.[39] France supports of India in the UN on Kashmir issue and Terrorism speaks about their bilateral relations. The International Solar Alliance has been started by India and France is another level of bilateral tie between the two. This kind of bilateral efforts is a challenge to the India–EU relations.

The French president came with high ambitions: to make France India's gateway to Europe, and to make India France's first strategic partner in Asia, an ambition he made clear during the presidential campaign last year.[40] With Germany, Italy, and the UK weakened by varying degrees of domestic political turmoil, Macron seeks to position himself as the most credible interlocutor in Europe. And with China tilting toward dictatorship and the US foreign and economic policy in chaos under Donald Trump, France – and its charismatic president – is an increasingly attractive partner on the world stage.[41] India has had strong relations with Germany, the UK, and France. Trade with Eastern Europe has also increased in the past decade. Trade with Germany is expected to increase further given PM Modi's new emphasis on wind power, science and technology and engineering. It means it is decreasing the importance of the India's relations with the EU as a whole. In a DW interview, Dr. Shazia Aziz Wülbers, Europe expert at the Germany-based University of Applied Sciences in Bremen, says that while the EU is likely to continue to be one of India's top trade partners, both sides should join forces in other areas to fully realize the partnership's potential.[42]

India has a very good bilateral trade relation with the UK, Germany, Italy, and many EU's countries which do not allow the India–EU relations to grow. Therefore, the relations between the two have seen many ups and downs and have not achieved its desire goals.

---

[38]Embassy of India Paris, https://www.eoiparis.gov.in retrieved on 20.01.19.
[39]Petersen, B. (2012, Aug 26) Growing Beyond the Bilateral, Observer Research Foundation, of online/expert-speak/growing –beyond-the-bilateral.
[40]Varma, T. (2018, Mar) Macron's Passage to India: A Missed Opportunity for Europe, European Council on Foreign Relations, ecfr.eu.
[41]Varma, Macron's Passage to India.
[42]https://www.dw.com

1.11   PROSPECTS

India and the EU have many things common which make them closer to each other and provide opportunities to grow simultaneously with protecting their own interests. Both are historically connected with each other having diversities in almost all fields of life. Both believe in multi-culturalism, multilingualism, multilateralism, and democratic values for good governance. Both support human rights, liberty, and equality and believe in rule of law. They have transformed their relations from normal relationship to a strategic partnership. Whereas India is the fastest growing economy in the world having a huge market economy, EU is the largest trade partner of India having largest FDI from it to India. Irrespective of that the both are unable to convince each other to avail the following opportunities. The following points display the opportunities where both should cooperate each other.

1.11.1   INDIA IS A YOUNG COUNTRY

India is going to be the most populous country by 2027 surpassing China has been projected by the UN report as "World Population Prospects" released on June 18, 2019.[43] Again, India is the youngest nation in terms of population among the BRIC countries. The working population of India is more than 60%. It reflects that how India can be very useful for the European Union in terms of chief labor for economic development of both India and the EU. Indian population has always helped in the growth of the West. The following facts show that India which is a young country having youth above 60% of the total population are playing a very important role in the growth of India as well as the world.

In terms of population, India is a young country where it contributes 17.5% of the world population and among them 30.6% is under 15 years of age group and only 4.9% is above 60 years. It means 64.5% of population is under the age in between 16 and 59 years of age. This working population is the strength of India's growth and prosperity as this provides chief labor force to the world economy and the European Union can avail this working population for its growth.[44] The labor force in India is a huge

---

[43]The Hindu Business Line, June 17,2019, thehindubusinessline.com/economic
[44]http://europa.eu/rapid/press-release_STAT-12-80_en.doc

market for the world and the European Union can avail this opportunity to enhance the economic relations. India is a huge market for chief labor among all the BRIC nations. It means India and the EU has a great opportunity in this field to enhance the relation and cooperation.[45]

According to Ruchir Sharma "the slowdown of economic growth in the USA was due to the collapse in population growth. In the USA, by the official numbers, productivity grew at an average pace of 2.2% between 1960 and 2005 before slowing to just 1.3% in the past 10 years. In the five decade before 2005, the US labor force grew at an average annual pace of 1.7%, but slowed to just 0.5% over the past decade. In short, the clearest explanation of the missing economic growth in the USA is roughly 1% decline in labor force growth, which is largely a function of growth in the population of working-age people, between 15 and 64".[46] From the above discussion, it is clear that population matters a lot and the working population of India can be a huge assert for the economy of both India and the EU.

1.11.2   FREE TRADE AGREEMENT

Indian economic growth is fastest in the world which is supporting for the creations of jobs and investments prospects for other nations. According to the EU's top ten trading partners list India stands ninth in terms of import and ninth in terms of export in 2018.[47] The scope of signing the Free trade Agreement between India and the EU will enhance their economic capacity and it will strengthen their bilateral relations. Both should try to sign the Business Trade and Investment Agreement as early possible. Both will be benefited out of it. It will increase their import and export capacity. If we observe the two Asian economic powers India and China, for EU, India is a natural and better choice than the communist China. China's policy is always a dominating and influential in nature which creates problem for both India and the EU. EU's ambassador to India Tomasz Kozlowqski said that "Brexit will not have any impact on Indo–EU relations. EU–India trade in goods and services reached 141 billion USD, our investments 90 billion USD. Trade is balanced, our economies are complimentary. Still

---

[45]http://europa.eu/rapid/press-release_STAT-12-80_en.doc
[46]Sharma, R. (2016) *The Rise and Fall of Nations*, Penguin Random House, pp. 24–25.
[47]http://trade.ec.europa.eu/doclib/doc

he said the potential is higher and we could do much more".[48] Both India and the EU have large domestic market, a large number of entrepreneurs. Both can be benefitted if the FTA is signed. India has a huge market and favorable conditions for investments with a high rate of economic growth provide huge opportunities for the EU. On the other hand, the EU enjoys the status of the largest trading bloc in the world. It provides enough opportunity for both to go for FTA.

1.11.3 GLOBAL CHALLENGES- CLIMATE CHANGE, UN REFORM, TERRORISM, PARIS AGREEMENT, SUSTAINABLE DEVELOPMENT

In 2016, a Memorandum of Understanding on the Indo–EU Water Partnership was signed. Under the Indo–EU Clean Energy and Partnership both have agreed to implement Paris Agreement. Under the EU–India Climate Change Dialogue and Partnership both are agreed to cooperate in climate change related problems that India faces. The 14th India–EU Summit was held in 2017 and one of the most important agreements that were concluded on Climate and Energy, UN Reforms, Declaration on Combating Terrorism, Paris Agreement, Sustainable Development, etc. But they have not achieved the desired goals. The EU–India Resource Efficiency Initiative funded by the EU was launched in 2017 with an aim to develop resource efficiency in Transport, buildings, renewable energy, waste recovery, and other sectors.[49] This is a multipolar world having global challenges which need to be solved with global efforts. The Agenda for Action 2020 which was adopted during the 13th EU–India Summit has a separate section on Climate Change. In this Action Plan, they have decided to cooperate on clean and renewable energy like solar and wind power and establishment of Smart Grids and energy research and innovations. India and the EU can join hands to solve these problems. It may be in terms of continuance with the Paris Agreement on Climate Change or to achieve sustainable development goals. Terrorism is an international problem which is threatening to both India and the EU for which joint efforts is needed to combat terrorism, while the EU is reaching out to China in terms of renewable technology and policy coherence, the engagement

---

[48]Business Standard-Brexit will have no impact on EU-India ties: Envoy, April 15,2019,
[49]India-EU Partnership for Sustainability, Clean Energy & Climate Action-eeas.europa.eu/sites/eeas/files/sustainability

with others players has been restrictive and limited to commerce and trade largely.[50] It means India–EU needs to do more in these fields of global issues. It is a fact that no nation can solve these problems unilaterally. It needs global effort to find a long-term solution where both India and the EU can contribute to erase the differences. It will help in the global peace and existence of human being itself. The reform of the UN is a prime area of concern where both can join hands. The permanent members of the UN Security Council enjoy special status in the UN and India is always in support of reforming UN. India's candidature is supported by all permanent members except China. The G4 nations Brazil, Germany, India, and Japan are stressing on the reform of UNSC. The EU and India should work for a more democratic based UN with equal treatments for all. The platform of the UN must not be used to fulfill interest of the powerful nations rather to establish peace and security in the world. So both India and the EU should join hands to reform the UN for the larger benefit of the humanity.

1.12   FINDINGS AND ANALYSIS

Indo–EU relations have always gone through ups and downs. It was a smooth sailing of relationship between the two from 2000 to 2012. India and the EU met regularly in all the Annual Summits till 2012. But after that there were no summits held till 2016. In between 2012 and 2016, there were no meetings between the two was organized which created a deadlock situation in their relationships. But after the Annual Summit of 2016, it seems that both have decided to move faster to face the challenges. But the inability to sign FTA and giving importance to bilateral relations between India and other countries of the EU has put questions to the relations of the two regions. People to people contact needs to be practiced vigorously. India is one of the largest trade partners of the EU but Free Trade Agreement is yet to be signed. Both should try to sign FTA. In issues like climate change, global warming, sustainable development, human rights, international trade and agreement and international peace and security both should try to fight jointly. In short, India needs the EU to achieve sustainable modernization, climate change and clean energy, trade investment (FDI) and innovation through people to people contact. The

---

[50]Rattani, V. (2017) Can India-EU Strategic Partnership Focus on Climate Change, Clean Energy? *Down to Earth*, October 6, 2017. Downtoearth.org.in/news/climate-change

EU needs India because India is Young country having chief labor force, fastest economy in the world, and a gateway to Asia. Dr. Manmohan Singh, India's former Prime Minister observed that the concurrent geopolitical re-emergence of China and India has initiated a period of "cooperation and competition" in the Indo–Pacific region: "it is an era of transition and consolidation. Inclusive economic growth remains the bedrock of our country's future. Infrastructure, education, development of skills, universal access to healthcare must be at the core of our national policies. Being a strong and diversified economy will provide the basis for India playing a more important global role. Hence, the primary focus of India's foreign policy has to remain in the realm of economic diplomacy."[51] India and the EU need to address the issues of each other so that both can avail the opportunities.

In international politics, it is said that "a nation without a foreign policy is just like a ship without a captain which drifts aimlessly" and to protect the national interest is the prime duty of all nations. In fact, national interest plays like a pole star for the nations to decide their foreign policies. The India–EU relation is not an exception to it. Both are trying to protect their national interests, but at the same time they should try to fight for the common interests. The recent developments in their relations reflect a positive approach on both side which will help both to solve their bilateral issues and challenges. It will allow them to achieve the desired goals. Both India and the EU should join hands to transfer the challenges into prospects. Their relations have not devalued rather it has advanced though it has miles to go.

KEYWORDS

- multipolar world
- bilateral relations
- free trade
- environment issues

---

[51]Singh, Dr. Manmohan, Strained Ties between India, Pakistan Affecting Growth of South Asia, *The Economic Times*, 1st Oct 2015.

BIBLIOGRAPHY

Books, Articles, Journals, News Papers, and Web Pages.

Arora, P. *Indian Foreign Policy*; Cosmos Bookhive's: Gurgaon, 2002.

Baroowa, S. The Emerging Strategic Partnership between India and the EU: A Critical Appraisal. *European Law Journal* 2007, *13*, (6), 732–749.

Basham, A. L. *The Wonder That was India*; Pan Macmillan Ltd.: London, 2004.

Baru, S. *Strategic Consequences of India's Economic Performance*; Academic Foundation: New Delhi, 2006.

Bhaskar, C. U. *Indian Foreign Policy Orientation in the Twenty-First Century: Continuity and Change*; Anmol Publications: New Delhi, 2001.

Casarini, N.; Bengalia, S.; Patil, S. *Moving Forward EU-India Relations*; Gateway House, Indian Council on Global Relations: Mumbai, 2017.

Chandra, P. *International Relations: Foreign Policies of Major Powers and Regional Systems*; Vikas Publishers: New Delhi, 2006.

Chaisse, J.; Chakraborty, D. The Evolving and Multilayered EU-India Investment Relations- Regulatory Issues and Policy Conjectures. *Eur. Law J.* 2014, *20* (3), 385-422.

Chopra, P. *Foreign Policy Issues*; Commonwealth Publishers: New Delhi, 1996.

Dutt, V. P. *India's Foreign Policy Since Independence*; National Book Trust: New Delhi, 2011.

Giri, D. K. *European Union and India-A Study in North – South Relations*; Concept Publishing Company, 2001.

Jaffrrelot, C. *India and the European Union*; SciencesPo, 2006. sciencespo.archieves-ouvertes.fr.

Jain, R. K. *India-EU Strategic Partnership: Perceptions and Perspective*; NFG Research Group: Berlin, 2014.

Kavalski, E. The EU and India Strategic Partnership: Neither Very Strategic, Nor Much of a Partnership. *Cambridge Review of International Affairs* 2015, *29* (1), 192–208.

Kumar, R. India as a Foreign Policy Actor—Normative Redux, Center for European Policy Studies Working Document, No.285/February 2008.

Kurian, N. India-EU Economic Relations: Problems and Prospects. *Contemporary Europe and South Asia,* Vivekananda, B.; Giri, D. K., eds. Concept Publishing Company: New Delhi, 2001.

Malhotra, V. K. *International Relations*; Anmol Publications Pvt. Ltd.: New Delhi, 2003.

Mohan, G. *Politics over Trade: A Revival of the EU-India Partnership*; GPPi. gppi.net, 2018.

Mukherjee, B. *India and the European Union: An Insider's View*; Vij Book India Pvt. Ltd.: New Delhi, 2018.

Nehru. *India's Foreign Policy: Selected Speeches*; September 1946–April 1961; New Delhi, 1961.

Qingjian, J. The EU's Relations with Developing Countries-The New Development since the Cold War, Europe, 2002. en.cnki.com.cn.

Sharma, R. *The Rise and Fall of Nations*; Penguin Random House: UK, 2016.

Singh, Dr. Manmohan. Strained Ties between India, Pakistan affecting growth of South Asia. *The Economic Times*, 1st Oct 2015.

Solana, J. The European Union and India. https://www.brookings.edu, retrieved on 11th Dec 2018.

Tharoor, S. *An Era of Darkeness*, Rupa Publication: New Delhi, India, 2016.

Varma, T. Macron's Passage to India: A Missed Opportunity for Europe, European Council on Foreign Relations. ecfr.eu. 2018.

Winand, P.; Vicziany, M.; and Datara, P. *The European Union and India; Rhetoric or Meaningful Partnership?*; Edward Elgar: London, 2015.

Wolf, S. O.; Casaca, P.; Flanagana, A. J.; Rodrigues, C. *The Merits of Regional Cooperation, the Case of South Asia*; Springer International Publishing: Switzerland, 2014.

Zajaczkowski, J.; Schottli, J.; Thappa, M. *India in the Contemporary World*; Routledge: New Delhi, 2004.

Business Standard

https://ec.europa.eu

https://www.dw.com

https://www.eoiparis.gov.in

The Economic Times

The Hindu

The Indian Express

The Times of India

www.eeas.europa.eu

www.gppi.net

www.indianembassybrussels.gov.in

www.mea.gov.in

www.nriol.com

ANNEXURE 1: INDIA–EU ANNUAL SUMMITS

No.	Years	Place	Declarations
1	2000	Lisbon	Strategic partnership in areas of Politics and Economy
2	2001	New Delhi	Counter Terrorism, IT Vision Statement, Agreements on S&T and Universalisation of Elementary Education (SSA)
3	2002	Copenhagen	Combating terrorism, support the Transitional Authority in Afghanistan, Strengthening the high-level economic dialogue and multilateral trade regime of WTO
4	2003	New Delhi	Signing of Customs Cooperation Agreement, a Financing Agreement for the India–EU Trade and Invest Programme, Support of UNSC Resolution 1373, EU–India Action Plan and Joint Political Declaration
5	2004	The Hague	Strategic Partnership, global and multilateral issues

No.	Years	Place	Declarations
6	2005	New Delhi	Forming a High Level Trade Group (HLTG), India's participation in Galileo satellite and International Thermonuclear Experimental Reactor Project, EU's support to NRHM and SSA, Joint Action Plan and Strategic Partnership
7	2006	Helsinki	Counter-Terrorism and energy, Acceptance of recommendations of the HLTG
8	2007	New Delhi	Joint Statement and Jap Implementation Report were issued, Partnership at global level for peace, security and sustainable development
9	2008	Marseilles	Broad-based trade and investment agreement and strengthening economic relations, Cooperation in ITER, energy research and climate change, Lunching of European Business & Technology Center in India.
10	2009	New Delhi	Reform in UN, fighting Terrorism, Signing Nuclear fusion energy research, Broad-based Trade & Investment Agreement, Maritime Transport Agreement
11	2010	Brussels	Cooperation in BTIA, Security & Defense, fighting Terrorism, Declaration on Culture, Clean Energy, Climate Change, India-EU Business Summit held
12	2012	New Delhi	Comprehensive bi-lateral relations, Joint Group on Counter Terrorism, Cyber Security, Joint Work Group on Energy, Clean Development and Climate change, Joint Declaration on Research & Innovation Cooperation
13	2016	Brussels	The EU–India Agenda for Action-2020, European Investment Bank, Counter Terrorism, India–EU Water Partnership, Clean Energy and Climate Change, Joint Declaration on Migration and Mobility
14	2017	New Delhi	Declaration on Counter Terrorism, Climate & Energy, Smart & Sustainable Urbanization, Strategic Partnership, Counter Terrorism, Global Migration and Refugee Crisis, UN Reform, Paris Agreement, Sustainable Development Goal, Re-engagement on BTIA

Source: www.indianembassybrussels.gov.in, mea.gov.in

Comparison and Evaluation of the Policies and Pattern of Port-Based Industries in Odisha with European Countries

ALAKA PANDA[1*] and SMRUTI REKHA SAHOO[2]

[1]*Research Scholar, Utkal University, Bhubaneswar, India*

[2]*P.G. Department of Commerce, SCS (A) College, Puri, India*

Corresponding author. E-mail: panda.alaka05@gmail.com

ABSTRACT

The key issues of India, in the existing scenario, as an emerging economy, are being able to create globally competitive India and ably surge ahead to become the leading economy of the world. The question is what India needs to do in order to mature into a developed economy from an emerging economy. It discusses the efficacies of the policies relating to the economic aspects the port, and whether it has the capacity to unlock the economic potentials of the state; whether this can be a valuable way to bring transformative investments in the business using local resources. The very traditional role of ports was limited to import and export has undergone changes and now includes activities like transshipment and logistics provider. It was marked that the ports and the hinterland coast have become the most preferred and highly congested space for public and private investments. Odisha coast is suitable for modern ports having the capability of adequate depth and vast surroundings for further development of the ports and coast. There are many evidences where many economic benefits have accrued too many countries and made them prosperous. Empirical results show that the countries have found that their trade volume has increased significantly because of rising efficiency of the ports. The ports play an important role in global supply chain and act as a facilitator of trade. Economic activities of the ports provide value addition to the economy. Do our policies confirm to this?

2.1 INTRODUCTION

A port becomes the backbone of an economy if it runs in an efficient manner. In the present scenario, the function of a port is not limited to trade only but also has expanded to a platform providing logistic services, which is also an important aspect in spreading international trade for a country.

Seaports are a passage point for trade, authorizing the import of goods that the country is not able to produce enough and export of those items that the country has a competitive edge to produce, contributing to the economic development of the country. Apart from these, a port is also a place that provides auxiliary services and adds significance to the products transported and thus facilitates the increasing demand of trade alongside supporting the small and medium enterprises (SMEs) in the vicinity of the port and facilitates trade along with services. The globalization of the world economy into one has led to tremendous rise in the exchanges of goods and services across the world. The main reason behind acceleration of trade is the decreased cost of shipping due to the development of technology and economies of scale. In order to cope with the increasing trade, ports in India will continue to play pivotal role in providing the economical mode of transportation.

The study is relevant with regard to establishment of plants and utilization of resources of coastal areas properly where the major aim is to promote regional development and industries relating to port along the coastline. The imperative of this study lies with the logic that how Odisha can harness the opportunities from the initiatives taken up by the government. Investment in port sector will further lead to the development of infrastructural facilities like roads and railways for quicker and competent handling of the cargo shipment. The very traditional role of ports was limited to export and import; however, over a period of time, it has undergone changes and now includes transshipment and provision of logistics like activities. This study is based on new and improved technological developments in the scenario of global shipping, especially a new layout of the port and also container handling equipment in order to accommodate container traffic. New institutional setup with the help of the latest technology is the need of the hour in order to grasp the flow of major investments in the ports of Odisha. The port locations and the constant water bodies of Odisha are strategically located which can ideally adapt to the latest developments in the area of technology, communication, automation, and cargo handling.

The main objective behind this study is:

1. To boost Odisha's allocation in the export, import sector, trade, and commerce by taking advantage of the policies of liberalization and globalization.
2. To find out the scope of establishment of emerging industries with a focus on infrastructure and enabling environment.

2.2   REVIEW OF LITERATURE

Through a study, links could be established between port activity and global firms, in particular maritime services relating to finance, insurance, law, and consultancy. The location and connectivity of multioffice firms in these sectors are closely following global city hierarchies alongside port hierarchies. For such economic activities, urban attractiveness in port areas is more important (Jacobs et al. 2010). Changes in the economy lead to boost the seaborne trade, spatial relocation of production, and growing importance of logistics. The role of ports is also evident in the industrial organization of transport industry by increasing cooperation in the form of strategic alliance, M&As, and vertical integration. As per the study, all these changes impact the port by increasing demand for new ports and focus on the efficacy of transport infrastructure (Ferrari 2011). In a study, it has been found out that the growth of port is directly proportional to employment in that area. According to an analysis of European port regions an increase of 1 million tonnes of port throughput is linked with an increase in employment in the port region of 0.0003%, which means that in a region with 1 million employees, employment would increase by 300 units, subsequently putting its impact in the long run by 7500 units (Feerari et al. 2012) Turnaround time is an important determinant of port competitiveness as quick turnaround allows for the reduction of port congestion and larger port throughputs. As per study, the most time-efficient ports can be found in East Asia, Europe, and Caribbean, and the least time-efficient ports are located in Africa and South Asia. An evaluation of vessel turnaround times swiftly increases in time efficiency of the ports (Ducruet et al. 2013). Innovative measures of increasing ocean port efficiency through simple statistical tools using US data on import flows were shown in a study (Blonigen et al. 2006). It also provided port efficiency compared on a commodity by commodity basis. This study also provided procedures of measuring port efficiency that can be used by future researchers to examine countless of new concerns, including progress of port efficiencies over time and its impact on international trade flows and country-level growth.

2.3   RESEARCH GAP

Till date, the economic importance of coastal belt adjacent to the port in the eastern zone of India has not been understood well. The primary reason behind this can be pointed as that the western coast of India has become vibrant leaving the eastern coast neglected. It can be pointed out by taking the example of a comparative performance of Mundra Port (Adani group) with SEZ Ltd., which shows that it is significantly superior to the port of eastern coast clearly indicating that developmental activities like increasing industrialization, tourism, and other port activities are not happening in the eastern coastal areas. The ports in Odisha will have to play a crucial role in the large development of ports in the Eastern region of the country and that its natural maritime and cultural endowments and industrial resources are to be optimally utilized. Seabound transport is one of the most cost-efficient and environmental conducive means of transport for the conveyance of raw materials, as well as finished products, in bulk. Such an infrastructure acts as a pillar for attracting multinational companies along with large-scale industries. An integrated port policy for the state should be encouraged which will lay down the trail for the growth, expansion and for promoting industry, trade, and commerce.

It remains a fact that till date the Government of India, along with the state of Odisha, has not been able to give importance to this ocean. But the recent economic policy of Make in India and the like, which are projected to enhance the investment in manufacturing industry, create an opportunity for the states with coastal belt and port facility. It is postulated that the industries would like to set up their plants in the proximate area of the ports from which the state of Odisha will be immensely benefitted. For that matter, the states will have to modernize their ports and provide the required infrastructure and facilities.

It is a fact that ports play critical roles in local and regional economies alongside the prosperity of the nation. Not only that, a large number of workforce is engaged in port-related activities not only directly but also in an indirect way, thus paving way to huge employment opportunities. One example of indirect employment is like supplying goods and services to companies engaged in port activity. Similarly, induced employment is also associated with expenditure resulting from those who derive income from port. By putting the related businesses in groups that surround the port area will create cluster area that will accelerate economic activities through competition, innovation, and creation of new business opportunities. This will also bring in new investment, new technology that will match the current and future requirements.

The problem of the state is that despite having plenty of resources both natural and human, it is not been able to grow economically. When comparisons are made even among the other states of India, it appears that the state still lacks proactive policies and effective implementation. Therefore, it necessitates an economic model that will be successful in coast-based economies and may be emulated with suitable modifications, so that the desired result can be achieved.

2.4   MATERIAL AND METHODOLOGY

This study has been done using secondary data that has been collected from various articles, journals, research publications, annual reports, books, and Internet. The data has been analyzed by using various different statistical tools and presented graphically using charts.

2.4.1   IMPERATIVES OF PORT INDUSTRIALIZATION POLICY

In India, Odisha is at the peak in terms of the total value of mineral resources. Odisha is the largest producer of chromite (98%), bauxite (59%), nickel (93%), graphite, dolomite, and manganese. It is also the fourth largest producer of coal and the fifth largest of iron ore in India. Odisha has enormous reserves of around 45,000 MT power grade coal deposit in the area of Talcher. Odisha is home to some of the leading

PSUs such as HAL, NALCO, and MCL and private companies such as Tata Steel, Vedanta Aluminium, Aditya Birla, and Jindal. Odisha receives unprecedented investments in steel, aluminum, power, and refineries. This opportunity is an ideal platform and presents a colossal opportunity for downstream and ancillary industries and also MSME sectors.

According to a survey, the primary goals for the port- and coastal-based industrial policies are:

- To attract FDI
- To create job and generate income
- To set up export processing unit
- To transfer the technology
- To create backward linkages through sourcing of raw materials
- Backward linkages through subcontracting

Odisha Policy Resolution 2015:

1. SEZs (Special Economic Zones)
   a. The Government of Odisha recognizes the prospective role of SEZ in driving industrial/economic growth that expedites exports where employment generation and export promotion remain some of its strategies. The State Government shall create a conducive environment for establishment and smooth conduct of SEZs at various locations in different parts of Odisha. Special thrust shall be given to promoting several other priority sectors ancillary to it. The state shall continue to support the implementation of the SEZs in a time-bound manner.
   b. The State Government shall issue a separate policy for SEZs proving fiscal and nonfiscal incentives to SEZs.
2. NIMZ (National Investment and Manufacturing Zones)
   a. The Government of India came out with the National Manufacturing Policy (NMP) in October 2011 where one of the distinct features of NMP is the organization of NIMZ. The state shall take adequate measures to proclaim and develop an NIM and has recognized Kalinga Nagar Industrial Complex, Dhamara, and Gopalpur as the proposed locations. The NIMZ shall be developed as a Greenfield/Brownfield industrial cluster having state-of-the-art infrastructure and offering business-friendly policies or services. This infrastructure

would include logistics, power, skill development, public utilities along with environment protection, which are essential requirements of a competitive manufacturing foundation. The infrastructure in NIMZ shall be supported by business-friendly means and operating policies. The development of NMIZ will provide attractive opportunities to investors across the world.

3. PCPIR (Petroleum, Chemicals and Petrochemicals Investment Region)

   a. The Government of Odisha has initiated steps to construct MEGA integrated PCPIR ON 284 sq. km. in the districts of Jagatsinghpur and Kendrapara. This will be the fourth PCPIR in the country and IOCL, being an anchor tenant is setting up a 15 MMTA grassroot refinery cum petrochemical complex. An SPV "Paradip Investment Region Development Limited" has also been formed for the implementation of state-of-the-art infrastructure in the region. Setting up of PCPIR would help units to get the benefits of networking and greater efficiency through the use of common infrastructure and support services.

   b. The SPV shall discover and attain land for the said purpose and identify potential tenant industries based on the feedstock available from anchor industries. The State Government agencies concerned and Central Institute of Plastic and Engineering Technology (CIPET) shall also be involved in this project. The SPV shall identify and acquire land for the purpose and identify potential tenant industries based on the feedstock available from anchor industries.

2.5 DISCUSSION

The scope of the study is limited to analysis of specific objectives in order to contribute to a better understanding of the process of reforms in port sector and its macrolevel workings in the state. This study also focuses on the unfolding traffic dynamics at various major and minor ports and the development of regulatory policy framework for the port globally. It is one of the important objectives of generating more interest at macrolevel issues and concerns that impact the future development of port sector.

A seaport is the transit point for this trade, permitting the export and import of goods. Besides, a port is also a place that provides further services and adds worth to the products transported and thus helps the increasing demand of trade along with encouraging the SMEs to these areas and facilitates trading in both goods-related transactions along with services.

The globalization of the world economy has brought about immense rise in exchanges of goods and services across the world. The world trade also accelerated as the cost of shipping has decreased due to the introduction of economy of scale and the development of technology in shipping.

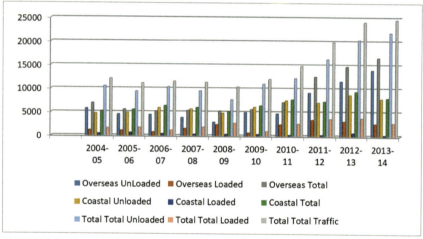

FIGURE 2.1   Graphical presentation of Table 2.1.

Table 2.1 represents the average growth, loading and unloading of coastal and overseas growth during the years from 2004–2005 to 2013–2014 in India. The number of overseas unloading presently reached to 13,987 in coastal points, whereas, in costal unloading, 7912 vessels have been engaged. The total traffic indicated 24,664, which is marked some extent declining from the previous period.

India's port and shipping sector saw a spectacular growth in the first four decades of postindependence period under the scheme of planned development and active government support. More than two-thirds of the cargo handling capacity and more than half of India's national shipping tonnage were established during this period.

TABLE 2.1 Shows Overseas and Coastal Scenario of Ports in India.

Year	Overseas				Coastal				Total		
	Unloaded	Loaded	Total	Unloaded	Loaded	Total	Total Unloaded	Total Loaded	Total Traffic
2004–2005	5782	1168	6950	4751	442	5193	10,533	1610	12,143
2005–2006	4519	1086	5605	4901	650	5551	9420	1736	11,156
2006–2007	4441	765	5206	5952	422	6374	10,393	1187	11,580
2007–2008	3840	1520	5360	5686	317	6003	9526	1837	11,363
2008–2009	2893	2376	5269	4813	334	5147	7706	2710	10,416
2009–2010	4971	646	5617	6092	337	6429	11,063	983	12,046
2010–2011	4730	2411	7141	7539	195	7734	12,269	2606	14,875
2011–2012	9196	3421	12,617	7102	228	7330	16,298	3649	19,947
2012–2013	11,630	3131	14,761	8759	678	9437	20389	3809	24,198
2013–2014	13,987	2613	16,600	7912	152	8064	21899	2765	24,664

However, looking from the perspective of the economic policy that lays more stress on self-reliance and strategies that aimed at import subsidization, the overall growth of trade and technology remains constricted. However, with the paradigm shift in economic policy since early 1990s, the government has liberalized the port sector by opening it to private sector investments.

As a result, ports have now begun to assume a more responsible role as a facilitator of trade with a wide range of value-added services in terms of cargo handling and seeking to improve their performance and relations with international ports.

2.6   EUROPEAN TRADE DRIVES CONTAINERIZATION

A steady rise has been seen in the European merchandise trade that has been growing at compound annual growth rate (CAGR) of 10.3% in terms of value during 2001–2005, which was the highest average growth rate of world merchandise trade in the last three to four decades, leading to pushing of container traffic worldwide. In 2005, it was estimated that world merchandise trade has witnessed an excellent growth rate of 13% in volume terms and container traffic has registered an estimated growth rate of 13.89%. Containerization, which accounts for over 50% of world merchandise trade, is expected to go up further.

Maritime transport is composed of two things—shipping and the port dimensions. The focus area includes establishing a vision for the future of maritime transport, identifying innovative technologies, business models and policies which will lead to change, overcoming barriers from innovation, and establishing governance structure at the global and national levels to foster innovation in different areas that our society will need for better performance—that our societies will need for a more sustainable and better performing future transport system. Innovations in policy, technology, and business practices will lead to the improvement of the performance of transport systems and other related activities in the long run. Doing so will require consideration of the present status and how systems are likely to evolve based on current drivers of demand of policy objectives that would seek to alter these projected trends and means of moving closer to policy aspirations. One of the elements of the debate is how much government needs to intervene and how much they are self-sufficient. Market-based innovations provide the transport system keeping in mind the needs and requirements of the society in future. A further question is with regard to various policy initiatives that would be needed to stimulate innovation in transport. Europe has adopted a policy of blue economy that conceptualizes ocean as a development space where planning integrates conservation, sustainability, extraction of mines and quarries, production of sustainable energy, and marine transport. The blue economy breaks the mold of the business to brown development model where the oceans have been perceived as means of free resource extraction and waste dumping place with cost externalized from economic calculations. The blue economy will incorporate ocean values and services into economic modeling and decision-making processes.

2.7 CONCLUSION

The study concludes that the concept of port and port hinterland during the last few decades has changed in a significant way. The very traditional role of port that was limited to export and import has undergone changes and now includes activities like transhipment and logistics provider. It was marked that the port has become the most preferred and highly congested space for both public and private investments. From the literature review, it was revealed that during the early 1970s, most of the port activities were undertaken in Europe. But nowadays it has been changed dramatically when more than half of the world port activities took place in Asia. The ports play an important role in global chain and act as facilitator of trade. The port policies increase the effectiveness of economic corridors of the ports and port hinterland that can unlock the economic potentials of the state.

KEYWORDS

- **port**
- **port hinterland**
- **transshipment**
- **logistics**
- **value addition**

BIBLIOGRAPHY

Ashar, A. Factor Analysis and Benchmarking Ports' Performance. *Maritime Policy Manage.* **1995,** *22* (4), 389–390.

Baltazar, R.; Brooks, M. R. In *The Governance of Port Devolution: A Tale of Two Countries,* Paper Presented at the World Conference on Transport Research, Seoul, Korea, July 2001.

Bontekoning, Y. M.; Macharis, C.; Trip, J. J. Is a New Applied Transportation Field Emerging? A Review of Intermodal Rail-truck Freight Transport Literature. *Trans. Res. A* **2004,** *38* (1), 1–34.

Goss, R. O. Economic Policies and Seaports: The Economic Functions of Seaports. *Maritime Policy Manage.* **1990a,** *17* (3), 207–219.

Goss, R. O. Economic Policies and Seaports: The Diversity of Port Policies. *Maritime Policy Manage.* **1990b,** *17* (3), 221–234.

Goss, R. O. Economic Policies and Seaports: Are Port Authorities Necessary? *Maritime Policy Manage.* **1990c,** *17* (3), 257–271.

Goss, R. O. Economic Policies and Seaports: Strategies for Port Authorities. *Maritime Policy Manage.* **1990d,** *17* (3), pp. 273–287.

Hayuth, Y. Containerisation and the Load Centre Concept. *Econ. Geogr.* **1981,** *57,* 160–176.

Hayuth, Y.; Roll, Y. Port Performance Comparison Applying Data Envelopment Analysis (DEA). *Maritime Policy Manage.* **1993,** *20,* 153–161.

Heaver, T. D. The Evolution and Challenges of Port Economics. In *Port Economics, Research in Transportation Economics No 16;* Cullinane, K., Talley, W., Eds.; Elsevier: Oxford, 2006; pp 11–41.

Macharis, C.; Bontekoning, Y. M. Opportunities for OR in Intermodal Freight Transport Research: A Review. *Euro. J. Infrastr. Res.* **2003,** *153* (2), 400–416.

Ogundana, B.Patterns and Problems of Seaport Evolution in Nigeria. In *Seaports and Development in Tropical Africa;* Hoyle, B. S., Hilling, D., Eds.; Macmillan: London, 1970; pp 167–182.

Pallis, A. A.; Vitsounis, T. K.; De Langen, P. W. Port Economics, Policy and Management: Review of an Emerging Research Field. *Trans. Rev.* **2010,** *30*(1), 115–161.

Slack, B. Pawns in the Game: Ports in a Global Transport System. *Growth Change* **1994,** *24* (4), 597–598.

Song, D.-W.; Cullinane, K. P. B. Efficiency Measurement of Container Terminal Operations: An Analytical Framework. *J. Eastern Asia Soc. Trans. Stud.* **1999,** *3*(2), 139–154.

Stahlbock, R.; Voss, S. Operations Research at Container Terminals: A Literature Update. *OR Spectrum* **2008,** *30* (1), 1–52.

Steenken, D.; Voss, S.; Stahlbock, R. Container Terminal Operation and Operations Research: A Classification and Literature Review. *OR Spectrum* **2004,** *26* (1), 3–49.

Taaffe, E. J.; Morrill, R. L.; Gould, P. R. Transport Expansion in Underdeveloped Countries: A Comparative Analysis. *Geogr. Rev.* **1963,** *53,* 503–529.

Tongzon, J. L. Systematizing International Benchmarking for Ports. *Maritime Policy Manage.* **1995,** *22* (2), 171–177.

CHAPTER 3

Productivity Sustenance with Effectiveness of Work Circles: A Study on the "Happy Hormones"

ANITA PAREEK[1*] and SANJAY KUMAR SATAPATHY[2]

[1]Research Scholar, Ravenshaw University, Cuttack, India

[2]Dean, School of Commerce & Management, Ravenshaw University, Cuttack, India

*Corresponding author. E-mail: anitapareek005@gmail.com

ABSTRACT

Productivity and effectiveness are the two wheels of sustainability. Survival is not just a dream. Right nurturing can support survival and lead to growth and achieving excellence. Exclusive knowledge can motivate the employees for greater accomplishment and goals but implicit knowledge can connect employees with organizational goals, human factors to humane factors. Happy employees have the driving shaft to carry an organization to be a learning, living, and laudable organization. Happiness at workplace is the most vital goal of today's organizations. Happiness has been recognized and acknowledged as a significant factor by researchers and practitioners to enhance the bottom line of organizations. Advancements and progress in neuroscience have imprinted important knowledge on brain and its related neurotransmitters that play a key role in happiness namely—DOSE (dopamine, oxytocin, serotonin, and endorphins). Triggering these neurotransmitters naturally can enhance their flow and make work more pleasant and enthusiastic. This chapter efforts to put light on these happy hormones, the catalyst of positivity, and enhancing productivity through ignited work circles, the proposed model for this study

"Work Circles-Satisfaction-Productivity-Sustenance Model." This chapter also paves way for self-development for both managers and employees.

3.1　INTRODUCTION

Effectiveness is "Doing Right Things" and efficiency is "Doing Things Right" said Peter Drucker. The employees in an organization are trained to do tasks in right manner. They are groomed and organized in the organizational frame. But the temperament of doing right things ignites the happiness flame within the employees and collectively contributes to the sustenance with a craving for excellence, not dwindling between survival and growth.

Happiness is the most fundamental and essential emotion for all human beings. In all the grounds, happiness ranks the highest in our professional as well as personal to-do list. Thus, it is normal tendency of humans to find happiness in anything and everything they do. Same case applies in professional front; employees constantly look for peace and happiness in their work environment, so that it may raise interest to work as well as enhance the individual and organizational productivity. For this reason, scholars and practitioners have been focusing studies regarding happiness at work as it is the ultimate way to enhance the productivity of the firm. Various studies have been conducted frameworks, theories, and empirical assessments on employee engagement, employee satisfaction, and work–life balance to help managers and employees get insight to resolve stress and dissatisfaction issues. But another answer to this issue can be *neuroscience* (the study of nervous mechanism to understand emotions) and *organizational neuroscience* (implications of brain science for workplace behavior); these studies have given several linkages between human brain as well as its effect on behavior, which ultimately projects the connection of brain in driving one's happiness.

Thus neuroscience aims to help managers in resolving certain organizational issue by offering solutions in the light of organizational neuroscience, which can prove to be highly effective if utilized with correct direction and guidance. Studies like psychology and neuroscience along with technologies like neuroimaging have shown the effect of neural connection on happiness. Along with this, the neurotransmitters released by brain or the brain chemicals have led to scientific conclusions about happiness and well-being (Suardi et al., 2016). The primary aim of this article is to promote sustenance and self-development via awareness and also to bring forth the information on the neurotransmitters that cause the reaction of happiness or the happy hormones of the body and also provide ways to enhance them for better productivity and well-being at workplace.

Certain day-to-day simple activities, fooding habits, and environmental influence the neural pathway to get stimulated and forms new neural connections. The behavioral activities and brain secretion are closely related to each other which affects mood and well-being. Work is an important part of individual's life, not only people earn to fulfill their economic needs but also for psychological satisfaction. This shows that being happy at work is no less important as it is the success key to business endeavors. A study suggested that happy people are 12% more productive (Oswald et al., 2015). On this light, happy employees are positive, enthusiastic, and deals customers better. Neuroscience advancements have clearly shown that there exist a relationship between neural links and actions. The feelings generated by humans are an outcome of the chemical reaction taking place in the brain, which are being transmitted as emotions/reactions. The chemical reactions generate both good and bad feelings, out of which DOSE—dopamine, oxytocin, serotonin, and endorphin are the happy hormones (Bergland, 2012).

DOSE in brain are known as the "happiness hormones" and also called "success hormones" because, apart from a peaceful mood, they provide energy, optimism, better connection with people, and greater focus and ultimately elevate one's drive, leadership skills, and confidence at work. Though one does not have a control on work environment or the coworkers, the good news is that certain activities and food habits trigger the right hormones and facilitate in every situations.

Dopamine: This hormone is often linked with the reward system and satisfaction/pleasure. It is initiated when one reaches the goal for which it can be also named as *"Eureka hormone"* (Satapathy and Pareek, 2019). Dopamine motivates one to do work and gain satisfaction, motivation to work more (Baixauli, 2017).

Oxytocin: This hormone is linked with social belongingness. It promotes building of relationships, trust, social bonding, prosperity, and empathy. This hormone can be named as *"Affinity hormone"* (Satapathy and Pareek, 2019) as it beings about love harmony and cohesiveness among people. The deficiency of this hormone can create depression anxiety and unwillingness to work and show deviant and unproductive behavior at workplace (Zak, 2013).

Serotonin: This hormone is linked with mood of an individual. People with high serotonin are usually calm and peace loving by nature; they have clarity of thoughts and are socially active ones. The deficiency of this *"Pacifying hormone"* (Satapathy and Pareek, 2019) can lower the self-esteem, elevate anger, anxiety, and depression, which results in poor performance at work. As a calm and creative mind can be more productive than a disrupted one, serotonin is also a forerunner to the sleep hormone melatonin (Watanabe and Yamamoto, 2015).

Endorphins: This hormone is linked with healing effect or decreases the feeling of pain, for example, endorphins are released during physical exercise to help body bear the pain. It also leads to the state of intense happiness or excitement (euphoria). Thus, exercising or any related activity becomes enjoyable. This *"Relieving hormone"* (Satapathy and Pareek, 2019) frees one from pain and helps them to bring enthusiasm and excitement that ultimately makes them happy. Endorphins can be boosted naturally to make oneself happier and more productive at workplace (Stoppler, 2018).

The happy hormones, the scientists, and some natural ways to boost them are presented in Table 3.1.

Figure 3.1 shows the happy hormones (dopamine, oxytocin, serotonin and endorphins) and their role in enhancing happiness level of human being.

FIGURE 3.1   Hormones-happiness set (proposed).

TABLE 3.1 The Happy Hormones.

Hormones	Impact	Enhancing supplements/activities
Dopamine (Dr. Carlsson, 1950) (Eureka hormone)	Dopamine effect makes one "want" to do things (that are related with happiness/pleasure). Its inadequacy causes slower reaction time and also anhedonia (unwillingness to do a task) and even depression. Dopamine is released when the doing action is connected with pleasure. It influences the level of motivation and plays a crucial role in how an individual perceives reality. Inefficiency in dopamine transmission is associated with a state called psychosis, a severely distorted form of thinking which is characterized by hallucinations and also sometimes delusions. It also plays a major role in the brain's reward system.	Eating food rich in protein Consuming less saturated fats Eating more of velvet beans Exercise Increased consumption of tyrosine (almonds, avocados, bananas, green tea, milk, water melon) Phenylalanine rich foods that contain protein like eggs, fish, meat, nuts Avoiding sweeteners Have good social circle Getting right sleep Exposing yourself to morning sunlight Meditation and yoga Listening music Listing down small-to-do talks
Oxytocin (Sir Henry Hallett Dale, 1906) (Affinity hormone)	Oxytocin helps individuals to create social bonds and also maintain them, and it causes the feelings of belongingness and connection (also love). Its deficiency lowers the productivity, ability, and capacity to communicate. Oxytocin is released during physical and also eye contact with other people. The high level of this chemical makes persons happy.	Consuming food rich in vitamin C and D Undertaking acupuncture therapy Consuming caffeine contents Keeping pets Listening to soothing music Eating dark chocolates Using fragrance of jasmine and lavender Massage therapy Incorporation of yoga Exposing oneself to both warm and cool temperatures can also help enhance oxytocin levels Positive social encounters and gatherings

TABLE 3.1 *(Continued)*

Hormones	Impact	Enhancing supplements/activities
Serotonin (Vittorio Ersplamer, 1940) (Pacifying hormone)	Serotonin causes the feelings related to safety, calmness, joy, and also self-confidence. Its scarcity leads to lowered self-esteem, high obsessive thoughts, quick compulsive behavior, impulsiveness and aggression. Serotonin is released when carbohydrates are consumed (e.g., sweets and chocolate). Serotonin gives a feeling of calmness and confidence. Not just happiness but it is calmness. Precisely is "relaxed happiness." Serotonin also helps in regulating sleep, appetite/hunger, moods, and also inhibits pain. Certain research supports the idea that depressed people tend to have a reduced level of serotonin transmission. Thus, lower levels of a serotonin by products have been associated to a higher risk for suicide.	Consuming soy products Taking a quality probiotic, hydrating body, and eating a brain-healthy diet Spend time with nature Gratitude: Scientific studies show that gratitude affects the brain's reward system positively. It is correlated with the secretion of dopamine as well as serotonin. Gratitude has been directly linked to increased levels of happiness and satisfaction Essential oils: Have medicinal properties. Studies have revealed that bergamot, lavender, and lemon essential oils are useful in therapeutic. Using these oils prompts brain to secrete serotonin leading to calmness Happy memories are formed in anterior cingulate cortex, as it is the region of the brain associated with attention. People who relive in sad memories produce less serotonin in that region. Thus, people dwelling on happy memories produce more serotonin. Psychotherapy is often proved to be helpful in improving mood. Such therapies can possibly raise one's serotonin levels. Exposure to bright light. Consumption of B6, B12, and folate related foods (green leafy vegetables, broccoli, cabbage, and whole grains.) Increase magnesium intake (dark greens, bananas, and fish) Less sugar intake Thinking positive

TABLE 3.1 *(Continued)*

Hormones	Impact	Enhancing supplements/activities
Endorphins (Choh Hao Li, 1960) (Relieving hormone)	Endorphins lead to really good/happy mood (also euphoric) and gives the surplus energy to "go an extra mile," with decreased feeling of tiresomeness. This chemical is considered very vital since stone age, as endorphins saved the life of nomads, which kept them going in spite of hunger and tiredness. The lack of endorphins can cause mood swings and also extremely contrasting emotions. It is also released during physical exercises and movement and tends to decrease the perception of pain.	Consuming chocolates. As cocoa contains mood-boosters such as phenethylamine, endorphin, and theobromine, a chemical which decreases pain and makes one feel more pleasant. **Eating one's favorite food.** Studies suggest that not only chocolate but all palatable foods can make brain secrete endorphins to elevate mood and excitement. **Exercising,** pumps out endorphins to cope with the pain released. Laugh aloud, it releases endorphins and creates happiness. **Not just listening but also** *making music* **boosts** endorphins secretion. Yoga and meditation. Giving: Volunteering, donating, and helping others may also make a person feel good. Researchers at the National Institutes of Health found that people who gave money to a charity activated pleasure center in their brain. This may lead to improved endorphin levels Dancing to the music Getting some morning sunrays Breathing exercises enhances endorphins production

Figure 3.2 shows the model proposed by authors, portrays the role of happy hormones in affecting work circles, so as to attain better productivity and sustainability at workplace.

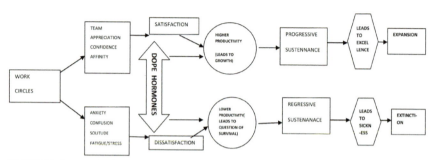

FIGURE 3.2   Work circles–satisfaction–productivity–sustenance model (propose).

The biological objectives of business comprise survival, growth, and excellence. The infant mortality in case of businesses is higher than that of human beings. Many business ideas face sudden demise for multiple reasons. Surviving ones only strive for growth and ultimately toward unending quest for excellence. Machines, money, and material-like resources do not beget a thrive for excellence. The living resource can do. The living resource can also push an excellent organization to see its doom. So nurturing HR can create a bonding of satisfied employees, which will lead to progressive sustenance. The reverse may put the red light on, in the path of progress. Figure 3.3 shows the Endocrine gland of human body, portraying various gland and their respective secretions, having various functions. The secretion of happy hormones is from the hypothalamus which helps in secretion other important neurotransmitters as well and regulates body temperature.

The real power of human resource is not in the muscles but in the hormones. Ignorance of getting abounding pleasure through work creates unknowingly a knack for laziness. Being positive, work circles give a leverage to productivity and make the organization shine. Self-knowledge is the super knowledge. Self-development is platinum development.

As shown in Figures 3.4 and 3.5 the congruency of management, organizational and subordinate goals leads to high degree of goal attainment thus, goal congruency leads to better productivity.

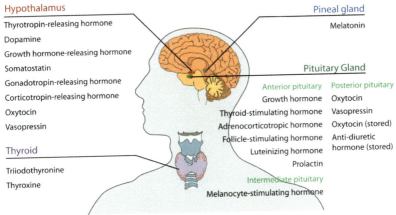

FIGURE 3.3   Various hormones produced by endocrine gland.
Source: https://en.wikipedia.org/wiki/Endocrine_gland.

FIGURE 3.4   Goal congruence.
Source: knowledgegrab.com › Glossary.

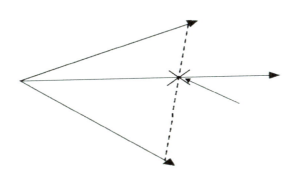

FIGURE 3.5   Achieving goal congruence.
Source: www.oocities.org/lionelpineda/ADMON/dir/dir17.htm.

Goals differ, work circles differ. The degree of attainment depends on the congruence of group goals. The individual goals need to be integrated to group goals like rivulets enrich and form a river (Table 3.2).

TABLE 3.2   Literature Review.

Author and topic	Website	Key findings
Marie Miguel (January 2, 2019). Happiness article	https://www.betterhelp.com/advice/happiness	Definition of happiness and how it helps one build socially, physically, and emotionally.
Medical University of Vienna (August 31, 2019). "Dopamin" far more than just the happy hormone	https://www.sciencedaily.com/	The importance of dopamine neurotransmitter, the related activities to it, and a correct balance in the body
Seana (2014). Happy hormones: how training makes you happy.	https://www.freeletics.com	Benefits of happy hormones and how they are enhanced after exercise and workouts.
Joanna Smykowski (January 2, 2019). Aristotle and Plato—how their views on happiness help us today.	https://www.betterhelp.com/advice/happiness	The value of happiness from Plato and Aristotle. The cardinal values which they gave for the world to be happier place.
Dolores Garcia (May 2, 2017). Happy or sad the chemistry behind depression	https://www.jax.org	The severity of depression and hormones that help reducing it.
Harvard Health Publishing (June 2009). What causes depression?	https://www.health.harvard.edu	Depression, its cause, regions getting affected, hormones affecting depression.
Timothy J. Legg (May 25, 2018). What are the benefits of sunlight?	https://www.healthline.com/health/depression/benefits-sunlight	Benefits of sunlight, happiness hormones during sunlight, and other health benefits of sunlight.
Sawaram Suthar (May 23, 2016). 6 scientific ways to increase productivity	https://visme.co/blog/how-to-increase-productivity-at work/#FSbtkkOCfEiPGAv4.99	Simple ways to improve productivity by managing temperature, light color etc. at workplace.

TABLE 3.2 *(Continued)*

Author and topic	Website	Key findings
ET Bureau (December 10, 2018). Boost these hormones to succeed as a leader at work	https://economictimes.india-times.com	DOSE happy hormones and how they help enhancing leadership skills.
Jordan Fallis (March 30, 2019). 25 effective ways to increase oxytocin levels in the brain	https://www.optimal-livingdynamics.com/blog/25-effective-ways-to-increase-oxytocin-levels-in-the-brain	Oxytocin, its effects and 25 ways to enhance it.

Outlooks differ, opinions vary. People think differently on the same subject also. The unmatching mental wave very often results in different interpretations. Gaps are many, and locating a gap leads to new thoughts, new visions, new versions and innovations. Sustainability is a dream of every individual and corporate. Making the dream true needs a congruence of different factors in a societal frame. Figure 3.6 shows the factors that impact corporate sustainability, as to what organizations should look for in order to bring about more sustainability.

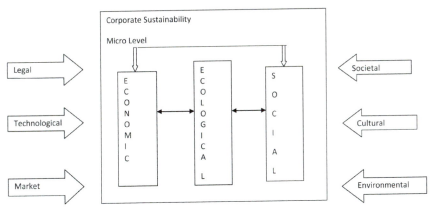

FIGURE 3.6 Corporate sustainability and its interdependences
Source: Modified from Baumgartner and Ebner, 2010).

Day-to-day events may help triggering of many of these neurotransmitters and raise the natural flow of these happy neurotransmitters. Thus, individuals engage in activities, of which they themselves have little or no knowledge as to what effect it has on the brain. Ample neuroscientific researchers have provided validation to certain activities in order to promote positive culture in today's organization.

- *Stay peaceful and consistent:*
  Endorphin is an important bliss hormone. It enhances mood and lowers physical pain and emotional strain. It amplifies cognitive power. At workplace, endorphins can be boosted with fun activities, for example, laughing triggers an instantaneous endorphin release. Similarly, listening music while working can also enhance endorphin levels. Going out for a short walk with a colleague during breaks with combination of stretching exercise, a good company and, also the sunlight all are contributors to heighten endorphin levels. Try out mini-exercise and take short deep breaths instantly releases both adrenaline and endorphins.

- *Be the captain:*
  The hormone that builds leadership within is serotonin hormone. It elevates will power, self-esteem, inner satisfaction, and confidence; thus, it needs to constantly battle with its opposite hormone cortisol (stress hormone). To enhance serotonin, natural sunlight acts as a booster. Saying thank you and expressing gratitude also builds serotonin.

- *Set and achieve goals:*
  Dopamine is otherwise known as reward/achievement hormone. Dopamine levels determine alertness, concentration, long-term memory, and innovation. Whenever a task is assigned to an employee, instead of completing the entire task (which is tuff), it should be broken into small milestones; thus, achieving those small milestones also triggers dopamine, which ultimately helps in completing the entire task enthusiastically. It is also important to recognize that what reward motivated oneself. Recognition and emotional awards also help us to boost dopamine levels.

- *Dedication and trust:*
  Oxytocin is the primary attachment molecule. It enhances interpersonal relations, boosts security, and reduces stress. Helping and encourage others and mentoring or compliment people at office are activities that boosts oxytocin. Positive interactions, smiling, and sharing jokes and stories help supplement oxytocin level. All these activities help us to bring productivity at work.

- *Have some natural light:*
  ✓ Enhances mood
  ✓ Elevates concentration
  ✓ Restore sleep mechanism
  ✓ Renew the body's biological clock to work efficiently
  ✓ Cutbacks chances of irritation and headache
  ✓ Lifts both physical and mental health

- *The right temperature:*

The ideal temperature to generate higher employee productivity lies between 70 and 73 °F (21.1–22.8 °C). Other experts have suggested that employee productivity is greatest at room temperature around 77 °F (25 °C). It is also seen that there is decrease by 2% in performance level for each °C increase in temperature between 25 and 32 °C. Just by adjusting light and temperature, drastic change can be seen in the productivity and performance of employees.

- *Choosing the right colors:*

  ✓ The color "blue" is calming. It boosts intercommunication and trust levels while increasing efficiency and balancing heart rate.
  ✓ The color "green" is soothing. It elevates harmony at workplace, decreases anxiety, and is relaxing to the eyes.
  ✓ The color "orange" boosts energy. It elevates the oxygen flow to brain, thus enhancing brain activity.

Warm (i.e., orange, red, and yellow) and cold (i.e., blue, green, and purple) colors affect human brains differently. The color red can be painted on the office walls of employees who have detail-oriented jobs or tasks. Whatever the job, there is a color that works best, just certainly not white, off-white, or gray!

- *Ergonomics at workplace:*

The word "ergonomics" has its roots from the two Greek words *ergon* that means "work" and *nomoi* that means "natural laws." Ergonomics is the science of designing and organize things in such a way, so that people can utilize them more efficiently, without getting injured or stressed. People spending majority of time sitting in front of a laptop/computer have been marked with a significant rise in musculoskeletal disorders (MSDs). Such work-related impairments results into significant costs to organization as well as nations.

Simplicity in designing the workplace, like,

- ✓ Convenient points must be chosen for location of switches with systematism.
- ✓ Equipment should be placed in such way so that they are easily reachable.
- ✓ Comfortable workstations, like easy chairs and ample leg space while sitting.
- ✓ Placing "most-often" used things/equipment to easily accessible places.

Adopting ergonomics to workplace can lead to the following benefits:

- Enhances comfort level at work.
- Improves the performance/productivity.
- Reduces workplace issues and injuries.
- Reduces the chances accidents at workplace.
- Enhances interest/enthusiasm and willingness to work.
- Elevates the overall level of job satisfaction.

- *Short daytime naps and sleep:*

    Better known as *"afternoon siesta"* is boost up for mental health and improved performance as it is a way to refresh oneself. Lack of sleep affects people both mentally and physically too which disrupts productivity at work. Sleep deprivation degrades performance and increases susceptibility to diseases like obesity, heart issues, and psychological disorders. Employees when given short breaks remain refreshed and accept new challenges at work.

Studies relate that,
- 40% Alertness can be enhanced with a 40 min nap.
- A 20-min afternoon nap is more effective than 20 min of sleep.

Benefits of napping:

- Naps refresh mind and boosts creativity.
    - ✓ It elevates positive mood.
    - ✓ Improves psychological health.

✓   Equalizes blood pressure.
✓   Enhances cognitive functions.
✓   Reduces the chance of heart disease.
✓   Maximizes information processing.

- *Take short breaks:*

Taking short breaks in between working hours helps us to refresh body, relieves joint pains, and calms eyes.

✓   "Microbreak" of as small as 30 s to 5 min increases mental activity by 13%.
✓   Fatigue can be reduced by 50% with a 15 s break every 10 min.
✓   Pressure and pain in forearm wrist, forearm, hand and legs can be decreased with 5 min break every hour.

A regular break in every 15 min has the chances of enhancing productivity at workplace by 6.45%.

- *Incorporation of yoga:*

Yoga must be incorporated into daily lives in order to lessen the mental and physical burdens. A study by the American Council on Exercise stated that more than 11 million Americans who practice yoga, find that the poses of yoga (i.e., *Asanas*) and breathing exercises strengthen mind and body by relaxing anxieties.

Yoga benefits:

✓   Yoga reduces anxiety and improves concentration.
✓   It boosts immunity.
✓   It increases flexibility at work.
✓   Reduces the stress level by balancing the cortisol hormone.
✓   Increases energy to work.

- *Music is an equally effective medicine:*

Studies have revealed the in-depth relationship between playing of slow background music during repetitive tasks and the efficiency of the employee increases in performing such works. The result shows that music is efficient in building efficiency during such type of work.

- *Laughter is the best health booster:*

  ✓ Laughter allows body to produce the serotonin, happy chemicals of endorphins, growth hormones, and other beneficiary hormones.

  ✓ It equalizes the level of stress hormones like cortisol and epinephrine.

  ✓ It helps body to generate endorphin, which is a natural opiate and natural painkiller.

  ✓ It improves blood circulation, relieves, and brings a pleasant physical state to work efficiently.

3.2   CONCLUSION

The Factories Act and many other laws and practices make it mandatory to maintain a comfortable environment for the employees. These are more about physical comfort, social comfort, financial comfort, logistics comfort, family comfort and growth comforts. These are understood as the parameters of sustenance. Men are not machines; this living resource needs to be happy to beget better productivity and excellence as well. The neuroscience provides us insight about scientific validation of the activities one do and how can it consciously cultivate a culture of serenity and happiness within the organization, thus creating enthusiastic employees and a happy workforce and providing innumerable opportunities, benefits, and sky-high possibilities of competitiveness, growth, tranquillity, and well-being.

KEYWORDS

- **effectiveness**
- **sustenance**
- **happiness**
- **productivity**
- **neurotransmitters**

- **hormones**
- **work circles**
- **self-development**
- **excellence**

REFERENCES

Baixauli, E. Happiness: Role of Dopamine and Serotonin on Mood and Negative Emotions. *Emerg. Med.* **2017,** *7,* 350.

Baumgartner, R. J.; Ebner, D. *Corporate Sustainability Stratergies: Sustainablity Profiles and Maturity Levels, Sustainable Development;* John Wiley & Sons: London, 2010.

Bergland, C. The Neurochemicals of Happiness: 7 Brain Molecules That Make You Feel Great. *The Athlete's Way. Psychology Today,* Nov 29, 2012. Retrieved from: https://www. psychologytoday.com/us/blog/the-athletesway/201211/the-neurochemicals-happiness.

Oswald, A. J.; Proto, E.; Sgroi, D. Happiness and Productivity. *J. Labor Econ.* **2015,** *33* (4), 789–822.

Satapathy, S.; Pareek, A. *Emotion, Empathy and Education: e-Trident for Excellence,* 2019, unpublished.

Stoppler, M. C. Endorphins: Natural Pain and Stress Fighters; Shield, W. C., Ed.; Medicine Net.com News Letters, 2018. Retrieved from: https://www.medicinenet.com/ endorphins_natural_pain_and_stress_fighters/views.html.

Suardi, A.; Sotgiu, I.; Costa, T.; Cauda, F.; Rusconi, M. L. The Neural Correlates of Happiness: A Review of PET and fMRI Studies Using Autobiographical Recall Methods. *Cogn. Affect. Behav. Neurosci.* **2016,** *16* (3), 383–392. DOI: 10.3758/s13415-016-0414-7.

Watanabe, N.; Yamamoto, M. Neural Mechanisms of Social Dominance. *Front. Neurosci.* **2015,** *9,* 154. DOI: 10.3389/fnins.2015.00154.

Zak, P. J. The Top 10 Ways to Boost Good Feelings, Lab-Tested Methods to Raise Oxytocin, and Feel Better about Yourself and Others. *Psychology Today,* Nov 7, 2013. Retrieved from: https://www.psychologytoday.com/us/ blog/the-moral-molecule/201311/ the-top-10-ways-boost-good-feelings.

WEBSITES

Alban, D. How to Increase Endorphins Naturally. Nov 15, 2018. Retrieved from: https:// bebrainfit.com/increase-endorphins.

Berry, J. Endorphins: Effects and How to Increase Levels. Feb 6, 2018. Retrieved from: https://www.medicalnewstoday.com/articles/320839.php.

Brown, L. 11 Ways to Increase the Serotonin in Your Brain (Naturally). Mar 13, 2019. Retrieved from: https://hackspirit.com/11-increase-serotonin-brain-naturally.

ET Bureau. Boost These Hormones to Succeed as a Leader at Work. Dec 10, 2018. Retrieved from: economictimes.indiatimes.com/articleshow/66988190.cms?from=mdr&utm_ source=contentofinterest&utm_medium=text&utm_campaign=cppst.

Fallis, J. 25 Effective Ways to Increase Oxytocin Levels in the Brain. Mar 30, 2019. Retrieved from: https://www.optimallivingdynamics.com/blog/25-effective-ways-to-increase-oxytocin-levels-in-the-brain.

Garcia, D. Happy-or-sad-the-chemistry-behind-depression. May 2, 2017. Retrieved from: https://www.jax.org/news-and-insights/jax-blog/2015/december/happy-or-sad-the-chemistry-behind-depression.

Gibb, B. J. A Quick Guide to Brain Chemistry. Nov 2017. Retrieved from: https://bigpictureeducation.com/chemicals-brain.

Good Therapy. Glutamate. May 24, 2017. Retrieved from: https://www.goodtherapy.org/blog/psychpedia/glutamate.

GoodTherapy.org Staff. 10 Best Ways to Boost Dopamine and Serotonin Naturally. Dec 12, 2017. Retrieved from: https://www.goodtherapy.org/blog/10-ways-to-boost-dopamine-and-serotonin-naturally-1212177.

Harvard Health Publishing. What Causes Depression. Updated: June 24, 2019, Published: June 2009. Retrieved from: https://www.health.harvard.edu/mind-and-mood/what-causes-depression.

Joe Cohen, B. S. Beneficial Effects of Oxytocin + 34 Ways to Increase It. July 25, 2019. Retrieved from: https://selfhacked.com/blog/the-social-chilled-out-and-empathetic-genes-oxytocin-receptor-snps/.

Julson, E. 10 Best Ways to Increase Dopamine Levels Naturally. May 10, 2018. Retrieved from: https://www.healthline.com/nutrition/how-to-increase-dopamine#section4.

Kuczyńska, D. Short Story about the Brain Chemicals and How They Affect Players. Dec 23, 2016. Retrieved from: https://blog.daftmobile.com/short-story-about-the-brain-chemicals-and-how-they-affect-players-d078792139ec.

Medical University of Vienna. "Dopamin" Far More Than Just the Happy Hormone. Aug 31, 2019. Retrieved from: https://www.sciencedaily.com/releases/2016/08/160831085320.htm.

Miguel, M. Happiness Article. Jan 2, 2019. Retrieved from: https://www.betterhelp.com/advice/happiness.

Nanda, A. Hormones and Chemicals That Influence Emotions. Dec 2016. Retrieved from: https://www.mokshamantra.com/hormones-chemicals-influence-emotions/.

Psychologies Boost Your Natural Feel Good Chemicals. Apr 14, 2018. Retrieved from: https://www.psychologies.co.uk/self/how-to-boost-your-natural-feelgood-chemicals.html.

Rayner, G The Emotion Centre is the Oldest Part of the Human Brain: Why is Mood So Important? Sept 26, 2016. Retrieved from: http://theconversation.com/the-emotion-centre-is-the-oldest-part-of-the-human-brain-why-is-mood-so-important-63324.

Santos, G. #3 Ways to Increase Dopamine to Boost Your Productivity. Mar 15, 2018. Retrieved from: https://helloendless.com/10-ways-to-increase-dopamine-to-boost-your-productivity.

Seana Happy Hormones: How Training Makes You Happy. 2014. Retrieved from:https://www.freeletics.com/en/blog/posts/happiness-hormones-training-makes-happy.

Smykowski, J. Aristotle & Plato—How Their Views on Happiness Help Us Today. Jan 2, 2019. Retrieved from: https://www.betterhelp.com/advice/happiness/aristotle-and-plato-how-their-views-on-happiness-can-help-us-today/.

Suthar, S. 6 Scientific Ways to Increase Productivity. May 23, 2016. Retrieved from: https://visme.co/blog/how-to-increase-productivity-at work/#FSbtkkOCfEiPGAv4.99.

Timothy, J. L. What Are the Benefits of Sunlight. May 25, 2018. Retrieved from: https://www.healthline.com/health/depression/benefits-sunlight#benefits.

Wu, K. Love, Actually: The Science Behind Lust, Attraction, and Companionship. Feb 14, 2017. Retrieved from: http://sitn.hms.harvard.edu/flash/2017/love-actually-science-behind-lust-attraction-companionship/.

CHAPTER 4

Global Research Output on Sustainable Development: A Scientometric Analysis

HEMANTA KUMAR BISWAL*, DESUL SUDASANA, JYOTSHNA SAHOO, RAJ KISHOR KAMPA, and MRUTYUNJAY SETHY

Department of Library and Information Science, Khallikote University, Berhampur 760001, Odisha, India

Corresponding author. E-mail: hemantab@gmail.com

ABSTRACT

This chapter presents a scientometric analysis of publications on sustainable development (SD) spanning a period from 2000 to 2018 as reflected in Web of Science (WOS) database. Basing upon the records retrieved from the database, it provides useful insights on several dimensions of SD publications. Results indicate that, though there is a steady growth in the quantity of publications, the citations have seen a steep decrease after 2013. China emerged as the leading country in terms of publications, whereas United States found to be the country with most impactful research with high link strength, and it has a strong relationship with other countries, especially with China and England. As per the productivity and influence of the leading researchers identified in author's collaboration network analysis, Yong Gengleads the other researchers both in number of publications and link strength, whereas Wei Wang found to be the author with high citations. The journal Sustainability appeared to be the leading journal in terms of productivity, whereas Journal of Cleaner Production was found to be the most cited journal. The chapter also reports the intellectual structure of sustainable SD research depicting the research hotspots as well as the research forefronts.

4.1 INTRODUCTION

The emergence of sustainable development (SD) has gained globally in recent years which had enhanced its implementation in every aspect and boost the healthy environment and economy growth. However, there have been issue and challenges in meeting some of the doorstep of SD due to the constraint imposed by the social issues, technological advancement and the knack of the ecosystem to accommodate human path. The Brundtland report *"Our Common Future"* in 1987 has brought an attention on SD worldwide and link the issues of economic development and environmental stability, and it defined the most frequently cited definition of SD as "development that meets the needs of the present without compromising the ability of future generations to meet their own needs" (United Nations General Assembly, 1987). The concept of needs here does not merely contains material needs but includes values, relationships, freedom to think, act, and participate, all amounting to sustainable living, morally and spiritually. The 30-year journey of four World Summits from Stockholm to Nairobi and from Rio to Johannesburg has put the worldwide notice that achieving SD in the 21st century is not an option but is inevitable. Over the last three decades, there have been numerous studies, research publications, and a proliferation of subdisciplines relating to SD. However, the bibliometric profile of SD in the literature is still unknown. Bibliometrics is a statistical analysis of written communication in science and science policy (Mayr and Scharnhorst, 2014) and is frequently used to provide quantitative analysis of academic literature. The present study reports the scientometric analysis based on SD research output data during 2000–2018. Such study would position researchers better placed in understanding the research being carried out worldwide in the domain of SD and would be useful in guiding the researcher in choosing appropriate scholarly journals for publication and for identifying prospective collaborators. This analysis would also be helpful in identifying the productive institutions, authors, and directions the research in the domain of SD.

4.1.1 OBJECTIVES OF THE STUDY

The objectives of this study were included as follows:

1. To study the characteristics of publication output on SD;

2. To evaluate the productivity and connectivity of countries, institutions, authors, and journals; and

3. Identify and visualize the emerging hotspots and the intellectual structure of SD field.

4.2 METHODOLOGY

The source of data for the present chapter is WOS database produced by Clarivate Analytics. This database covers nearly 19,000 titles from over 3500 publishers, of which 13,000+ are peer-reviewed journals in the fields of scientific, technical, medical, and social sciences (including arts and humanities) disciplines. We used the advance search box in WOS database where publication year was chosen for 19 years, that is, {P Y= (2000–2018) and all the related papers (17,115) published only in English language in the form of journal articles, and reviews were retrieved and compiled into MS Excel spreadsheet for detail analysis. The scientometric indicators like co-occurrence analysis have been employed to analyze the author co-occurrences, country co-occurrences, and institution co-occurrences as well as co-occurrences of keywords. These techniques have been recommended by previous studies of a similar nature (Song et al., 2016). Along with this, two visualization tools namely CiteSpace and VOSviewer (Chen, 2015; Van Eck and Waltman, 2009, 2010) were employed in the current study to visualize the intellectual structure of SD field and to highlight the emerging areas of research.

4.3 RESULTS AND DISCUSSION

4.3.1 CHARACTERISTICS OF PUBLICATION OUTPUTS

The search in the WOS database resulted in 17,115 documents in the field of SD during the period from 2000 to 2018. It is reflected that, more than half (8891; 52%) of publications were published in the last 4 years that is in between 2015 and 2018 and the year 2018 had the highest number of publications (3164; 18%) as shown in Table 4.1. It is also observed that there is a sharp decrease in the average citations for paper after 2013. Though the reason for such a drop is not clear, the possibility is that the recent research takes time to get cited. The *h*-index (as seen in Table 4.1) was sharply increased from 2001 to 2005 and remained constant in the period from 2005 to 2007 and shown a sharp decrease from 2014 onwards.

TABLE 4.1   Year-Wise Distribution of Articles, Citations, *h*-Index, Average Citations Per Paper.

Year	Total number of research publications	%	Total number of citations (TC)	h-index	ACPP
2000	158	0.9	7009	40	44.36
2001	161	0.9	5174	32	32.86
2002	206	1.2	8665	45	42.06
2003	228	1.3	8882	49	39.91
2004	252	1.5	11,016	54	43.71
2005	310	1.8	13,488	64	43.51
2006	381	2.2	13,344	64	35.02
2007	486	2.8	18,695	64	38.47
2008	484	2.8	17,547	66	36.25
2009	656	3.8	20,983	72	31.99
2010	728	4.3	22,056	73	30.3
2011	814	4.8	22,485	65	27.62
2012	982	5.7	20,825	62	21.21
2013	1165	6.8	20,624	60	17.7
2014	1213	7.1	20,179	59	16.64
2015	1507	8.8	19,519	51	12.95
2016	1802	10.5	16,307	45	9.05
2017	2418	14.1	12,081	38	5
2018	3164	18.5	3908	17	1.24

4.3.2   *AUTHORS' PRODUCTIVITY AND CONNECTIVITY ANALYSIS*

This section analyzes coauthorship network and provides the names of the most productive researchers in the global SD research, in terms of publications, citations, and collaboration network, as measured by VOSviewer.

Figure 4.1 displays the visualization of most productive authors and their collaboration network. For this visualization, we kept the threshold value of five as a minimum number of publication for an author, and it is seen that 47,899, 576 authors met this threshold which was used for visualization, where each node represents an author's productivity and the links between the authors denote the collaboration established through the coauthorship in the articles. The size of frames represents the quantum of the publications of the authors, and thickness of the line represents the frequency of collaboration among the authors. The color of the frames remains the same for the authors in the same cluster. In the term of publications, Yong Geng ($n = 45$) was most productive researcher in this domain.

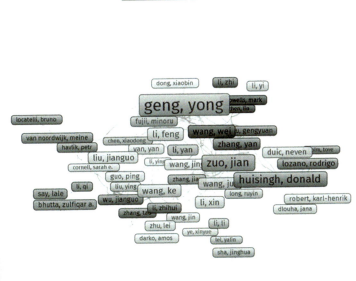

FIGURE 4.1   Coauthorship network visualization. The merged network contains 359 nodes and 818 links. The size of frames represents the quantum of the publications of the authors, and thickness of the line represents the frequency of collaboration among the authors.

Even though visualizations give a clear picture of several authors, Table 4.2 also illustrates a detailed analysis of most productivity authors.

TABLE 4.2 The Top 10 Productive Authors in Terms of the Publications.

Rank	Author	No. of publications	Country
1	Yong Geng	45	China
2	Jian Zuo	28	Australia
3	Donald Huisingh	25	United States
4	Xiaoling Zhang	24	China
5	Feng Li	18	China
6	Walter Leal Filho	17	China
7	Ke Wang	17	China
8	Wei Wang	17	Germany
9	Jun Wang	16	China
10	Bing Xue	16	China

Here we can notice that out of the 10 productive authors in terms of publications; the most highly productive author in the network is Yong Geng with 45 publications. Yong Geng is a Professor of Environmental Science and Engineering at Shanghai Jiao Tong University, China, followed by Jian Zuo, (28 publications) who is an Associate Professor of Architecture and Built Environment, in the University of Adelaide, Australia. Next is Donald Huisingh (25 publications), who is the founder and Editor-in-Chief of Journal of Cleaner Production and belongs to University of Tennessee, United States. From the rest seven authors, Wei Wang the eighth ranked author belongs to Germany where as the all the six authors are from China.

TABLE 4.3 The Top 5 Productive Authors in Terms of the Citations.

Rank	Author	Citations
1	Wei Wang	1197
2	Yong Geng	1195
3	Rodrigo Lozano	1150
4	Donald Huisingh	947
5	Jun Chen	841

Table 4.3 depicts the top 5 ranked authors in terms of citations received to their articles. It is seen that Wei Wang is the most highly cited author with 1197 citations in the network followed by Yong Geng (1195 citations), Rodrigo Lozano (1150 citations), Donald Huisingh (1150 citations), and Jun Chen (841 citations).

TABLE 4.4 The Top 5 Collaborative Authors.

Rank	Author	Total link strength
1	Yong Geng	98
2	Jian Zuo	55
3	Huijuan Dong	46
4	Tsuyoshi Fujita	45
5	Donald Huisingh	43

For additional connectivity analysis, we have observed the top collaborative authors based on coauthorship pattern as depicted in Table 4.4. Yong Geng (LS = 98), Jian Zuo (LS = 55), and Huijuan Dong (LS = 46) are the top 3 researchers who had strong connection link with others in the field. It is seen that productivity, influence, and connectivity are not connected.

Visualization in Figure 4.2 shows the authors who have strong citation bursts and the respective years in which it took place. It can be seen that Kamil Kaygusuz (2000) from Karadeniz Technical University, Turkey, has strong burst among the top 5 authors since 2001. Liu (2000) has the second strong burst, which took place during the period from 2016 to 2018. Following him are Hepbasli (2000) from "Yasar University, Turkey," Ibrahim Dincer (2000) from "University of Ontario Institute of Technology, Canada" and X Wang.

Authors	Year	Strength	Begin	End	2000 - 2018
KAYGUSUZ K	2000	15.5607	2001	2009	??????????????????
LIU Y	2000	11.6978	2016	2018	?????????????????????
HEPBASLI A	2000	8.5971	2004	2009	???????????????????
DINCER I	2000	7.0637	2001	2011	?????????????????????
WANG X	2000	7.0389	2016	2018	?????????????????????

FIGURE 4.2   The top 5 coauthors associated with strong citation bursts. The time interval is depicted as a blue question mark symbols. The period in which an author's work was found to have a burst is shown as a red question mark symbols segment, indicating the beginning year and the ending year of the duration of the burst.

4.3.3 PRODUCTIVITY AND CONNECTIVITY ANALYSIS OF COUNTRIES

Analysis of productivity and connectivity among the countries based on the affiliations of author's contribution to the global SD research was performed by VOSviewer. A threshold value of 5 was prescribed as a minimum number of research publications coming out of any given country. Out of the 187 countries from where publications have come, 132 met the given threshold. The connectivity among the countries is presented in Figure 4.3. Each node represents the country's productivity and the links between the countries denote the collaborations established through the authorship in the articles. The size of the node is proportional to the number of publications of the country and the thickness of the line representing the intensity of the collaborations between the countries. The color of the frames stands for the countries in the same cluster.

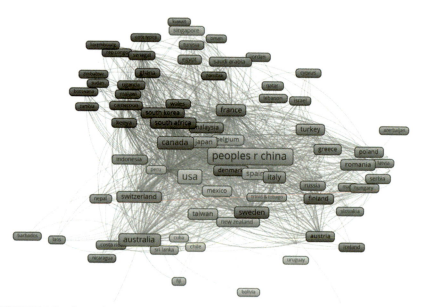

FIGURE 4.3 Countries network of 132 nodes and 2695 links. The size of the node being proportional to the number of publications of the country and the thickness of the line representing the intensity of the collaborations between the countries. China is the highly publication node, whereas United States and England are having more collaboration with other countries.

TABLE 4.5 The Top 10 Productive Countries in the Terms of the Publications.

Rank	Country	Number of publications
1	China	4009
2	United States	2393
3	England	1291
4	Germany	873
5	Australia	849
6	Canada	826
7	India	699
8	Italy	650
9	The Netherlands	639
10	France	607

We performed an analysis in terms of quantum of publications associated with the country. Table 4.5 represents the top 10 countries based on publications. China tops the list with 4009 publications followed by United States and England. It is also encouraging to note that India occupies seventh position with 699 publications in the field of SD.

TABLE 4.6 The Top 5 Highly Cited Countries.

Rank	Country	Citations
1	United States	57,666
2	China	50,773
3	England	31,167
4	Germany	21,751
5	Canada	18,576

When citations are taken into consideration, a new trend is observed. Though China occupied first rank in terms of publications, as per citations, it is United States that occupies the leading position followed by China. It reveals that articles produced from United States are more impactful than other countries.

Table 4.7 depicts the connectivity analysis of top 5 countries having strong collaboration link strength with others. It is interesting to note that

United States and China with total link strengths 2963 and 2179, respectively, are having more collaboration with other countries. United States played a core role in the collaboration network and has good collaborations with other counties in general and in particular with China and England.

TABLE 4.7   The Top 5 Countries in Term of the Collaboration.

Rank	Country	Total link strength
1	United States	2963
2	England	2179
3	China	1856
4	Australia	1294
5	Germany	1293

4.3.4 INSTITUTIONS PRODUCTIVITY AND CONNECTIVITY ANALYSIS

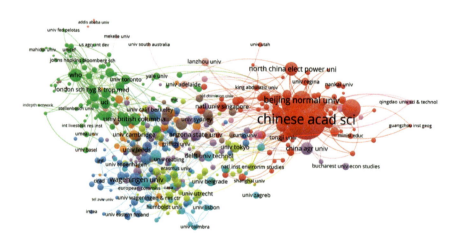

FIGURE 4.4   Institutions network of 500 nodes and 7716 links. The size of the node being proportional to the number of publications of the institutions and the thickness of the line representing the intensity of the collaborations between the institutions. Chinese Academy of Sciences is the highly publication node, whereas Chinese Academy of Sciences and University of Chinese Academy of Sciences are having more collaboration with other Institutions.

Research publications that came out in the period indicated that 11,008 institutions around the world engaged in the SD research and the top 10 productive institutions are listed in Table 4.8. Among the top 10 institutes, seven are from China, and the remaining one each from the Netherlands, Switzerland, and Canada. This reveals that China has the maximum contributors to the research publications among all the countries. As far as the number of publications is concerned, "Chinese Academy of Sciences" took the first place with 867 publications, followed by "Beijing Normal University" and "University of Chinese Academy of Sciences." When it comes to citations from institutions (as represented in Table 4.9), Chinese Academy of Sciences was the most cited institution with 13,208 citations, followed by "University of Leeds" and "Arizona State University."

TABLE 4.8   The Top 10 Productive Institutions in the Terms of the Publications.

Rank	Institution	Country	No. of Publications
1	Chinese Academy of Sciences	China	867
2	Beijing Normal University	China	231
3	University of Chinese Academy of Sciences	China	217
4	Tsinghua University	China	137
5	Peking University	China	131
6	North China Electric Power University	China	117
7	Wageningen University	The Netherlands	117
8	World Health Organization	Switzerland	106
9	China Agricultural University	China	101
10	University of British Columbia	Canada	98

TABLE 4.9   The Top 10 Highly Cited Institutions.

Rank	Institution	Citations
1	Chinese Academy of Sciences	13,208
2	University of Leeds	4098
3	Arizona State University	3829
4	Wageningen University	3687
5	Harvard University	3352

Like the country's connectivity analysis, institutions connectivity analysis was also carried out using VOSviewer and presented in Figure 4.4 and Table 4.10. It can be inferred from the figure,

- Overall, the cooperation relationships in 500 institutions were relatively intimate.
- "Chinese Academy of Sciences" and "University of Chinese Academy of Sciences" are having a large number of links in the network and have good collaboration with most of the institutes, especially with "Beijing Normal University" and "Lanzhou University."

TABLE 4.10   Top 5 Institutions in Terms of Collaboration Strength.

Institution	Total link strength
Chinese Academy of Sciences	878
University of Chinese Academy of Sciences	323
Beijing Normal University	266
World Health Organization	243
University of Washington	210

4.3.5   JOURNALS PRODUCTIVITY AND CONNECTIVITY ANALYSIS

Research output in the domain of SD is scattered through 2126 journals. The top 20 journals in the domain of SD are shown in Table 4.11. The top-ranked journals based on the count of the number of the published articles are, Sustainability, with a record of 1234, followed by Journal of Cleaner Production, with 1126 publications. It can be inferred that these two are the core journals where research relating to SD are published. It is interesting to note that as per SCImago Journal Rank (SJR) level (http://www.SCImagojr.com), the journals, Energy Policy and Ecological Economics had a higher rank (1.99 and 1.66) indicating better influence in the related research. The journals Journal of Cleaner Production and Renewable and Sustainable Energy Reviews occupied top positions in the most cited (23,986 and 20,413, respectively) journals, indicating that better quality of research being published in these two journals.

TABLE 4.11   Top 5 Journals in Term of Articles and Citations.

Articles					Citations	
Rank	Name	Articles	Country	SJR	Name	Citations
1	Sustainability	1234	Switzerland	0.54	Journal of Cleaner Production	23,986
2	Journal of Cleaner Production	1126	The Netherlands	1.47	Renewable and Sustainable Energy Reviews	20,413
3	Renewable and Sustainable Energy Reviews	569	The Netherlands	3.04	Ecological Economics	10,920
4	Energy Policy	311	United Kingdom	1.99	Energy Policy	8925
5	International Journal of Sustainable Development and World Ecology	289	United Kingdom	0.69	Journal of Environmental Management	5532

To get information about the connectivity of journals, journals' network was constructed by VOSviewer, with a threshold value of 5 as a minimum number of research publications coming out of any given journal. A simplified picture of journal connectivity is shown in Figure 4.5. It can

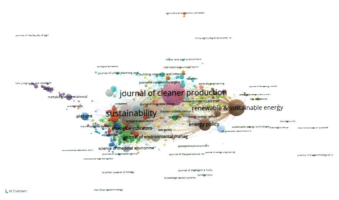

FIGURE 4.5   Journals network of 60 nodes and 5716 links. The size of the node being proportional to the number of publications published by journal and the thickness of the line representing the intensity of the collaborations between the journals. Sustainability is the highly publishing node, whereas the Journal of Cleaner Production and Sustainability are having more collaboration with other journals.

be seen from the figure that some nodes had connected with a large thick line, which indicated strong bonding between them. The journals, Journal of Cleaner Production, Sustainability and Renewable and Sustainable Energy Reviews, had strong relationships among them and had relations with almost all the journals.

4.3.6 RESEARCH HOTSPOTS AND EMERGING TREND BASED ON KEYWORDS

The keyword can be a single word or phrase that is more suitable for providing a high level of description of a document (Sudarsana et al., 2018). The analysis of keyword co-occurrences could reflect research hotspots, whereas burst words represent new research frontiers that represent words that are cited frequently in a period of time, and these parameters were analyzed for the domain of research in SD. Both CiteSpace and VOSviewer were employed to visualize analysis of keywords co-occurrence from the articles collected in the study. The hotspots of the research in the field of SD in the past decades were identified. It is to be mentioned here that WOS provides two types of keywords, namely, author keywords and keyword plus. Author keywords are prepared by collecting author-assigned keywords in the articles, whereas keyword plus is prepared by WOS for the retrieval and indexing purpose. In the present work, authors' assigned keywords were used for arriving at the keyword co-occurrence network as they reflect the author's thoughts. The keyword co-occurrence network of SD (Fig. 4.6) was constructed by the VOSviewer software. It is to be noted that (1) the size of the nodes and words in Figure 4.6 denotes proportionality to the co-occurrence frequency of that keyword, and (2) the distance between the nodes reflects the strength of the relation between them. A shorter distance generally reveals a stronger relationship. The line between the two keywords represents the co-occurrence of the words, and thickness of the line denotes frequency of the co-occurrence of the two keywords. The nodes with the same color indicate that they belong to a cluster, and all the members in the cluster can be considered as more related to each other. As can be seen in the map (Fig. 4.6), nodes such as "SD $(f = 3667)$," "sustainability $(f = 1070)$," "china $(f = 479)$," "climate change $(f = 441)$," "renewable energy $(f = 387)$," "environment $(f = 249)$," "SD goals $(f = 240)$," "energy $(f = 202)$," and "ecosystem services $(f =$

162)," have the highest frequency and these can be represented as research hotspots in the SD. The small nodes without the name reflect the fewer occurrences of these subjects in the research papers pertaining to the SD.

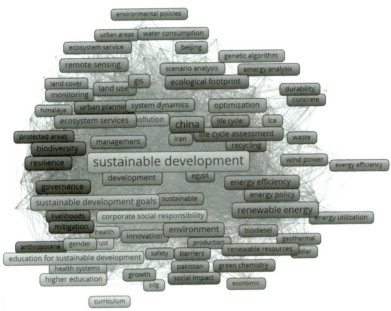

FIGURE 4.6 Keywords network of 500 nodes and 10,412 links. The size of the node being proportional to the frequency of keyword co-occurrences and the thickness of the line representing the intensity of the collaborations between the journals. SD is the highly co-occurrence node.

As per CiteSpace analysis for detecting emerging trend (as presented in Fig. 4.7), a total of 92 of the 643 keywords have occurred as citation bursts. The time interval is depicted as a blue question mark symbols. The period in which a keyword was found to have a burst is shown as a red question mark symbols, indicating the beginning year and the ending year of the duration of the burst. It can be concluded that the top 5 burst keywords were "economic growth," "sustainable development goals," "clean development mechanism," "turkey," and "education for SD," whereas, "economic growth," "sustainable development goals," "data development analysis," "ecosystem service," "sustainability assessment," and "uncertainty" are forefronts of research in the recent years.

Keywords	Year	Strength	Begin	End	2000 - 2018
economic growth	2000	17.8684	2015	2018	????????????????????
sustainable development goals (sdgs)	2000	17.0282	2016	2018	?????????????????????
clean development mechanism	2000	14.6163	2007	2010	?????????????????????
turkey	2000	14.0505	2004	2013	?????????????????????
education for sustainable development	2000	12.9302	2013	2015	?????????????????????
india	2000	11.0642	2008	2012	?????????????????????
biofuel	2000	10.7984	2008	2014	?????????????????????
higher education	2000	10.3209	2013	2016	?????????????????????
data envelopment analysis	2000	9.7065	2014	2018	?????????????????????
efficiency	2000	9.6212	2008	2011	?????????????????????
groundwater	2000	9.3029	2009	2012	?????????????????????
water quality	2000	8.9784	2011	2014	?????????????????????
exergy	2000	8.4683	2005	2009	?????????????????????
recycling	2000	8.3567	2012	2015	?????????????????????
ecosystem service	2000	8.1407	2016	2018	?????????????????????
biodiesel	2000	8.0295	2009	2011	?????????????????????
strategy	2000	7.4862	2009	2010	?????????????????????
review	2000	7.4828	2015	2016	?????????????????????
pollution	2000	7.4384	2009	2012	?????????????????????
hydropower	2000	7.3963	2007	2011	?????????????????????
environmental assessment	2000	7.3392	2003	2008	?????????????????????
agriculture	2000	7.2956	2007	2010	?????????????????????
vulnerability	2000	7.197	2015	2016	?????????????????????
conservation	2000	7.0712	2010	2013	?????????????????????
cleaner production	2000	6.9966	2004	2007	?????????????????????
management	2000	6.9744	2001	2012	?????????????????????
university	2000	6.966	2013	2015	?????????????????????
rural development	2000	6.7094	2012	2013	?????????????????????
decision making	2000	6.5143	2013	2015	?????????????????????
public policy	2000	6.4088	2002	2006	?????????????????????
environmental impact assessment	2000	6.1927	2007	2010	?????????????????????
renewable energy source	2000	6.1702	2011	2013	?????????????????????
natural resource	2000	6.0764	2006	2011	?????????????????????
energy consumption	2000	6.038	2014	2016	?????????????????????
biogas	2000	6.0266	2012	2015	?????????????????????
environmental policy	2000	5.7846	2000	2010	?????????????????????
eco-efficiency	2000	5.7397	2010	2013	?????????????????????
ecosystem	2000	5.7178	2000	2007	?????????????????????
evaluation	2000	5.6119	2008	2012	?????????????????????
tourism	2000	5.6093	2009	2010	?????????????????????
sustainability assessment	2000	5.6	2015	2018	?????????????????????
bioenergy	2000	5.5994	2008	2011	?????????????????????
social-ecological system	2000	5.5553	2014	2016	?????????????????????
mining	2000	5.4132	2003	2006	?????????????????????
modelling	2000	5.1933	2007	2012	?????????????????????
ecological footprint	2000	5.165	2009	2013	?????????????????????
sustainable building	2000	5.1284	2005	2006	?????????????????????
uncertainty	2000	5.1099	2014	2018	?????????????????????
ecosystem management	2000	5.0707	2000	2003	?????????????????????
resilience	2000	5.0621	2013	2015	?????????????????????
sustainability indicator	2000	5.0359	2001	2009	?????????????????????
brazil	2000	5.0009	2004	2007	?????????????????????
renewable resource	2000	4.9841	2008	2010	?????????????????????
eco-industrial park	2000	4.9164	2004	2009	?????????????????????
risk assessment	2000	4.8886	2005	2007	?????????????????????
regional development	2000	4.8789	2001	2009	?????????????????????
deforestation	2000	4.8789	2001	2009	?????????????????????
electricity	2000	4.8146	2009	2011	?????????????????????
simulation	2000	4.7933	2007	2012	?????????????????????
natural capital	2000	4.6107	2003	2010	?????????????????????
forestry	2000	4.5849	2002	2008	?????????????????????
decision support system	2000	4.5572	2000	2010	?????????????????????
environmental sustainability	2000	4.5171	2012	2014	?????????????????????
indigenous knowledge	2000	4.5023	2009	2010	?????????????????????
land use change	2000	4.4362	2015	2018	?????????????????????
mitigation	2000	4.4349	2001	2009	?????????????????????
decision-making	2000	4.4098	2000	2005	?????????????????????
sustainability science	2000	4.3867	2009	2013	?????????????????????

FIGURE 4.7 Keywords' burst-detection based on WOS data. The time interval is depicted as a blue question mark symbols. The period in which a keyword was found to have a burst is shown as a red question mark symbols segment, indicating the beginning year and the ending year of the duration of the burst.

4.3.7 DOCUMENT CITATION ANALYSIS

The most cited articles are usually regarded as landmarks due to their ground-breaking contributions (Chen et al., 2012). To identify the most influential research papers among in the field of SD, a total of 17,115 articles, in the time span of 2000–2018 and a threshold of 10 citations, were analyzed using VOSviewer.

The top 10 papers with the most citations were selected for further analysis. Table 4.12 shows the highly cited papers with the details like title, journal, authors, and year of publication and citations. There were five highly cited papers published in 2000–2006, and the rest were published 2007–2018. Among the 10 highly cited papers, 3 were single author publications and 7 were coauthored papers.

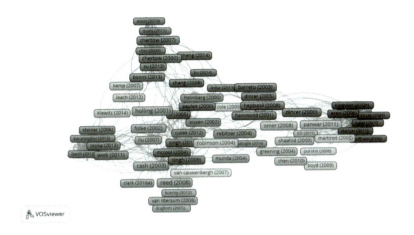

TABLE 4.12 The Top 10 Articles in the Terms of Citations.

Rank	Title	Journal	Authors	Year	Citation
1	Understanding the complexity of economic, ecological, and social systems	Ecosystems	CS. Holling	2001	1275
2	Stakeholder participation for environmental management: a literature review	Biological conservation	Mark S. Reed	2008	1226
3	Knowledge systems for sustainable development	Proceedings of the national academy of sciences of the United States of America	DW Cash et al.	2003	1212
4	Resilience and sustainable development: building adaptive capacity in a world of transformation	Ambio	C. Folke et al.	2002	827
5	Plant oil renewable resources as green alternatives in polymer science	Chemical society reviews	Michael A. R. Meier et al.	2007	785
6	Ecology—economic reasons for conserving wild nature	Science	A. Balmford et al.	2002	714

TABLE 4.12   *(Continued)*

Rank	Title	Journal	Authors	Year	Citation
7	Life cycle assessment part 1: framework, goal and scope definition, inventory analysis, and applications	Environment international	G. Rebitzer et al.	2004	654
8	Role of renewable energy sources in environmental protection: a review	Renewable and sustainable energy reviews	N. I. Panwar et al.	2011	652
9	Redefining innovation— eco-innovation research and the contribution from ecological economics	Ecological economics	R. Kennings	2000	590
10	Sustainable supply chains: an introduction	Journal of operations management	Jonathan D. Linton et al.	2007	590

4.4   KEY FINDINGS

The major outcome of the study carried out in the present work is summarized next:

Though there is a steady growth in the number of publications, the citations have seen a steep decrease after 2013. Citation per paper has also a continuous decrease after 2005. China emerged as the leading country in terms of publications, whereas United States found to be the country with most impactful research, and it has a strong relationship with other countries, especially with China and England. As per the productivity and influence of the leading researchers identified in author's collaboration network analysis, Yong Geng, Jian Zuo, and Donald Huisingh were the top 3 productivity authors in this field. Wei Wang, Yong Geng, and Rodrigo Lozano were the top 3 most cited authors. The most influencing author was found to be Yong Geng, which indicated that all highly productive researchers have received the same high level of influence. Among the top 10 institutes, seven are from China, and the remaining one each from the Netherlands, Switzerland, and Canada. With regards to the most productive and connectivity of the institutions, Chinese Academy of Sciences, Beijing Normal University, and University of Chinese Academy of Sciences were found to be the top 3 productivity institutions in terms of publications and Chinese Academy of Sciences being a top-cited institution. However, Chinese Academy of Sciences, University of Chinese Academy of Sciences, and Beijing Normal University are having good collaboration with most of the institutes. Journals such as Sustainability, Journal of Cleaner Production, Renewable and Sustainable Energy Reviews, and Energy Policy were found to be the top journals in which the research on SD is being published. Among these, Journal of Cleaner Production, Renewable and Sustainable Energy Reviews, and Ecological Economics have received high citations. With regards to emerging trends, "economic growth," "sustainable development goals," "data envelopment analysis," "ecosystem service," "sustainability assessment," and "uncertainty" are forefronts of research in recent years. Mapping of intellectual structure of SD research provides us useful insights to observe and consider the research focus of the scholarly publications. In this chapter, we used scientometric indicators and visualization tools to conduct a quantitative as well as visual study of SD research, and we hope it would be useful to those who are concerned about the issues of SD.

KEYWORDS

- **sustainable development**
- **CiteSpace**
- **VOSviewer**
- **intellectual structures**
- **scientometric analysis**

REFERENCES

Chen, C. *The CiteSpace Manual v1.05*; College of Computing and Informatics, Drexel University, 2015; p 102. http://cluster.ischool.drexel.edu/~cchen/citespace/manual/CiteSpaceManual.pdf[accessed 2020-09-18]

Cobo, M. J.; López-Herrera, A. G.; Herrera-Viedma, E.; Herrera, E. Science Mapping Software Tools: Review, Analysis, and Cooperative Study among Tools. *J. Am. Soc. Inf. Sci. Technol.* **2011,** *62* (7), 1382–1402.

Emas, R. *Brief for GSDR 2015 the Concept of Sustainable Development: Definition and Defining Principles*, 2015.

Fang, Y.; Yin, J.; Wu, B. Climate Change and Tourism: A Scientometric Analysis Using CiteSpace. *J. Sustainable Tourism* **2017**, *1* (1), 1–19.

Hassan, S.; Haddawy, P.; Zhu, J. A Bibliometric Study of the World's Research Activity in Sustainable Development and Its Sub-areas Using Scientific Literature. *Scientometrics* **2013**, *99*, 549–579.

Klarin, T. The Concept of Sustainable Development : From Its Beginning to the Contemporary Issues. *Zagreb Int. Rev. Econ. Bus.* **2018**, *21* (1), 67–94.

Office, T. H. E.; The, O. F., General, C., Patents, O. F., Marks, T., Indications, G. *Annual Report*, 2016.

Redclift, M. The Meaning of Sustainable Development. *Geoforum* **1992**, *23* (3), 395–403.

Shah, M. M. Sustainable Development Sustainable. In *Encyclopedia of Ecology*, Jørgensen, S. E.; Fath, B. D., Eds. 2008. Academic Press. http://doi.org/https://doi.org/10.1016/B978-008045405-4.00633-9

Song, J.; Zhang, H.; Dong, W. A Review of Emerging Trends in Global PPP Research: Analysis and Visualization. *Scientometrics* **2016**, *107* (3), 1111–1147.

Sudarsana, D.; Meenachi, N. M.; Venkatesh, T.; Gunta, V.; Gowtham, R.; Sai Baba, M. Method for Automatic Key Concepts Extraction: Application to Documents in the Domain of Nuclear Reactors. *Electron. Libr.* **2018**, *37* (1), 2–15. doi:10.1108/EL-01-2018-0012.

United Nations General Assembly. *Report of the World Commission on Environment and Development: Our Common Future*; United Nations General Assembly, Development and International Co-operation: Environment: Oslo, Norway, 1987.

Van Eck, N. J.; Waltman, L. Software Survey: VOSviewer, a Computer Program for Bibliometric Mapping. *Scientometrics* **2010**, *84* (2), 523–538. doi:10.1007/s11192-009-0146-3.

Van Eck, N. J.; Waltman, L. VOSviewer : A Computer Program for Bibliometric Mappin, 2009. http://hdl.handle.net/1765/14841.

CHAPTER 5

Case Study on Exploring Suitability of Sustainable Agriculture in Western Rajasthan

RAJASHREE BANERJEE[1], TAMOGHNA ACHARYYA[1*], and
PRERNA AGARWAL[2]

[1]*School of Sustainability, Xavier University Bhubaneswar, Odisha, India*

[2]*URMUL Seemant Samiti, URMUL Trust, Bikaner, Rajasthan*

Corresponding author. E-mail: acharyyat@xsos.edu.in

ABSTRACT

The scarcity of water has always been persistent all over the world; this has been witnessed more in western parts of Rajasthan that lie within the inhospitable area of the Thar Desert. The Thar Desert is one of the most densely populated deserts in the world with the main occupations of its inhabitants being agriculture and animal husbandry; the secondary occupation involves being labors in brick factory. Animal husbandry, trees and grasses, intercropped with vegetables or fruit trees, is the most viable model for arid, drought-prone regions. Owing to climate change, the rainfall in this area has been unpredictable and hence agriculture is becoming tougher in this region.

This report deals with the various initiatives taken by URMUL Seemant Samiti in the field of agricultural advancement and the adversity faced in the operation of seed bank and Azolla farming. It also deals with the future propositions of climate smart farming through in-house mushroom farming and growing their local crops like Sangri, local berries and set up an industry for food processing the said items.

The current venture of URMUL is to form an enterprise and all the project pertaining to agriculture will come under this enterprise.

The basic aim of this paper is to depict the initiatives of sustainable agriculture and hence depict the economic growth in the dry areas of Thar.

5.1 INTRODUCTION

Agricultural practices still continue to occupy pivotal position in the Indian dual economy in as much as it continues to be the main source of livelihood for majority of Indian. It contributes around 23% of the GDP and employs 65% of the work force in the country (https://www.omicsonline.org/ open-access/agriculture-role-on-indian-economy-2151-6219-1000176. php?aid=62176). Significant measures have been taken in the field of agriculture; green revolution is one such example. Now after 72 years of independence, this shortage of food has been changed into food surplus, and India is emerging as one of the major agricultural power.

Rajasthan is the largest state of India. Out of the total geographical area in the State, even 50% is not cultivable and within the 50% that falls under the cultivable land, soil fertility varies considerably across districts. The main difference for the varying soil fertility is a result of the sandy soil and varying amount of rainfall. The wide variation in land productivity indicates the difference in soil health across districts in the State.

Rajasthan is an agrarian state, where 80% of the total population resides in the rural area and largely dependent on agriculture as the source of their livelihood. The economy of state is mostly depended on agriculture. Nearly 22.5% of state's GDP comes from agriculture.

A chief requisite of agriculture is the availability of water which is not equally distributed in every parts of India. Majority of the districts of north-west Rajasthan, which include Bikaner and Jaisalmer, experience a tropical desert climate, thereby remaining extremely cold in the months of October to February while it is extremely hot (Temp range with average) from March to September. Rainfall in Rajasthan is very scanty; therefore, it suffers from drought. Monsoon occurs during the month of July and August, but western Rajasthan receives the scantiest rainfall. Bikaner is one of the districts to receive least annual rainfall, that is, 241 mm (climate-data.org). Therefore, agriculture is difficult and produce is less.

In northwest Rajasthan, only 20% of the total land can be cultivated. Droughts are common in the western part, and Rajasthan has received some of the severe droughts in the last few decades. Due to unstable, unpredictable, and scanty rain, farmers depend mainly on ground water agriculture. With the decreasing ground water level, the farmers in the state are increasingly depending on surface water received from the rivers of Punjab in the north, River Narmada in the south, and the Agra Canal from Haryana and Uttar Pradesh. Northwestern Rajasthan is irrigated by the Indira Gandhi Canal. Irrigation is done through electric pumps.

Indira Gandhi Canal—The Indira Gandhi Canal irrigates a vast amount of land in the Indian portion of the Thar. The canal begins at the Harike Barrage—at the confluence of the Sutlej and Beas rivers in the Indian Punjab—and continues in a southwesterly direction for some 290 miles (470 km). (https://www.britannica.com/place/Thar-Desert#ref138038)

5.1.1   TYPES OF CROP GROWN IN WESTERN RAJASTHAN

Rabi crops: These are basically crops that are dependent on ground water. Also known as winter crop, these are cultivated in the month of October–November and cultivated in March–April. The crops sown during rabi season are barley, wheat, gram, pulses, and major oil seeds include rape and mustard.

Khariff crops: These are the rainfed crops the seeds of which are sown in the months of June and July and harvested in the months of September and October. The availability of rain determines their production. The crops of this season include bajra, pulses, jowar, maize, and ground nuts.

5.1.2   EVOLUTION OF AGRICULTURE IN RAJASTHAN

Green revolution in Punjab and Haryana involved using high-quality seeds and pesticides in production. Therefore, after the construction of Indira Gandhi Canal in Rajasthan which ensured surface water in the north-west (NW) Rajasthan, Rajasthan started farming as per their neighboring states Punjab and Haryana. However, there lies a quality difference between the soil fertility of Punjab and Thar Desert. The desert soil is sandy and very porous, which can retain the fertilizers for a longer time degrading the soil quality further. When this problem was realized, in order to maintain agriculture sustainability in NW Rajasthan and mitigate the environmental ill-effects, measures such as water efficient irrigation (sprinkle/drip irrigation), organic farming, green manure, cultivating climate resilient crops, and maintaining healthy seed bank started to come into place. URMUL, a local NGO functioning from 1994, is trying to bring the theoretical practices of sustainable agriculture into practice. It has initiated several agricultural interventions in and around Bajju (an area which comes within 70 km of the Indo-Pak border) such as seed bank, organic and climate smart farming, zero expense farming, and circular economy. The main factor acting behind URMUL's intervention is to ensure a constant income and help maintain the livelihoods of the local. This book chapter gives an account of these interventions, analyzes its financial viability, and suggests future directions.

5.2   METHODOLOGY

The study was mainly conducted in Bajju Tehsil in Kolayat Taluk of Bikaner district of Rajasthan (Fig. 5.1) in collaboration with URMUL Seemant Samiti from December 1, 2018 to January 1, 2019 for a period of 1 month.

URMUL Seemant Samiti is a registered nongovernmental non-profit-making organization working in northwestern part of Rajasthan in India. URMUL Seemant Samiti, Bajju came into existence as an independent organization in 1994 and was formally registered in 1995. They mainly work for capacity building, the recent addition being their ventures in agriculture where they are trying to build models of natural farming and forming SHGs to implement the same.

5.2.1 OBJECTIVES

This study was conducted with the following objectives in mind, and the end result was a case study:

- To explore the challenges of agriculture in western Rajasthan
- To prepare the crop calendar for western Rajasthan.

- To document the traditional farming practices that is done and the ways this principles can be clubbed with the organic farming.
- To assess advantages, challenges and risks of seed bank pertaining to sustainable agriculture through SWOT analysis.
- To build an operational model of the seed bank that will operate from Bajju and the model of which will be implemented in other URMUL centers.

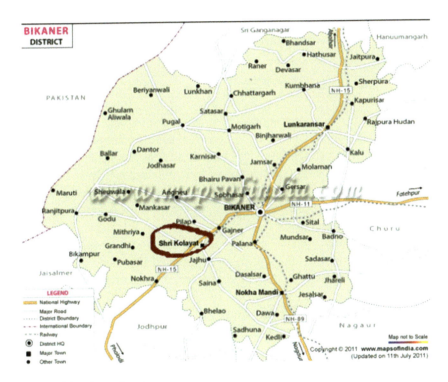

FIGURE 5.1 Area of study.

5.2.1.1 METHODOLOGIES

The following methodologies were used to conduct the study for primary and secondary data collections.

Primary data	Questionnaire: In order to collect primary data from the focus area, a questionnaire was developed to collect the information (Annexure 5.1).
	Focused group discussions (five members)
	Interview-based survey: Interview-based survey was conducted in the villages, and data was collected after conducting personal interviews with the residents of the three villages
Secondary data	Review of various reports and papers based on sustainable agriculture, pollination, indigenous knowledge in the western Himalayas, etc. was done to collect the information
PRA tools	Semi-structured interview (SSI)
	Resource map
	Crop calendar

PRA refers to participatory rural appraisal, which "is a growing combination of approaches and methods that enable rural people to share, enhance and analyze their knowledge of life and conditions, to plan and act and to monitor and evaluate. The role of the outsider is that of a catalyst, a facilitator of processes within a community which is prepared to alter their situation" (Cavestro). Elaborating on the tools used pertaining to the project under study were,

Semi-structured interview: A semi-structured interviewing and listening technique involves having a predefined boundary for questions to be asked but letting the flow of conversation go normally though carefully controlled.

Crop Calendar: The construction of crop calendar was done in order to determine the trends and patterns in the village with respect to agricultural utilities, such as the rainfall distribution, agricultural production, food availability, work distribution, etc.

Resource Map: The Village Resource Map is a tool that helps learn about a community and its resource base. The primary concern is not to develop an accurate map but to get useful information about local perceptions of resources".(Cavestro)

5.2.2 QUESTIONNAIRE

The following questions were asked during the interview to do a need assessment of the seed bank

1. Name and Village they belong to
2. Family Members Count
3. Sources of Income
4. Landholding
5. Crops they grow and pesticides and fertilizers they use
6. Member/Non Member of Seed Bank
7. If they are the member why did they invest in the seed bank
8. Why they did not buy seed from the seed bank inspite of investing in it
9. How do they procure seed
10. Where do they sell their produce

The discussions helped us to ascertain the crops they grow and the seed they want to take from the seed bank. Future forecasting for any form of transaction in seeds and the need assessment leading to eventual planning is required to reduce the hassles and uncertainties of the functioning of seed bank in the future.

Further the data collected of 98 farmers helped us to ascertain our findings and find feasible solutions to combat the underneath problems of agriculture. Some of the findings are mentioned underneath.

5.2.3 ANALYTICS OF THE TARGET GROUP

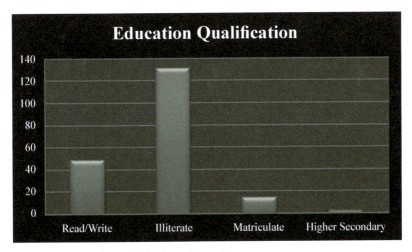

FIGURE 5.2   Education qualification of interviwee.

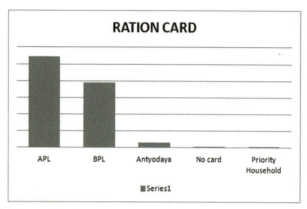

FIGURE 5.3   Income level.

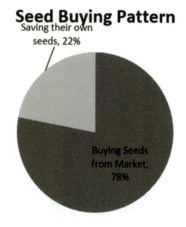

FIGURE 5.4   Seed buying pattern.

Land holdings	
No. of farmers	**Land holding (Bigha)**
39	0–10
24	10–20
25	20–30
4	30–40
3	40–50
2	50–60
1	90–100

5.3   RESEARCH AND DISCUSSION

- Farmers face a lot of difficulty in buying seeds because of the present of middlemen in the system. This vicious process of manhandling by middlemen is not limited to Rajasthan but whole of India. The scenario in Rajasthan is that farmers get very easy access to loans from the local money "lenders" but on one condition that is they will sell their produce to them, and when they sell it, they get much lower rate. Therefore, they have lesser amount of money to buy the seeds.
- The local money lender lends money at an interest of 2–3% compounded monthly, so by the time they pay their debt, their debt sums up to a humongous amount.
- Soil productivity varies widely in Rajasthan, and the situation has been worsened in the present time due to excessive use of fertilizers and even lesser rainfall as an effect of climate change.

Some of the ideas that were proposed to mitigate the solution and have been started and operating successfully are as follows:

5.3.1   *SUSTAINABILITY THROUGH MULTICROPPING AND ORGANIC FARMING*

Initially people in Rajasthan used to do Birani kheti, that is, they used to depend solely on rain water for their cultivation. But with the formation of Indira Gandhi Canal, they have started Nehri kheti (using both canal and rain water). So in this present condition, they have fixed source of water. Having a fixed supply of water empowered them to imitate Punjab and Haryana's way of agriculture.

In 2018, the water level of the canal has gone down and chemical fertilizers have done considerable harm to the soil. Another harm that has been caused is due to mono-cropping in the form of cultivation of cash crops. People now prefer growing crops that can be commercially sold, and as a result, the soil does not get replenished by the nutrients as only one crop is being grown. Traditional crop cycle was designed to ensure soil replenishment and ensuring fertility. A good example is the local crop grown like chena takes up a lot of nutrients from the soil, which is replenished by peanuts. But due to mono-cropping, crop rotation is not done, which decreases the soil fertility.

To mitigate the ill-effect, government has given impetus to sustainable farming, and URMUL Trust has incorporated sustainable agriculture as one of its pilot projects to ensure capacity building. It has also received grants from Oracle to promote off-grid sustainable Farming in north-west Rajasthan. Organic farming has been one of the priority areas of the state government in agriculture sector. Organic farming promotional activities have been taken up under state plan by the recent government as it reduces cost of production. Government has formed SHGs to promote organic farming implementation. Government is giving 50% assistance of up to Rs. 2000 at successful implementation site. For this mission, at least Rs. 50 lakh have been proposed by the government. To promote organic farming among farmers, an incentive of Rs. 8000 per ha per farmer will be provided as promised by the government. During 2015–2016, the pilot programme was done in 10 districts with 1630 ha area and provision of Rs 185.00 lakh.

The crop calendar is maintained to ensure crop rotation and a healthy crop growth.

Using organic fertilizers: Organic farming involves developing organic fertilizers and pesticides which is self-sustaining. Some of the fertilizers that have had a good result in parts of India are,

Jivamrita: Jivamrita is a fermented microbial culture. It provides nutrients, but most importantly, acts as a catalytic agent that promotes the activity of microorganisms in the soil, as well as increases earthworm activity; during the 48-h fermentation process, the aerobic and anaerobic bacteria present in the cow dung and urine multiply as they eat up organic ingredients (like pulse flour). A handful of undisturbed soil is also added to the preparation, as inoculate of native species of microbes and organisms. Jivamrita also helps to prevent fungal and bacterial plant diseases. The maker, Sulabh Palekar, suggests that Jivamrita is only needed for the first 3 years of the transition, after which the system becomes self-sustaining. To prepare Jivamrita, 200 L of water in a barrel, 10 kg fresh local cow dung and 5–10 L aged cow urine, 2 kg of pulse flour, a handful of soil from the bund of the farm, and 2 kg of jaggery (a local type of brown sugar) are added, and the solution is stirred well and let to ferment for 48 h in the shade to be ready for application. An amount of 200 L of Jivamrita is sufficient for one acre of land. Jivamrita can be applied to the crops twice a month in the irrigation water or as a 10% foliar spray (http://www.fao.org/3/a-bl990e.pdf)

Crop	Jan	Feb	Mar	Apr	May	June	July	Aug	Sept	Oct	Nov	Dec
Guvar	–	–	–	–	–	Sowing	Sowing	Growth	Growth	Growth	Harvesting	–
Peanut	–	–	–	–	Sowing	Sowing	Growth	Growth	Growth	Growth	Harvesting	–
Bajra	Harvesting	–	–	–	–	–	Sowing	Sowing	Growth	Growth	Growth	Growth
Moth	–				–	Sowing	Growth	Growth	Growth	Growth	Harvesting	–
Til	–				–	Sowing	Growth	Growth	Growth	Growth	Harvesting	–
Moong	–	–	–	–	–	Sowing	Growth	Growth	Growth	Growth	Harvesting	–
Makki	Growth	Growth	Growth	Harvesting	–	–	–	–	–	–	Sowing	Growth
Chana	Growth	Growth	Harvesting	Harvesting	–	–	–	–	–	Sowing	Growth	Growth
Sarson	Growth	Growth	Harvesting	Harvesting	–	–	–	–	–	Sowing	Growth	Growth
Gehu	Growth	Growth	Harvesting	Harvesting	–	–	–	–	–	Sowing	Growth	Growth
Jeera	Growth	Growth	Harvesting	Harvesting	–	–	–	–	–	Sowing	Growth	Growth
Methi	Growth	Growth	Harvesting	Harvesting	–	–	–	–	–	Sowing	Growth	Growth

Bijamrita: It is a treatment used for seeds, seedlings, or any planting material. Bijamrita is effective in protecting young roots from fungus as well as from soil-borne and seed-borne diseases that commonly affect plants after the monsoon period. It is composed of similar ingredients as Jivamrita—local cow dung, a powerful natural fungicide, and cow urine, a strong antibacterial liquid, lime, and soil. Bijamrita is added to the seeds of any crop: coating and mixing by hand; drying them well and using them for sowing (http://www.fao.org/3/a-bl990e.pdf)

5.3.2   SUSTAINABILITY THROUGH SEED BANK

Seed forms the fundamental and integral part of food chain, and any disruption will result in a catastrophic event. It is the basis of regeneration and holds the power of biodiversity. These are primary reasons why it's necessary to preserve the seed, and it is this need through which the concept of 'seed bank' emerged. In Rajasthan, therefore, it becomes a necessity to build a seed bank to maintain the diversity of crops that grow here but not in any other region. Seed banks help the small and marginal farmers in growing local crops thus saving indigenous species with the help of farmer community. Community seed banks assist local farmers to barter local seed, thereby facilitating informal seed distribution that has been practiced in villages since ancient time. This distribution of seeds maintained by local farmers helps in their socio-economic development and also local seed quality is maintained

URMUL is a well-known nongovernmental organization with a substantial presence in the remote villages Bikaner district. URMUL is already involved in activities related to organic farming and dairy farming; it has good connections with farmers of the nearby villages. The main agenda of these seed bank initiatives to facilitate farmers with various livelihood support options to increase their income. The process of seed bank in this case involved initial buying and storing of seeds by the community in large quantity at the Bajju premise to ensure that planting material is available and then in the following years maintaining the seed flow in the farmer community. Bajju community seed bank thought of dealing only with indigenous seed to ensure local seed security and converse their traditional way of farming. It will help in maintaining the ecological biodiversity as a result.

URMUL put forward certain conditions to functionalize its seed bank. General conditionality's of seed bank:

- Making organic farming compulsory
- Maintaining nearly 10% of the agricultural land to double the seed productivity
- Having a fixed amount deposited (Rs. 1000 per annum in case of URMUL) which acts as an asset while taking seeds
- Maintaining the seed flow in the seed bank.
- Communication among stakeholders for smooth functioning.

Prerequisite for setting up a seed bank:

- Using non-hybrid non-GMO seed
- Storage at a cool place
- Avoid humidity, that is, storing seeds at dry places
- Seeds should be stored away from direct sunlight

In case of URMUL, the community seed bank is 1 year in running. They had procured nearly 50 quintals of Guar seed to initiate the process but failed to capture the market despite of interest among the local communities due to interventions of middle men.

5.3.3 SUSTAINABILITY THROUGH DIARY

URMUL has a diary within a campus and trying to run the model of circular economy. The cows present in the campus help in making fertilizers, and they get the fodder through the produce.

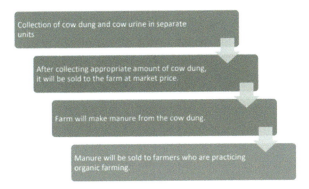

Collection of cow dung and cow urine in separate units

After collecting appropriate amount of cow dung, it will be sold to the farm at market price.

Farm will make manure from the cow dung.

Manure will be sold to farmers who are practicing organic farming.

5.3.4   SUSTAINABILITY THROUGH PROMOTION OF LOCAL PRODUCT AND CLIMATE SMART FARMING

5.3.4.1   CLIMATE SMART FARMING—INDOOR MUSHROOM CULTIVATION

Context:

Mushroom cultivation is very new concept when it comes to the western parts of Rajasthan, because of the existing weather conditions and because of the scarcity of water and lesser fertile land. If URMUL Seemant starts mushroom cultivation under sustainable farming, it will have a first mover advantage, since it will be the only supplier of mushroom in this region. Also being a pioneer helps to tap the tier 2 and 3 cities in Rajasthan without any existing competition. URMUL can start with tapping the local market in Rajasthan but not just limit itself to that. The shelf life of mushrooms is very limited and they get spoilt in a few days; however, if packaged properly, the shelf life of mushrooms can be increased and it can be sent to other major Tier 1 cities too. The market for mushrooms is huge, so even if the supply is more than the demand, URMUL can always move the yield to Delhi for sale where the mushroom demand exists in plenty already. This plan is based on organically growing mushrooms without the use of pesticides and other harmful chemicals. The organic production of mushrooms can become as a huge USP for URMUL Seemant as there is an ever growing acceptance toward everything organic in the cities these days. Also, if the mushrooms are marketed well and if nutritional facts and the impacts are spread in the villages, it will not be very difficult to create a market for mushrooms. An advantage about mushroom cultivation is the ease with which it can be grown by controlling the climatic conditions. Mushroom farming requires a humid temperature that can be created manually; hence, it is easy to manage the conditions in which mushrooms can be grown. Mushroom farming is easiest to implement and high-profit-making activity that can be performed with a limited amount of daily supervision. If done right, the profits margins in mushroom farming are huge; hence, it can be started by URMUL Seemant as a social entrepreneurship program where URMUL can train the local farmers and can help them in supplementing their already existing income to facilitate community and livelihood development.

5.3.4.1.1 Steps in mushroom farming

- Spawns of mushroom can be prepared or bought from market but at initial stage, buying is an economical option. One bottle of mushroom spawns of good quality comes at a price around Rs. 18 per bottle.
- To plant the mushroom, straw beds are needed. For making the straw bed, first the straw is treated with an aqueous solution of calcium carbonate and then dried. It is not necessary to completely dry the straw as it stores the moisture.
- The straws are packed closely and mushroom seeds are added in a circumferential way along with casing soil, manure and wheat flour, which promotes the rapid growth of mushroom. Up to three layers are stacked in one bed, yielding a minimum of 3 kg mushroom.
- After the layers are set, the whole system is wrapped in a polythene that maintains the humidity that is a prerequisite for the growth of mushroom.
- Small pores on polythene ensure humidity, which promotes growth.
- Temperature needed during fruiting should be around 28–35 °C.
- To ensure the quality of mushroom grown, everyday monitoring during the fruiting time is required. Water droplets on the healthy surface ensure good quality, but black patches on the straw bed is a clear indication that the mushrooms have rotten out and the complete bed must be removed to prevent further damage.
- As the mushroom grows, the pores are made big using knifes, and after 21 days, the polythene bags are removed to ensure total growth.
- Mushroom grows within a month. While picking up mushroom, care should be taken to choose only the healthy mushroom and not pick mushroom that have black edges or are excessive mushy.

5.3.4.1.2 Mushroom Cultivation Cost Analysis

Assumptions for the calculation: The following points have been kept in mind for undertaking the calculations presented previously:

1. The following calculations have been done for 8 months, that is, (August–March) when the mushroom farming has been considered the most suitable keeping in mind the weather conditions.

2. In the calculations following, it is assumed that there will be 100 beds of mushroom; each of these 100 beds will yield 3 kg of mushroom in a month; therefore, 300 kg of mushroom will be the yield per month.

3. The overall yield for 8 months is taken at 2400 kg (refer to the previous point).

4. The selling price used for the calculation is Rs. 50/kg which is taken as the most competitive market price.

5. All the costs mentioned previously have been taken through competitive secondary sources and previous studies undertaken regarding mushroom farming.

5.3.4.2 SANGRI FARMING AND PACKAGING

Context:

Sangri or *Prosopis cineraria* is a small to medium-sized tree found mainly in the Thar Desert. Its trade name is kandi. It grows in dry and arid regions of India mainly Rajasthan, Haryana, and Punjab. Since it is local product found in abundance in this region, there was a thought of commercializing it and adding value by processing the same to create different products that can be widely sold in the market (epdf.tips).

URMUL Seemant can start the processing for Sangri, which will help them to have a first mover advantage in this region. This pioneer move will help to create a market and explore what products match the customer demands with minimum or no amount of existing competition in this area.

The biggest advantage of selling Sangri is the product diversification that is possible. Sangri is consumed as a vegetable in Rajasthan, but not only that, it can be used to make chutney, pickles, chips and since it has many inherent medicinal properties it has been used for pregnancy as well as for curing leprosy, dysentery, bronchitis, asthma, leukoderma, piles, and tremors of the muscles (http://rapidorganic.blogspot.com/2012/04/organic-ker-kumtiya-sangri-in-rajasthan.html).

Being a local product that has been found and grown in this region for years, there exists a lot of prior knowledge regarding how it needs to be grown and what its uses are, which acts as an added advantage for URMUL in terms of availability and procurement of the raw materials.

Apart from all the advantages mentioned previously, these products are widely accepted in the northern parts of India, so URMUL can market these products easily within and outside Rajasthan to begin with and will have a lot of scope for expansion.

Part of the yield of Sangri is used in vegetables, and the remaining yield is wasted since there is no way to store or process the entire yield. If URMUL starts this initiative, it can act as a processing unit where it buys the Sangri from the farmers and processes it for further sale, and this will help in facilitating the income of the farmers and will help URMUL achieve its objective of livelihood and community development.

5.4 CONCLUSION

Seeing the previous case, it can very easily be said that if conventional or inorganic farming involving a lot of pesticide continues to be used, the future is unsustainable. It is also not true that organic farming is not economically viable, but at the same time, a lot of work needs to be done to functionalize organic farming in India.

As of for Rajasthan, its climate supports the traditional crops like Sangri, mustard, and rape seeds, and hence to sustain agriculture maintaining the fertility, it becomes a necessity to shift to traditional way of farming which involved crop rotation.

KEYWORDS

- Thar
- Rajasthan
- sustainable agriculture
- animal husbandry
- crops

WORKS CITED

Cavestro, 2. (n.d.).
epdf.tips. (n.d.).
http://rapidorganic.blogspot.com/2012/04/organic-ker-kumtiya-sangri-in-rajasthan.html.
    (n.d.).
http://www.fao.org/3/a-bl990e.pdf. (n.d.).
https://www.britannica.com/place/Thar-Desert#ref138038. (n.d.).

CHAPTER 6

Exploration of a Sustainable Business Assessment Plan for Setting Up a Dyeing Plant: Discussions from the Case of Western Rajasthan

ISHITA GUPTA[1], TAMOGHNA ACHARYYA[1,*], and PRERNA AGARWAL[2]

[1]*School of Sustainability, Xavier University Bhubaneswar, Odisha, India*

[2]*URMUL Seemant Samiti, URMUL Trust, Bikaner, Rajasthan*

Corresponding author. E-mail: acharyyat@xsos.edu.in

ABSTRACT

The Thar is one of the most heavily populated desert areas in the world where the livelihood of the people mainly revolves around agriculture and animal husbandry. Agriculture is not a dependable proposition in this area because after the rainy season, at least one third of crops fail. Owing to climate change, the rainfall in this area has been unpredictable, too. Uttar Rajasthan Cooperative Milk Union Limited (URMUL), a registered, not-for-profit local organization started to facilitate the income of the communities situated in this area by diversifying their sources of income. Considering the locally available raw materials, human skills and markets, URMUL decided to focus on promoting the dyeing and block printing unit to aim at empowering women and making them independent. This research studies the set-up of a small natural dyeing plant in a village in Western Rajasthan (Runiya Barawas) which will provide a steady source of income and employment to the locals (Ojha, 2014). Our analysis shows that setting up of the dyeing plant is very much feasible and breakeven is expected to reach within 7 month. This unit will make optimal utilization of water and other locally available raw materials of organic origin. It can also help local women to be independent, thus, to be able to support their family through their own income.

6.1 INTRODUCTION

The scarcity of consumable water has always existed all over the world especially in the arid and semiarid regions (Bhandari, 2016; Chaudhry, 2013). Runiya Barawas is located in the west of Rajasthan where the scarcity of water has been a persistent problem. Agriculture is not considered to be the most reliable source of income. There was a need to provide the people with an alternative source of livelihood through which the economic status could be uplifted (Garrett, 2011) leading to overall improvement in the village. Given the harsh physical geography of the Thar Desert Uttar Rajasthan Cooperative Milk Union Limited (URMUL) Seemant Samiti, a registered, not-for-profit local organization initiated to offer food, fodder, and water security to the local people (Ojha and Mishra, 1982; 2011). Considering the locally available raw materials, human skills, and markets, URMUL began its first income-generating activity for enhancing the household income of the rural people of the region viz. the enterprise of spinning wool (Mahala, 2002). URMUL identified the poor families to be involved in the activity (Ojha and Mishra, 2011). The need for setting up a dyeing unit came about because the major source of income in the village "Runiya Barawas" was agriculture. URMUL decided to focus on promoting the dyeing and block printing unit to aim at empowering women and making them independent.

This research studies the setting up of a small plant which works on natural dyes with reduced water and electricity consumption to eliminate the hazardous effects of chemical dyes. In the Thar Desert of Rajasthan, India, the textile industry is being forced to reevaluate its water-intensive practices following increased public pressure and legal actions against the industry. It is important to tap into the right market because natural dyes are eco-friendly, biodegradable, and noncarcinogenic in comparison to synthetic dyes. They are made from all-natural ingredients and are easy to dispose of without causing environmental harm. Not only that, embroidery and dyeing have different sections of markets that they cater to. Embroidery caters to a slightly higher priced market and dying caters to affordable market segments. This gives more scope and demand for dyeing with lesser existing competition. Below, we discuss conventional process of dyeing and its likely consequences on environment.

6.1.1   PROCESS OF DYEING

The process of dyeing starts with the estimation of demand and by marking the target market. Post this, the size of the market is estimated to finalize the demand. Once the demand is known, the process for preparation of the dye is initiated; the dye is prepared in quantities similar to the demand, in order to promote resource efficiency. Once the dyes are prepared and the cloth is procured for dyeing, the cloth is then dipped into a mordant (Code, 2003). Mordant is a base which helps in fixing the color to the cloth. Once the mordant is used the cloth is dried and after that the dye is applied to the cloth. The dyeing is done once or twice based on the required color needed. The cloth is then put out to dry in the sun, where it is made sure that the color is fixed to the cloth. Once the color is fixed, it is given to artisans for block printing as the finishing touches. There are quality checks after that based on the market; there are minimum 3–6 quality checks for one cloth. After the cloth passes the quality check, the final product is sold in the market. The entire process has been outlined in Figure 6.1.

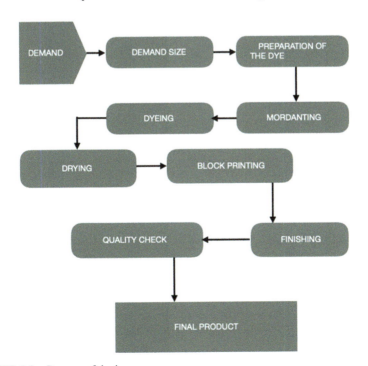

FIGURE 6.1   Process of dyeing.

6.1.2   BLOCK PRINTING

Block printing is a form of dying and coloring a fabric using wooden blocks (Fig. 6.2); sometimes, linoleum blocks are also used. From Gujarat, the art of block printing spread to Rajasthan. Some of the important centers are in Jaipur, Bangru, Sanganer, Pali, and Barmer.

6.1.3   ENVIRONMENTAL IMPACTS OF CHEMICAL DYES

Increase in the demand for textiles and the increase in their production along with the use of synthetic dyes have been major sources of pollution problems in current times. Greater part of the colors escape regular wastewater treatment procedures and persist in nature for a long time due to high thermal and photo stability(Choudhary, 2017).

6.1.4   WATER FOOTPRINT

The contamination and the overuse of water has become a concern in the textile industry; hence, economical and optimal use of water has gained attention. Water not only is misused, but also turns toxic and unfit for recycling or further consumption (Kant, 2012). Hence, the water footprint of proposed unit becomes an important factor that must be taken care of. Being a natural dyeing unit that is set up in a water scare zone in the western parts of Rajasthan (Husain, 2013), this unit does plan on making optimal use of water with minimal wastage. Not only that, since the dyes that will be used are natural dyes, the harmful impacts of this plant are close to zero (Rathore, 2011).

6.1.5   ECOLOGICAL AND LAND FOOTPRINT

The increasing scale of production and extensive use of synthetic dyes has led to a considerable environmental pollution, making it a serious concern. Legislation on the limits of color discharge has rightly become more rigid. As this process involves the use of natural dyes, there is a huge reduction in the amount of land and ecological pollution and the harm that is otherwise done to the environment by the disposal of chemical waste

(Trivedi, 2016). This unit thus helps in reducing environmental pollution to a great extent.

6.1.6   CARBON FOOTPRINT AND ENERGY CONSERVATION

Carbon footprint of textile industries is usually very high because of the large amount of fuel it uses for its boilers and for energy generation. However, since it is a small-scale plant, energy can be conserved by proper housekeeping, that is, by monitoring the unnecessary running of boilers, heaters, lights, and fans to reduce the excess energy consumption. Since the proposed plant will use biogas (easily obtainable locally) as a fuel, the carbon footprint will be considerably less.

6.2   OBJECTIVES

The study was conducted in the month of December 2018 keeping following objectives in mind:

Analyze and compare financial feasibility of setting up a dyeing and block printing unit in Runiya Barawas and Bajju.

Develop a dynamic pricing model for calculating the break-even point.

Understand the sustainability footprint of a dyeing and block printing unit.

Assess the challenges and risks of setting up the business.

6.3   STUDY AREA

Runiya Barawas is a small village situated in Bikaner Block of Bikaner district in Rajasthan, the northwestern parts of the Thar Desert (Fig. 6.2). The village consists of 352 families with a literacy rate of 35% (male and female literacy rate 45% and 24%, respectively).

6.4   METHODOLOGIES

The following methodologies were used to conduct the study:

FIGURE 6.2   Location of Runiya Barawas in western Rajasthan.

6.4.1   PRIMARY DATA

A primary survey was conducted through the questionnaire and a focused group discussion. Following questions were asked:

1   What are the sources of water in the village?
2   What are the existing sources of income?
3   What are the existing sources of electricity? Are there frequent power cuts?
4   Is the labor available there?
5   Are the locals satisfied with the training provided by URMUL?
6   Are the locals open to the dyeing unit?
7   Is there an availability of electricity and water?

PRA tools (Cavestro, 2003) like semi-structured interviews were also used in order to understand if the local community at Runiya Barawas is accepting the unit and if the resources needed for setting up the unit like labor, water, and electricity will be available as per requirements or not.

Daily activity survey was conducted to know how much maximum and minimum labor is available per day.

6.4.2   SECONDARY DATA

Various expense reports of the raw materials purchases, salaries, and wages were reviewed. Various sites were also visited to calculate the competitive pricing for material.

6.5   RESULT AND DISCUSSION

From the survey, it was found that bore wells and supplied water from the State Water Board are the sources of water in the village Runiya Barawas. Electricity is provided through grids, though occasional power cuts are common. Cattle rearing and agriculture are the major livelihood of the villagers. Requisite labors for the proposed dyeing plant will be available except in the months of June, July, and September because of their involvement in agriculture. Villagers were open to the idea of setting up of dyeing unit.

6.5.1   DAILY AVAILABILITY CHART

Daily activity of 60 women between 10 AM–6 PM has been plotted in Figure 6.3. This graph helped us to estimate how many minimum women will be available for the unit once it is set up.

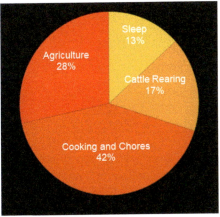

FIGURE 6.3   Average hours spent by women in the village on various activities. The breakup is based on hours spent on each activity among the total hours; n = 60.

6.5.2 SOURCES OF FUNDING

There are a lot of costs involved, like salaries and wages and other fixed costs for setting up a full-fledged dyeing and block printing unit. URMUL Seemant Samiti plans to raise funds from third-party sources or approaching companies for their CSR funds. Initial funds will be used for training costs and to meet other technical costs. The dyeing and block printing unit is expected to breakeven within a year; hence, it will be able to start making profits soon. In future, URMUL will opt for loans from the bank but for now the primary source of funding for all its fixed and variable expenses will be met from grants.

6.5.3 FINANCIAL ASPECTS

1. Fixed capital (machinery and equipment): Fixed capital is made up of long-term assets and capital investments that are needed to start up and conduct business, even at a minimal stage. Table 6.1 depicts fixed costs of the proposed dyeing plant.

TABLE 6.1   Fixed Costs.

S. No.	Description	Quantity	Rate (₹)	Amount (₹)
1	Boilers (Patilas)	5	1000	5000
2	Chulah	3	600	1800
3	Pit	1	400	400
4	Blocks for block printing	20	2500	50,000
5	Tables for block printing	2	15,000	30,000
	Total			87,200

2. Variable costs change with proportion to the production output. They increase as production rises and decrease as production falls. Variable cost examples include the raw materials and packaging (Table 6.2–6.5).

(1) Staff wages (per month)

TABLE 6.2   Staff Wages.

S. No.	Description	Quantity	Rate (₹)	Amount (₹)
1	Manager + accountant	1	10,000	10,000
2	Quality check	1	7000	7000
3	Designer	1	35,000	35,000
	Total			52,000

(2) Artisan wages (per month)

TABLE 6.3   Artisan Wages.

Description	Hours	Number	Rate (₹)	Amount (₹)
Artisans	8	5	220	33,000
Total				33,000

(3) Raw material (for 2 months, quantities are taken based on previous runs conducted)

TABLE 6.4   Raw Materials.

S. No.	Description	Units	Quantity	Rate (₹)	Amount (₹)
1	Indian Madder	Kgs	2	400	800
2	Madder TCR	Kgs	2	550	1100
3	Some lai leaves catan	Kgs	2	280	560
4	Gammirevanchini	Kgs	2	300	600
5	Myrobalan	Kgs	2	100	200
6	Pomegranate	Kgs	2	80	160
7	Allium cepa	Kgs	2	200	400
8	Alkanet	Kgs	2	550	1100
9	Sappar	Kgs	2	450	900
10	Lac	Kgs	2	600	1200
11	Kiker	Kgs	2	200	400
12	Arsumu	Kgs	2	200	400
13	Natural indigo	Kgs	2	1900	3800

TABLE 6.4 *(Continued)*

S. No.	Description	Units	Quantity	Rate (₹)	Amount (₹)
14	Alum	Kgs	2	50	100
15	Ferrous	Kgs	2	50	100
16	Copper sulphate	Kgs	2	220	440
	Sum Total				12,260
	GST@5%				613
	Gross Total				12,873

(4) Utilities

TABLE 6.5 Utilities.

Description	Amount (₹)
Electricity bill	300
Water charges	2100
Repairs and maintenance charges	2000
Transport and stay costs for artisans	2,20,000
Miscellaneous expenses	5000
Total	2,29,400

6.5.4 ASSUMPTIONS

The following were the assumptions for the calculations of financials:

Though all the variable costs (expenses, salaries, and wages) are mentioned per month, the same are calculated for 20 working days per month; therefore, for 240 days per year because 3 months in a year there is no availability of labor due to their involvement in agriculture. Hence, the approximate cost for 20 days is calculated from the costs mentioned for a month.

Artisans will be available for 8 h a day and only a maximum of five people will be available each day. The availability of artisans was calculated through the daily availability chart.

It is also assumed that an artisan can finish 6 m of cloth dyeing, printing each day.

The maximum capacity of the plant assuming all the variables like the workforce and raw materials remain the same at this present capacity will be 600 m per month which is the product of the number of available days, the workforce available, and meters of cloth dyed and printed by each artisan, that is, 20 × 5 × 6 m.

The water requirement per month is assumed to be 100 L, that is, 6 m/L, which is available through the State Water Board at ₹ 20.925/L.

The electricity usage is calculated on 5 LEDs that consume 5 W each and a fan which uses 75 W will be used for 8 h a day, that is, 800 WH or 0.8 kWh per day of electricity.

The rate taken for electricity is ₹7.55/unit. This was calculated as follows:

The selling price is calculated at ₹ 120/m, which is a competitive market price taken from the market pricing of the existing competitors.

The wages for artisans is calculated for a month at ₹ 220 per day taken keeping in mind the minimum wage act.

Repairs and maintenance and miscellaneous expenses are taken as approximate figures.

Depreciation costs are taken at 10% p.a. as an average.

6.5.5 FINANCIAL ANALYSIS

Cost of production (per year)

Yearly cost of production	
Particulars	Amount (₹)
Raw material expenses	51,492
Depreciation	8720
Labor costs	2,64,000
Total	3,24,212

6.5.6 NET PROFIT (PER YEAR)

Net profit per year	
Particulars	Amount (₹)
Sales	8,64,000
Less: fixed expenses	1,02,920
Variable expenses	7,50,692
Profit	10,388

6.5.7   TURNOVER (PER YEAR)

Yearly turnover	
Particulars	**Amount**
Selling price	₹ 120
Quantity produced per month	600 m
Number of months	12
Total (₹)	₹ 8,64,000

6.5.8   NET PROFIT RATIO

TABLE 6.6   Net Profit Ratio.

Net profit ratio (NPR)	
Particulars	**Amount**
Net profit (₹)	10,388
Turnover (₹)	8,64,000
Net profit ratio	11.294%

Therefore,

Net profit ratio for the proposed dyeing plant = net profit/turnover = $(10,388/8,64,000) \times 100 = 1.202\%$.

6.5.9   BREAK-EVEN POINT

The main use of break-even analysis is for the determination of the level of production or a targeted desired sales mix. This is done to decide whether to invest in a project/investment. It looks at the level of fixed costs relative to the profit earned by each additional unit produced and sold, that is, (fixed cost/per unit sales price—per unit variable cost).

TABLE 6.7   Break-Even Point.

Break-even point	
Particulars	Amount (₹)
Fixed costs	87,200
Selling price per meter	120
Variable cost per meter	106.44
Breakeven in meters	6431

Therefore, for Runiya Barawas, considering 600 m is produced in 20 working days of a month, the project should breakeven in 214–215 days of its function.

Break-Even Point (in Rupees) = 6431* ₹ 120 = ₹ 7,71,720

6.6   RISKS AND CHALLENGES

However, the proposed organic dyeing and block printing may face some potential risks and challenges in the future. Some of those probable challenges and risks are mentioned below.

6.6.1   CHALLENGES

Competition: The current situation of setting up a dyeing and block printing unit in Runiya Barawas is done keeping in mind that the dyes used are organic; however, there exist a lot of chemical versions of the same production the market, which can be sold at a cheaper cost because of the lesser cost of production, this gives rise to a lot of substitutes and competition in the market.

Resource Management: The biggest challenge any business/unit faces is effectively and efficiently managing its resources so that the unit does not harm the environment and can sustain for a long time. When it comes to the dyeing and block printing unit in Rajasthan, the issue of resource management needs to be looked at because of the location of the unit.

Dealing with Artisans: The biggest challenge that this unit would face would be dealing with artisans because the most important asset of any business is its human resource and the same stands true here. Getting at least five artisans to work every day is very important for the unit to run.

6.6.2 RISKS

Product Risk/Market Risk: Is the risk that relates to how the market reacts to its products. The fact that the market demand will exist for the natural tie and dye products has been taken from secondary sources; however, it is a risk for the business unless it actually starts market interaction.

Financial Risk: Is the risk that the financial resources of the business could be misused in the future or the business could run short of the finances.

People Risk: Is the risk that relates to dependency on employees. This risk is huge because the business cannot function unless the artisans are willing to work.

Competitive Risk: Is the risk that the competing product will be able to surpass the unit's product. Currently, the competition the unit faces is from the chemical and mass production tie and dye units; however, it needs the company's aim to surpass this competition and capture the larger market through its USP of natural dyeing.

6.6.3 PROSPECTS

TABLE 6.8 Future Predictions.

Scenario-based profit and loss account			
Particulars	**Worst case**	**Ideal**	**Best case**
Sales	8,64,000	12,09,600	17,28,000
Less: variable expenses	7,50,692	9,39,449	11,38,984
Less: fixed expenses	1,02,920	1,12,680	1,27,680
Profit	10,388	1,57,471	4,61,336

Notes:

The scenarios mentioned above have been calculated by changing one variable, that is, the number of artisans; costs and sales have changed according to the change in the number of available artisans; therefore, leading to varied profits. The number of artisans in the worst-case scenario is 5, whereas that for the ideal and best case is taken at 7 and 10, respectively.

To further illustrate the prospect, a dynamic model for breakeven and profit and loss has been designed, where the variable factor is the number of units. Graph for break-even analysis for both the locations is shown below (Fig. 6.4). The dynamic models for the calculation of the break-even point and the profit provide a sense of flexibility which can be used with the ever-changing demand and prices applicable for a block printing unit. The model can also help in accommodating the varied number of workers which will have a direct impact on the capacity of the unit.

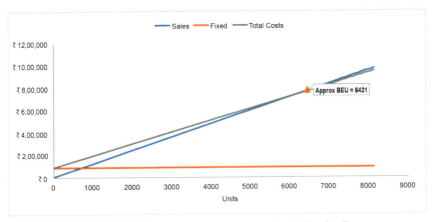

FIGURE 6.4   Break-even point analysis of the dyeing plant in Runiya Barawas.

6.7   CONCLUSION

Textile dyeing industries consume a huge amount of water, steam, and electricity and substantial quantities of complex chemicals. Moreover, these textile dyeing houses operating in this sector are facing significant challenges to reduce their energy and water footprint along with taking proper measures of how the chemical waste from these dyes is disposed, since it can be hazardous to the health and fertility of the land. Therefore, there is a lot of scope to improve from the current scenario. With agricultural uncertainty existing at its peak, the need for provision of an alternative livelihood source is at its best. The textile industry is often associated with environmental pollution problems and this industry is also considered as ecologically one of the most polluting industries in the world. Rajasthan holds a special place in textile dyeing and printing. Dyeing units of the textile industry are water and chemical intensive and hence generate huge amounts of effluents with toxic components. With the growing need to sustain our resources, NGOs like URMUL take special measures to reduce the toxicity of the effluents by using all naturally available ingredients. The unit needs to ensure proper use and disposal of water, so that no harm is caused to the locals and their land. Optimization of resources will help in making the unit more profitable which can in turn lead to more community development. It is extremely important to market the product right using its USP to stand out.

KEYWORDS

- **Western Rajasthan**
- **Thar**
- **dyeing plant**
- **block printing**
- **URMUL**

REFERENCES

Bhandari, A.; Aggarwal, P.; Bhagat, K.; Malik, B. Promoting Sustainable Agriculture, Agroforestry and Livelihood Enhancement in Thar Desert, Rajasthan, 2016.

Cavestro, L. P.R.A.-Participatory Rural Appraisal Concepts Methodologies and Techniques. Universita' degli Studi di Padova Facolta' di Agraria, 2003.

Chaudhry, T. Understanding Water Scarcity in the Socio-Cultural Context in Thar Desert of Pakistan Tehreem CHAUDHRY. *J. Int. Dev. Cooperation* **2017,** *23*(1), 1–1. http://s-ja. hiroshima-u.jp/upload_files/download_files/2.Tehreem CHAUDHRY_0.pdf

Code, P.; Preparation, O. F.; By, P. Bleaching and Dyeing of Cotton Knitted Fabric, 2003.

Choudhary, M. P.; Saiful Islam, I. Assessment of Environmental Impacts during Operational Phase of a Textile Industry, 2017.

Garrett, B. Evaluation of Textile Treatment and Treatment Alternatives for the Village of Jasol in Rajasthan, India, 2011.

Handa, B. K. Treatment and Recycle of Wastewater in Industry; National Environmental Engineering Research Institute: Nagpur, 1991.

Husain, I.; Husain, J.; Arif, M. Environmental Impact of Dyeing and Printing Industry of Sanganer, Rajasthan (India). *Turkish J. Eng. Environ. Sci.* **2013,** *37*(3), 272–285. https://doi.org/10.3906/muh-1310-8

Kant, R. Textile Dyeing Industry an Environmental Hazard. *Nat. Sci.* **2012.**

Mahala, V. Impact of URMUL Trust in the Development of Farm Women in Western Rajasthan, 2002.

Ojha, J. K.; Mishra, B. Building Capacities of Rural Women Artisans: Case Studies of Women Empowerment from Thar Desert of Western Rajasthan. *J. Rural Dev.* **1982,** *32*(3), 291–300. http://nirdprojms.in/index.php/jrd/article/view/93326

Ojha, J. K.; Mishra, B. Traditional Artisans in Global Market: Experience of Weavers' Collective from Western Rajasthan **2011,** *2*(2), 247667.

Ojha, J. K. Weaving Threads of Development: A Case Study of Urmul Marusthal Bunkar Vikas Samiti-Phalodi, Rajasthan, 2014.

Rathore, J. Assessment of Water Quality of River Bandi Affected by Textile Dyeing and Printing Effluents, Pali, Western Rajasthan, India, 2011.

Sabir, E. C. Modeling of Textile Dyeing-Finishing Mill Production Cost and Time Under Variable Demand Conditions With Simulation. *Tekstil ve Konfeksiyon* **2014,** *24*, 371–379.

Sutra, D.; Museum, B.; East, F. (n.d.). History of Block Printing in India.

Trivedi, R. Threat to Aquatic Biodiversity of Arid Regions: A Review on Dyeing Units in Rajasthan, 2016.

CHAPTER 7

Accessibility of Water, Electricity, and Fuel to the Households in India: Evidence from IHDS (2011–2012)

SANGRAM CHARAN PANIGRAHI*

F.M. (Autonomous) College, Balasore, Odisha, 756001, India

E-mail: spsangramjrf@gmail.com

ABSTRACT

Access of natural resources (i.e., water, electricity, and fuel) is essential means for improving the welfare of individuals and households both in the short and long run. In the short run, the use of resources helps to increase the standard of living of the people and, in turn, reduces the adverse socio-economic shocks. In the long run, the availability of resources facilitates the development of human capital, thereby raising economic growth in a sustainable approach. Keeping the abovementioned importance of resources, this chapter highlights about use of water, electricity, and fuel by the households living in India using empirical data of Indian Household Development Survey (IHDS-II, 2012). The result shows that more proportion of households living in rural areas belong to below poverty line families, and backward castes are more vulnerable in the accessibility of resources as against their counterparts.

7.1 INTRODUCTION

Natural resources are important prerequisites after food, cloth, and shelter for the development of human beings vis-à-vis the economic growth of a country. It refers to all elements in the physical sphere, plants, and animals, including human beings in the biological sphere. The renewable resources are created automatically to fulfill the need of human generation. On the other hand, nonrenewable resources are formed after millions of years, and once used, they cannot be replaced. The depletion of nonrenewable resources obstructs the process of economic development on a sustainable basis. The economic growth of developing countries depends upon the availability and use of natural resources. It provides income support to the poorest people in developing countries. There is a need for the proper use of natural resources for sustainable development. Sustainable development refers to the use of natural resources at an optimum level while keeping the importance of the same for the future generation. In the present context, sustainable development of air, water, and fuels are highly essential for the survival of physical and biological spheres.

Conventionally speaking, food, clothing, and shelter are considered as the basic needs in economics. However, next to air, water, and fuel is the fundamental basic need of mankind. And, therefore, now the provision of adequate and safe drinking water is considered as a human right. Health, hygiene, and development of human capital are critically dependent on the availability of safe and adequate water. Instead of the abovementioned benefit of resources, developing countries are unable to supply an adequate amount of natural resources especially water, electricity, and fuel to the households. Water is needed for both domestic work and agricultural practices. In India, nearly 60% of the population is engaged in agricultural activities, and it contributes only 16% of GDP. Nearly 76 million people are using unsafe drinking water in India. The time incurred by households to get access of drinking water ranges between 15 min and 6 h/day. Contaminated water has contributed to 88% of illness worldwide.

The availability and accessibility of energy help in the socioeconomic development of individuals and communities. Nearly 1.1 billion people lack access to electricity globally, and 300 million of these live in India. More than 2.9 billion people depend on traditional biomass for cooking. This figure touches to 800 million in India where households use firewood, dung cakes, charcoal, or crop residue cooking. All the abovementioned metrics indicate the effective policy implementation in order to address the energy need of the population. The slow village electrification rate and limited availability of liquefied petroleum gas (LPG) hinder the improvement in energy accessibility of households.

7.2 REVIEW OF PAST STUDIES

The census of 2011 found the 86% of people have access to safe drinking water. The people living in urban areas have more access to safe drinking water than rural households (92 vs. 83%) (Census, 2011). More people in rural areas (63.4 million) are living without access to clean water in India. Similarly, very few proportions of households (16%) have piped water in the rural area. Iron was found in the drinking water of nearly one in every three (30%) rural households. Similarly, one in every five (21%) household's drinking water is contaminated with arsenic, known to cause skin lesions and cancer (Hindustan Times, 2019). The role of water and energy became an important aspect for day-to-day life and expected to grow with the increasing population and economic growth (Tana and Zhib, 2016). Water is used for domestic activities, irrigation, transport, and power generation (CEC, 2005; Kahrl and Roland-Holst, 2008; Mielke et al., 2010; Siddiqi and Anadon, 2011). The limited availability of water influences the choice of energy facilities (Mielke et al., 2010). The growth of population leads to an increase in water use for energy developments (Pate et al., 2007; Healy et al., 2015), and major research are being carried to cut the water consumption of energy to save the stock of energy.

The availability of energy is a vital input for the socioeconomic development of any nation. An increase in agricultural and industrial activities leads to increases in demand for energy. There is a need for allocation and production of energy from different sources (viz., solar, wind, bioenergy) in order to meet the needs of the future generation. The study carried out by the World Bank (1993) indicated that with low energy prices and with the present state of technology, a saving of 20–25% of the energy consumed could be achieved economically in many countries with existing capital stock. If investments were made in new more energy-efficient capital equipment, a saving on the order of 30–60% would be possible. The study concludes that the main element of existing bank policy for achieving energy efficiency in the developing world will remain in force while every additional opportunity to improve energy efficiency is fully exploited. The relationship between energy and poverty was clearly highlighted in a number of the World Bank's reports (World Bank, 1996). By 2008, the World Bank could claim that the investment in rural electrification helps in improving the standard of living of the households on a sustainable basis. The provision of lighting facilities in rural areas helps in improving possibilities for education, accessibility of an urban job by raising skills, and increasing prospects of rural nonfarm employment (Gibson and Olivia, 2009). Different studies found the decline and degradation of natural resources affected the poor, increases in food and energy prices, environmental pollution, and climate change. All the past studies highlight theoretical aspects on the availability of natural resources toward the socioeconomic development of the households. The lack of primary data on the use and availability of resources obstruct the formulation of sound policy and programs toward the proper use of natural resources for sustainable development. Therefore, there is the need to develop strategies for management of natural resources to improve the welfare of the poor and sustain economic growth in order to achieve Millennium Development Goals. It would help to enhance the ability of poor women and men to contribute to and benefit from growth based on the reverse of trickle-down approach.

The present study used empirical data on the accessibility of natural resources using Indian Household Development Survey (IHDS-II, 2012).

It highlights the living pattern of households by focusing on their pattern of consumption by analyzing the access to clean water, fuel, and electricity. The provision of piped water, electricity, and availability of fuel reflect a household's quality of life. For example, the supply of clean water helps in improving the health status of the family member. The availability of electricity enables more reading and improves the skill and employment of the youth section. The accessibility of LPG or kerosene stove for cooking reduces the time women spend in fuel collection, which could be devoted to other activities. New fuels and improved stove/chulha provide a cleaner environment and better health of the society. All the abovementioned facilities improve the quality of life and are considered as signs of social status.

This chapter does not comment on aiming to strengthen the relationship between natural resources and sustainable economic development through environmental policy, programs. In fact, we want to examine the impact of the abovementioned program at the grassroots level. This will raise some questions in our mind like, what is the value of theories and policies formulated by the planners for sustainable use of natural resources? To what extent policies and plans have solved the problem existing between natural resources and economic development? Has there been accompanying progress in access of water, fuel, and electricity to the people of India? Are the policy planners formulating suitable policy for green accounting? In order to bridge the gap in access of energy, water, and electricity as well as to examine the relationship with socioeconomic aspects, the present study used IHDS-II. The general objective of the study is to give proper importance toward access of resources for sustainable development in India. The specific objectives of the study are as follows:

7.3 OBJECTIVES

To explore the consumption patterns of basic amenities such as clean water, fuels, and electricity to the households in India.

To examine the interrelation between accesses of resources with respect to socioeconomic status and area of living of the households.

To suggest some measures on the availability of the natural resources for sustainable development of the people.

7.4 ECONOMETRICS AND DATA ISSUES

In order to examine the research objectives, the present chapter used "India Human Development Survey-II" (IHDS-2012). The IHDS-II is a nationally representative, multi-topic panel survey of 42,152 households in 384 districts, 1420 villages, and 1042 urban neighborhoods across India. Most of these households had been interviewed for IHDS-I (2005). Both surveys cover all states and union territories of India except for Andaman/Nicobar and Lakshadweep. The survey asked a few questions related to employment, income, expenditure, credit, assets, marriage, fertility, gender relations, and social capital, and other general welfare indicators. It also provides information on the availability of natural resources in India. The present study highlighted the use of different resources viz., sources of water, time to collect water, use of fuel and electricity, etc. by the households in India. We applied the crosstab technique to examine the significant relationship between access of resources based on region and economic status of the households. The accessibility of resources by people residing in different states has been examined to assign the rank. Using the technique, we are able to make the prediction about the status of people regarding the use of water, fuel, and electricity and the problem associate with the same. This study addresses three major themes: First, it provides a brief description of the standard of living of households measured by basic facilities, such as access to water, fuel, and electricity. Second, it highlights the inequalities in the possession of these facilities, with a particular focus on regional inequalities. Third, it analyzes the challenges of providing basic services by documenting the reliability (and lack thereof) of electricity and water supply.

7.5 RESULTS AND FINDINGS

7.5.1 ACCESSIBILITY OF WATER

Conventionally speaking air, water is the fundamental basic need of mankind. Therefore, now the provision of adequate and safe drinking water is considered as a human right. Health, hygiene, and development of human capital are critically dependent on the availability of safe and adequate water.

TABLE 7.1 Sources of Water Supply for Drinking.

Categories	Piped public supply		Tube well/ hand pump		River, canal, other		Total	
Residence	*N*	*%*	*N*	In %	*N*	In %	*N*	In %
Rural	10,888	50.18	12,935	81.85	4355	73.96	27,478	65.43
Urban	10,115	49.82	2869	18.15	1533	26.04	14,517	34.57
Poverty								
APL	13,401	66.06	10,479	66.33	3806	64.67	27,686	65.97
BPL	6885	33.94	5319	33.67	2079	35.33	14,283	34.03
Caste								
General	6191	30.57	4244	26.89	1385	23.57	11,820	28.20
OBC	8109	40.05	6300	39.91	2570	43.74	16,979	40.51
SC/STs	5949	29.38	5240	43.74	1921	32.69	13,110	31.28
Sources of income								
Agriculture	5731	28.24	6849	43.35	2290	38.92	14,870	35.42
Nonagriculture (labor, artisan, shop)	7357	36.25	5905	37.37	2123	36.08	15,385	36.65
Other (business, salary, profession)	7207	35.51	3046	19.28	1471	25.00	11,724	27.93
Total (All India)	20,303	48.35	15,804	37.63	5888	14.02	41,995	100

Source: Computed based on IHDS-II (2012); percentages are based on column for each category.

Table 7.1 informs about sources of drinking water supply to the households in India. It shows that nearly half of the households (48.3%) collected water from the piped supply by government, followed by one-third of the households (37.63%) depend upon hand pump or tube well. A few proportions of the population (14%) depend upon rivers and canals to collect water for drinking. Disaggregating the data based on residence, we observed that an equal percentage of households (50%) depend upon the piped public supply of water in both rural and urban areas. More propor-tion of people living in the rural area are relying on tube well or hand pump or river/canal as against urban area. For example, one in every five households (81.85%) living in the rural area were dependent upon tube well as against their urban counterpart (18.15). Similarly, nearly 73% of households residing in the rural area used river or canal water for drinking, which is 26% for the urban area.

The significant difference was found in access of drinking water based on the poverty status of the households. It can be seen from Table 7.1 that 66% of households belonging in above the poverty line (APL) have depended upon piped public supply, which decreases to 34% for the households belong to the below poverty line (BPL). The sound socio-economic position of the households in APL groups might be the reason to access of water from the piped public supply. The same proportion of households (66%) in APL categories were depended upon tube well or piped public supply for collection of water as against BPL category (33%). It clearly reveals about the inadequate provision of tube well for the areas where poor people live in India. The access of water from the piped public supply is higher for other backward castes (40%) as against generals (31%) followed by scheduled castes (SCs) and scheduled tribes (STs) (30%). More proportion of SC/STs (44%) were depending on tube well for the collection of drinking water, which is lower (24%) for households belonging to general castes. The sources of income of the family are strongly and positively associated with access of water supply for drinking. The proportion of households regarding piped public water supply steadily decreases from 36% for households, the main sources of income of which are nonagriculture or other to 28% for households, the main source of income of which is agriculture. More households with nonagricultural sources of income are capable to dig a bore well inside the house perimeter, might be the reason for the abovementioned find-ings. Similarly, two out of every five (43%) of households depend upon

Resource Efficiency, Sustainability, and Globalization

collected water from tube well for agriculture, which declines to 37% for nonagriculture (nonagriculture wage labor, artisan, shopkeeper) and 20% for others (business, salary, other professions).

The access of water inside of the households helps in saving the time and energy that could be used for other productive purposes. The availability of water inside the households depends upon the supply of water by the local institutional body and the standard of living of the people. An increase in the economic status of the households presumes on availability of water inside the house.

TABLE 7.2 Sources of Water Supply for Drinking is Inside or Outside of House.

	Outside		Inside		Total	
Residence	*N*	**%**	*N*	**In %**	*N*	**In %**
Rural	15,652	79.13	11,823	53.29	27,475	65.47
Urban	4127	20.87	10,363	46.71	14,490	34.53
Poverty						
APL	11,379	57.56	16,282	73.44	27,661	65.96
BPL	8390	42.44	5888	26.56	14,278	34.04
Caste						
General	3790	19.18	8024	36.27	11,814	28.21
OBC	8285	41.93	8677	39.22	16,962	40.5
SC/STs	7684	38.89	5419	24.50	13,103	31.29
Sources of income						
Agriculture	8803	44.52	6065	27.35	14,868	35.44
Nonagriculture	7556	38.21	7818	35.26	15,374	36.65
Other	3415	17.27	8292	27.91	11,707	27.91
Total (All India)	19,774	47.14	22,175	52.86	41,949	100

Source: Computed based on IHDS-II (2012); percentages are based on column for each category.

Table 7.2 reveals information about the access of water supply, that is, inside or outside of the households. A little bit higher proportion of households (53%) agreed on the availability of water supply inside of the households, which declines to 48% for who depend upon outside for collection of water in India. One in every five households (80%) residing in the rural area depends on outside sources of water supply. More proportion of households living in rural areas have access of water inside the house as against urban counterpart (53 vs. 45%). The higher income of the rural households might be the possible reason to have indoor piped water as against urban counterpart. About three-fourths (73%) of the most affluent (APL) households have indoor piped water, which declines to 26% for the poorest households (BPL). The majority of households belonging to the backward castes are depending upon the outside sources of water supply as compared to the forward caste. For example, 41% of households that belonged to OBCs depend upon outside sources for the collection of water, which declines to 39% for households of SC/STs. The collections of water from outside of the house are higher (45%) for households who mainly depend upon agriculture as compared to households, the main income sources of which are nonagriculture (38%) and others (17%).

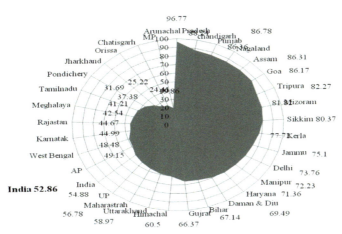

FIGURE 7.1   State-wise availability of water inside the house in %.

The availability of piped water inside the house is largely dependent upon the economic status of the household and the wealth of the state (see Fig. 7.1). Nearly half of the households (53%) in India have inside water facilities. For instance, 66% of households in Gujarat have indoor piped water as compared to Madhya Pradesh (MP) with 23 and 24% in Chhattisgarh. Nevertheless, the reliability of water service remains a significant problem throughout most of India. Most of northeastern states of India have water facilities within housing perimeters as against other states of India.

TABLE 7.3 Purification of Drinking Water.

	Never		Rarely		Usually		Always		Total
Residence	N	%	N	%	N	%	N	%	%
Rural	20,611	71.97	2367	61.37	1922	50.79	2405	44.11	27,305
Urban	8026	28.03	1490	38.63	1862	49.21	3047	55.89	14,425
Poverty									
APL	18,672	65.24	2037	52.87	2595	68.61	4201	77.11	27,505
BPL	9949	34.76	1816	47.13	1187	31.39	1247	22.89	14,199
Total (All India)	28,637	68.62	3857	9.24	3784	9.07	5452	13.06	41,730

Source: Computed based on IHDS-II (2012); percentages are based on column for each category.

Table 7.3 depicts about purification of water for drinking by the households in India. The majority of the households (69%) never purify water for drinking. Very few proportions of households (13%) purify drinking water regularly. Nearly one in every four households (72%) living in the rural area never purify drinking water that is lower for the households living in the urban area (28%). An increase in the economic status of the households leads to a high probability of the purification of water regularly. For example, nearly 77% of the households under APL categories purify water always that is 23% for households under the BPL category.

7.5.2 ACCESSIBILITY OF FUELS

The availability of fuels is an important resource as it provides food and lighting to the households. The extensive use of fuel wood for cooking in the last two decades led to extensive deforestation and severe health problems. The indoor air pollution leads to affect the health condition of the households in developing countries. In India, more proportion of households uses biomass traditional chulha followed by kerosene stove and LPG.

The IHDS found that Indian households use different fuels for cooking, lighting, and heating. The most widely used cooking fuel remains firewood, used by 51% of households followed by dung cake (31%). However, 15% of households use crop residue, that is, stalks left over after threshing and not used for animal fodder. Very few proportions of households (11%) use kerosene for cooking. About half of Indian households (40%) now use LPG for some or all of their cooking, and this figure has been increasing steadily. Nearly two out of every five households (43%) agreed on burning of stove/chulha for less than 2 h/day for cooking, heating water, etc. Majority of the households (58%) burn stove/chulha for 2–5 h/day.

TABLE 7.4   Types of Fuel Used for Cooking.

	Open fire (3 stone)		Traditional chulha without chimney		Improved chulha with chimney		Kerosene/ LPG		Total in %	
Residence	*N*	*%*	*N*	In %	*N*	In %	*N*	In %	*N*	In %
Rural	5654	83.22	14,636	87.08	2386	80.8	4724	30.83	27400	65.43
Urban	1140	16.78	2172	12.92	567	19.2	10599	69.17	14478	34.57
Poverty										
APL	3671	54.1	10,590	63.03	1636	55.42	11724	76.57	27621	66
BPL	3115	45.9	6212	36.97	1316	44.58	3588	23.43	14231	34
Caste										
General	1204	17.73	3824	22.77	620	21.03	6147	40.27	11795	28.22
OBC	2898	42.69	6759	40.25	1369	46.44	5903	38.67	16929	40.51
SC/STs	2687	39.58	6208	36.97	959	32.53	3214	21.06	13068	31.27
Sources of income										
Agriculture	3428	50.49	7766	46.22	1431	48.51	2203	14.38	14828	35.42
Nonagriculture	2395	35.28	6311	37.56	975	33.05	5669	37.01	15350	36.67
Other	966	14.23	2727	16.23	544	18.44	7447	48.61	11684	27.91
Total (All India)	6794	16.22	16,808	40.14	2953	7.05	15323	36.59	41878	100

Source: Computed based on IHDS-II (2012); percentages are based on column for each category.

The use of modern fuels—kerosene, LPG, or coal—is vastly greater in urban than in rural areas (Table 7.4). The use of traditional chulha without chimney plays a dominant role (40%) followed by kerosene/LPG (37%). More people living in rural areas used traditional chulha as against urban counterpart (87 vs. 13%). Nearly 70% of households residing in the urban area use kerosene/LPG, which declines 30% for rural households. The economic status of households significantly influences the use of kerosene/LPG for cooking. For example, three out of every four households (77%) that belonged in APL categories used kerosene/LPG for cooking. It declines to 23% for households under the BPL categories. More proportion of households in general and OBC caste (40%) use some modern fuel for some of their cooking. The reverse situation appears as only 20% of households belonging to SC/STs caste use LPG for their cooking.

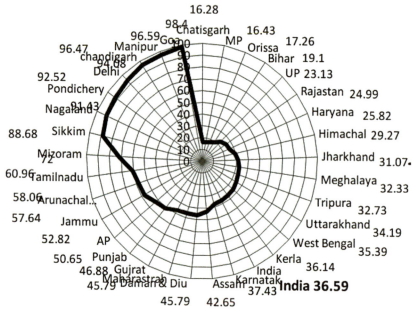

FIGURE 7.2   State-wise use of LPG by households in %.

States also differ widely in the use of modern fuels (Fig. 7.2). More than one-third of households (37%) use LPG for cooking in India. Over half of rural households belonging to different states, viz., Jammu and Kashmir (57%), Himachal Pradesh (53%), Punjab (51%), the North-East (54%), Gujarat (47%), and Maharashtra (46%) use LPG for cooking. Less than 1 in 20 rural households in Chhattisgarh (16%), MP (16%), Odisha (17%), Bihar (19%), and Uttar Pradesh (23%) have LPG connection in the house. These differences might be inequalities in the income of the households residing in different states. For example, the household in the wealthiest category uses modern fuels, while the poorest rural households depend on biomass. This may be due to two reasons: first, the easy accessibility of modern fuel in cities and the better financial position of households living in the urban area; second, the easy availability of biomass fuel in rural households as compared to the urban area.

7.5.3   TIME SPENT ON COLLECTION OF WATER AND FUELS

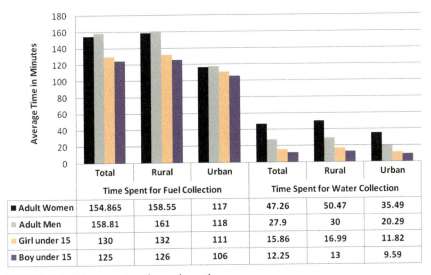

	Time Spent for Fuel Collection			Time Spent for Water Collection		
	Total	Rural	Urban	Total	Rural	Urban
■ Adult Women	154.865	158.55	117	47.26	50.47	35.49
▨ Adult Men	158.81	161	118	27.9	30	20.29
▨ Girl under 15	130	132	111	15.86	16.99	11.82
■ Boy under 15	125	126	106	12.25	13	9.59

FIGURE 7.3   Time spent on domestic work.

The collection of water for domestic purposes is time consuming for the women in the society. Figure 7.3 provides information about time spent for collection of fuel/water in India. The average time for the supply of water is 240 min. Similarly, the average time of walking for one way collection of water is 11 min. The Indian household without indoor water spends 48 min/day collecting water. The graph suggests that women spend nearly twice as much time fetching water as men (48 vs. 28 min). A similar ratio exists between girls and boys in the time devoted to the collection of water (15 vs. 12 min). As might be expected, the time spent collecting water is substantially greater in rural areas (51 min/day) than in urban areas (36 min/day). This substantial loss of time could be used for other productive purposes. The collection of firewood requires longer trips and households spend an average of 52 min, or more than 6 h/week on this activity. The role of men in the collection of fuel is a little bit higher than women (158 vs. 154).

7.5.4 AVAILABILITY OF ELECTRICITY

TABLE 7.5 Access of Electricity in the Households.

	Yes		No		Total	
Residence	*N*	**In %**	*N*	**In %**	*N*	**In %**
Rural	22,569	61.52	4898	92.36	27,467	65.42
Urban	14,116	38.48	405	7.64	14,521	34.58
Poverty						
APL	24,462	66.72	3222	60.78	27,684	65.97
BPL	12,199	33.28	2079	39.22	14,278	34.03
Caste						
General	10,896	29.77	921	17.38	11,817	28.2
OBC	14,830	40.52	2147	40.61	16,977	40.52
SC/STs	10,876	29.71	2232	29.71	13,108	31.28
Sources of income						
Agriculture	12,301	33.55	2563	48.34	14,864	35.41
Nonagriculture	13,204	36.01	2180	41.12	15,384	36.65
Other	11,165	30.45	559	10.54	11,724	27.93
Total (All India)	36,685	87.37	5303	12.63	41,998	100

Source: Computed based on IHDS-II (2012).

The Indian government is trying to provide adequate electricity for all segments of the society. Different programs and policies have been implemented to achieve the objectives within the stipulated time period. However, a significant number of households lack electricity, especially in developing countries like India. The IHDS found that 87% of households have electricity. The people living in rural areas have suffered in lack of electricity. For example, more than 9 out of 10 households living in rural area (93%) do not have electricity. The households with APL have electricity as against BPL households (67 vs. 33%). Out of total households with access of electricity, 40% belong to OBC followed by 29% in the general category. The households depend upon agriculture as a source of income and have less access of electricity as against who depends upon nonagriculture-related activities (33 vs. 36%)

7.6 CONCLUSION

Conventionally speaking, food, clothing, and shelter are considered as the basic needs in economics. However, next to air, water is the fundamental basic need of mankind. And, therefore, now the provision of adequate and safe drinking water is considered as a human right. Health, hygiene, and development of human capital are critically dependent on the availability of safe and adequate water, availability of electricity, and modern fuel to the households. Looking into the results of the abovementioned study, there is the call for the provision of safe water in rural areas, awareness on the purification of water, and indoor water facilities to the households that belonged to the BPL category and backward castes. There is a need for the provision of smokeless cooking for improvement in the health status of women. Different states, viz., MP, Chhattisgarh, Odisha, Bihar, and Rajasthan need to give attention on the provision of indoor water facilities and supply of LPG to the households. It would help in the development of human resources in a sustainable approach with increases in economic growth.

KEYWORDS

- water
- electricity
- natural resources
- fuel
- sustainable development

REFERENCES

Census. 2011. Retrieved from https://data.gov.in/catalog/households-access-safe-drinking-water.

Gibson, J.; Olivia, S. The Effect of Infrastructure Access and Quality on Non-Farm Enterprises in Rural Indonesia. *World Dev.* **2009**, *38* (5), 717–726.

Healy, R. W.; Alley, W. M.; Engle, M. A.; McMahon, P. B.; Bales, J. D. *The Water-Energy Nexus: An Earth Science Perspective*; No. 1407; US Geological Survey, 2015.

Hindustan Times. Retrieved Jan 18, 2019 from https://www.hindustantimes.com/india-news/6-3-crore-indians-do-not-have-access-to-clean-drinking-water/story-dWIEyP962FnM8Mturbc52N.html.

Kahrl, F.; Roland-Holst, D. China's Water-Energy Nexus. *Water Policy* **2008**, *10*, 51.

Mielke, E.; Anadon, L. D.; Narayanamurti, V. *Water Consumption of Energy Resource Extraction, Processing, and Conversion*; Belfer Center for Science and International Affairs, 2010.

Pate, R.; Hightower, M.; Cameron, C.; Einfeld, W. *Overview of Energy-Water Interdependencies and the Emerging Energy Demands on Water Resources*; Report SAND, 1349, 2007.

Siddiqi, A.; Anadon, L. D. The Water-Energy Nexus in Middle East and North Africa. *Energy Policy* **2011**, *39* (8), 4529–4540.

Tana, C.; Zhib, Q. The Energy-water Nexus: A Literature Review of the Dependence of Energy on Water. *Energy Procedia* **2016**, *88*, 277–284.

World Bank. *Rural Energy and Development, Improving Energy Supplies for Two Billion People*; World Bank: Washington DC, 1996.

CHAPTER 8

A Critical Analysis of Migration and Socioeconomic Development of Slum Dwellers: A Study of Twin City of Odisha

SOUMENDRA KUMAR PATRA[1*] and D. M. MAHAPATRA[2]

[1]*Department of Business Administration, Ravenshaw University, Cuttack, Odisha, India*

[2]*PG Dept. of Commerce, FM Autonomous College, Balasore, Odisha*

Corresponding author. E-mail: soumendra.patra@gmail.com

ABSTRACT

The socioeconomic status of slum dwellers is generally poor as a result of lack of basic social facilities: supply of education, financial benefits, sanitation, and health resources. They migrate from village to city in search of employment and stay in slum areas. Little attention is paid to the fact that the majority of slum dwellers are migrants to the city, who are victims of unbalanced development processes, social injustice, and inequalities. This study explores the socioeconomic development of slum dwellers relating to socioeconomic conditions and their migration from rural areas. This chapter is analytical in nature and also measures the economic status index and social status index of slum peoples in Cuttack and Bhubaneswar city of Odisha. Here, the requirement for an all-encompassing methodology that considers to the different elements of social, monetary, in framing any slum improvement policy/scheme ought to be stressed.

8.1 INTRODUCTION

Over the last few years, there has been an unprecedented rise in the process of industrialization followed by urbanization in India. India is one of the fastest developing countries with many metropolitan cities (e.g., Mumbai, Pune, Bangalore, Hyderabad, Delhi, and Chennai). Thus, during last two decades, migration from villages and small towns to metropolitan areas has increased tremendously in India. So the surround rural population has attracted toward nearer city or urban area. This urban provided all season employment. It leads the process of migration. Rural threshold has been migrated toward city or urban area in search of jobs. These migrants are low educated, unskilled, and skilled labor force for urban industrialization. Urban industrialization changes the face of urban area, its functions too. Due to urban industrialization, the city's previous functions are mainly services, suppliers. The city's traditional function is served to optimum threshold, but today it served more threshold through multifunctioning. It provides better income in compare of rural area. This leads to the degradation of urban environmental quality and sustainable development especially in the metropolitan cities. The problems faced by the people living in the urban areas of India have become major concerns for the government. Slums are considered to be the major issue within many urban areas, particularly problems related to transportation, population, health, and safety. Considering today's poor urban environmental quality in India, the majority of families affected by urban development projects are located in slum areas that are under consideration for resettlement and/or rehabilitation. As a result, people migrate from rural areas to urban parts of India in lure of jobs to lead a good and comfortable life. Urbanization goes along with the need for increased investment in basic necessities such housing, roads, education and health services, water and sanitation, energy, among others. Thus, it ushers to the need to raise the socioeconomic status along with living standard, lifestyle, and all over development and progress of individuals. The education and occupation are the most important elements in the study of socioeconomic status of population. Besides these elements age, castes are also taken into consideration. Cities provide better income in comparison of rural area. So the rural population surrounding the urban areas is attracted toward nearer city or urban area. These urban areas provided all season employment. These migrants are low educated, unskilled, and skilled labor force for urban industrialization. Though the migration is for jobs, these type of jobs provided low income to the labor force. For accessible purpose, the labors are in search of shelters. But cities have higher land cost; due to this, the labor can't purchase their own house in city area. So they take shelter in public open land, other open places of the city, places nearer to industrial area, and also footpath. This process gives birth to formation of *slums*.

8.2 PROBLEM STATEMENT

- Increasing numbers of slums constitute a major challenge to development.
- Thus, there is a need to improve the physical environment of the dwelling places like basic amenities of toilets, proper drainage, sewerage system, and adequate water supply.
- The present study aims to examine the factors that attract slum dwellers to settle in slums and to know their economic activities and socioeconomic profiles.

8.3 REVIEW OF LITERATURE

A slum is a summary region of a city portrayed by inadequate lodging, griminess, and ailing in residency security (UN-HABITAT, 2003). A stunning number of individuals (around 65,494,604), which records for 5.41% of all out populace in India, lived in ghetto in 2011. During this time, 3.72% of absolute population in Odisha are slum tenants (Slum Population—Census 2011). Around 163,983 (out of 843,402) in Bhubaneswar and 163,766 (out of 610,189) live in slum areas. So around 20% of the population in Bhubaneswar and 26% in Cuttack live in slum zones (Slum Population—Census 2011).

Slum implies a vigorously populated region in city (Hossain, 2013). Slum is that pieces of the urban areas which are mostly occupied by needy people (Stokes). In the early period of modern revaluation, initially slum is made in the urban communities not so far of the focal point of the urban areas and close of plants' entryway (Kumar). In the beginning of industrialization, most minimal paid specialists of industrial urban areas of England and the United State lived in slums (Joshi, 2005). The last are devastated shanty settlements made and possessed by squatters, a considerable lot of whom are moderately late vagrants (Nautiyal, 1993). Slum territories represent high paces of neediness, absence of education, and awful wellbeing status. Slum occupants have low winning. Urban zones do not give them appropriate employments. They do not have any formal instruction offices. Occupants of slums are occupied with casual work through which they cannot acquire much. They work in conditions that are unsafe to them. This reality drives them to work in casual parts (Alamgir, 2009).

Lower financial conditions lead them to poor life. Despite the fact that the living state of slum occupants are more awful than that of country tenants, they are increasingly powerless against transmittable ailments and lack of healthy sustenance and simultaneously presented to more serious danger of mishaps at work (Ameratunga, 2006; Kamruzzaman, 2015). The vast majority of the slum tenants in developing nations are living underneath neediness line. They do not have great wellspring of pay. Inadequate supply of drinking water is essential human need (Ompad, 2007). Lamentably, a large portion of the families in slums do not even have safe drinking water. In certain regions, open water supply is accessible; however, the quality available water is not as per standard. Sanitation framework is exceptionally poor in slums (Kamruzzaman and Hakim, 2016).

Their lanes are thin and unpaved; slum inhabitants need to face water stagnation in stormy season. This makes the earth of that zone unhygienic. Such condition causes various infections in slums (Dziuban et al., 2010). One of the most significant attributes of slums is absence of responsibility for where they are living. Typically they make their homes on empty government or open land or minimal land bundles like railroad mishaps or unfortunate damp land. At the point when the land isn't in gainful use, they get it as a chance and settle there. They are defenseless against avalanche, flood inclined regions, and perilous condition (Siegel et al., 1997; Kamruzzaman, 2015). The summary of literature review is presented in Table 8.1.

TABLE 8.1 Major Summary of Literature Review.

Year	Author	Findings
2017	Nisanth M. Pillai and R. L. Jayagovind	Economic backwardness because of low income and unemployment forced people to stay in slums

TABLE 8.1 *(Continued)*

Year	Author	Findings
2016	Brijendra Nath Singh	Slum dwellers are the stock of the potential human resource, and it can be developed through skill enhancement programs initiated by the government and through appropriate public action relating to social provisions and redistribution social amenities
2013	Benjamin Marx, Thomas Stoker, and Tavneet Suri	Direct relationship between economic growth, urban growth, and slum growth in the developing world
2003	Sunil Kumar Karn, Shigeo Shikura, and Hideki Harada	Socioeconomic and environmental factors lead to morbidity
1999	David Vlahov, Nicholas Freudenberg, Fernando Proietti, Danielle Ompad, Andrew Quinn, Vijay Nandi, and Sandro Galea	Improving living conditions in slums as housing, employment, education, equality, quality of living environment, social support, and health services is central to improving the health of urban populations

8.3.1   RESEARCH GAP

• Review of past literature suggests that although a number of studies have been conducted on socioeconomic development of slum dwellers in Odisha, so far no study has been conducted in twin city of Odisha.
• Further none of these studies have made an attempt to measure social status index (SSI) and economic status index (ESI) of the slum dwellers.

8.3.2   OBJECTIVES OF THE STUDY

1. To study the migration of rural peoples.
2. To study the employment status of slum peoples in twin city of Odisha.

3. To study various types of economic activities undertaken by the slum dwellers of Cuttack and Bhubaneswar city of Odisha.
4. To measure SSI and ESI of slum dwellers.
5. To examine whether economic conditions of slum dwellers has improved due to their migration from their origin.
6. To suggest measures for improvement of socioeconomic conditions of slum dwellers.

8.3.3 HYPOTHESIS OF THE STUDY

1. H_o: There is no significant relationship between migrated from and economic index of slum people
   H_a: There is a significant relationship between migrated from and economic index of slum people
2. H_o: There is no significant relationship between migrated from and SSI of slum people
   H_a: There is significant relationship between migrated from and SSI of slum people

8.4 RESEARCH METHODOLOGY

8.4.1 SOURCES OF DATA

- Primary Data: Data collection using questionnaire from the slum people and communities those are engaged for development of people
- Secondary Data: Reports, publications, and websites

8.4.2 SAMPLING

- Method: Stratified random sampling.
- Size: Will be calculated based on pilot response quality.

8.4.3 RESEARCH INSTRUMENTS

- Questionnaire

8.5 DATA ANALYSIS

8.5.1 DEMOGRAPHIC DISTRIBUTION OF SAMPLES

The primary data is obtained through a well-framed questionnaire circulated among the slum peoples of twin city of Odisha (Cuttack and Bhubaneswar). The questionnaire comprises of personal details to be filled by the respondents. In particular, the study ascertains the gender, age, caste, education, and religion of the respondents. The percentage analysis is applied to identify different categories of respondents with different personal backgrounds.

The data pertaining to the demographic profile is relevant to an analysis of the understanding of respondents about the living styles and socioeconomic activities. The demographic characteristics of the respondents are given in Table 8.2. In gender majority are male, that is, 216 (78.30%), and the rest are females 60 (21.70%). The major age group is between 36 and 50, that is, 132 people (47.80%) per cent than coming 26–35 years, that is, 60 (21.70%) less than 25 years.

TABLE 8.2 Demographic Profile of the Respondents ($N = 276$).

Particulars		Frequency	Percent	Cumulative percent
Gender				
Male		216	78.3	78.3
Female		60	21.7	100
	Total	**276**	**100**	
Age				
Less than 25		36	13	13
26–35		60	21.7	34.8
36–50		132	47.8	82.6
More than 51		48	17.4	100
	Total	**276**	**100**	
Caste				
SC		132	47.8	50
OBC		84	30.4	81.8
General		48	17.4	100
Total		264	95.7	

TABLE 8.2   *(Continued)*

Particulars		Frequency	Percent	Cumulative percent
Missing		12	4.3	
	Total	**276**	**100**	
Education				
Illiterate		36	13	13
Primary		132	47.8	60.9
Secondary		84	30.4	91.3
Graduate		12	4.3	95.7
PG and above		12	4.3	100
	Total	**276**	**100**	
Religion				
Hindu		180	65.2	65.2
Muslim		96	34.8	100
	Total	**276**	**100**	

Further, in caste, majority of the respondents are in schedule caste 132 (47.80%) and then coming OBC 84 people (30.4%). Similarly, in education, maximum of the respondents are in primary category, that is, 132 people (47.8%) and then coming secondary levels 84 people (30.4%).

8.5.2 MIGRATION

Table 8.3 and Figure 8.1 present the migration of people from rural to urban areas and from urban to urban areas. The table reveals maximum migration from rural area to urban area, that is, 73.90% and from urban to urban 26.10%.

TABLE 8.3   Migration of People from Rural and Urban Areas.

Particulars	Frequency	Percent	Cumulative percent
Rural area to urban area	204	73.9	73.9
Urban area to urban	72	26.1	100.0
Total	276	100.0	

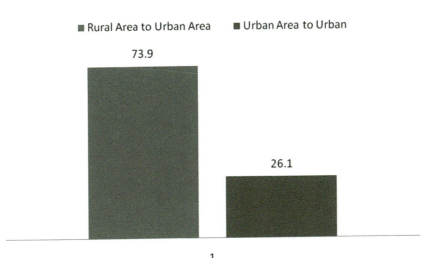

FIGURE 8.1   Migration of people from rural and urban areas.

Table 8.4 and Figure 8.2 represents the reasons of migration. The reasons is coming to others (in search of improvement of economic and social status) (91.30%) and then coming due to unemployment (26.10%) and low wage in rural areas (21.70%).

TABLE 8.4   Reasons for Migration.

Particulars	Frequency	Percent	Cumulative percent
Unemployment	72	26.1	28.6
Low wage	60	21.7	52.4
Debt	24	8.7	61.9
Drought	12	4.3	66.7
Conflict	36	13.0	81.0
Education	24	8.7	90.5
Marriage	24	8.7	100.0
Others	252	91.3	
Missing system	*24*	*8.7*	
Total	276	100.0	

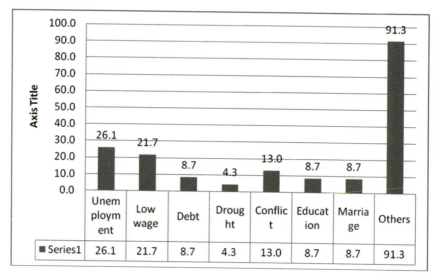

FIGURE 8.2 Reasons for migration.

Figure 8.3 and Table 8.5 shows the result of number of years slum peoples staying in Cuttack and Bhubaneswar city of Odisha. The table reveals that most of the people are staying more than 5 years (78.30%) and then coming 1–3 years (8.70%) and 3–5 years (8.70%).

TABLE 8.5 Number of Years of Stay in this Town/City.

Particulars	Frequency	Percent	Cumulative percent
0–1 year	12	4.3	4.3
1–3 years	24	8.7	13.0
3–5 years	24	8.7	21.7
More than 5 years	216	78.3	100.0
Total	**276**	**100.0**	

8.5.3 EMPLOYMENT STATUS OF SLUM PEOPLES

The employment profile of the surveyed households in the sample reveals that majority of them earn their livelihood by doing construction work in the city (43.5%). Then comes the self-employment (26.1%) of the sample households. The details of employment status of slum peoples is presented in Table 8.6 and Figure 8.4.

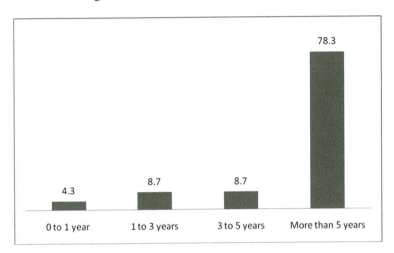

FIGURE 8.3   Number of years of stay in this town/city.

TABLE 8.6   Employment Status of Slum Peoples.

Sl. no.	Particulars	Frequency	Percent	Cumulative percent
1	No job	36	13	13
2	Construction labor	120	43.5	56.5
3	Self employed	72	26.1	82.6
4	Others	48	17.4	100
	Total	276	100	

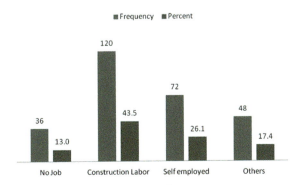

FIGURE 8.4   Employment status of slum peoples.

8.5.4 ASSOCIATION BETWEEN MONTHLY INCOME AND ECONOMIC INDEX OF SLUM PEOPLES

TABLE 8.7 Monthly Income and Economic Index Cross Tabulation ($N = 276$).

Particulars			Economic index			Total
			No change	Little change	Moderate change	
Monthly income	Less than 5000	Count	12	36	60	108
		%	11.10	33.30	55.60	100.00
	5000–10,000	Count	0	12	12	24
		%	0.00	50.00	50.00	100.00
	Above 15,000	Count	0	12	0	12
		%	0.00	100.00	0.00	100.00
Total		Count	12	60	72	144
		%	8.30	41.70	50.00	100.00

Table 8.6 represents monthly income with respect to corresponding economic index. The monthly income is subcategorized in three different ranges that is, less than 5000, 5000–10,000, and above 15,000. The economic index is classed in three broad categories, that is, no change, little change, and moderate change with respective weightage, that is, 0, 1, 2, 3, and 4.

From the data in Table 8.7, it is evident that the sample population earning above Rs. 15,000 has the highest percent (100%) of response that the social economic status have little changed. Whereas the sample population whose monthly income is below Rs. 5000, they consider moderate change in their economic index.

TABLE 8.8 Chi-Square Tests (Monthly Income and Economic Index).

Particulars	Value	df	Asymp. sig. (2-sided)
Pearson Chi-square	22.667	4	0
Likelihood ratio	28.868	4	0
Linear-by-linear association	3.828	1	0.05
N of valid cases	144		

The test was performed at 5% level of significance. The output of Chi-square test is as presented in Table 8.8. The Pearson Chi-square significance value is 0.000 and degree of freedom is 4. This reveals that there is a significant association between monthly income and economic index of the slum peoples. This proves the hypothesis, that is, *there is a significant relationship existing between monthly income and economic index of slum peoples*. In other words, these two factors are significantly associated. From the last row of the same table, it is also seen that Cramer's V value is significant with 0.000, and there is a degree of association between these two variables.

TABLE 8.9 Association between Migrated from and Economic Index of Slum Peoples ($N = 276$).

Particulars			Economic index			Total
			No change	Little change	Moderate change	
Migrated from	Rural area to urban area	Count	0	72	84	156
		%	0.00	46.20	53.80	100.00
	Urban area to urban	Count	12	0	12	24
		%	50.00	0.00	50.00	100.00
Total		Count	12	72	96	180
		%	6.70	40.00	53.30	100.00

Table 8.9 represents the association of migration and economic index. To measure the association, migration is subclassified into rural area to urban area and urban area to urban, whereas for economic index three classification were made no change, little change and moderate change.

It can be observed that the sample populations that have migrated from rural area to urban area felt moderate change in their economic index having the highest percent (53.8%), whereas the sample population that moved from urban area to urban area has the highest percent (50%) who have felt no change in the economic index.

The following hypothesis can be formed to verify the test results of the tabulated values:

H_{o1}: There is no significant relationship between migrated from and economic index of slum people

H_{a1}: There is significant relationship between migrated from and economic index of slum people

TABLE 8.10   Chi-Square Tests (Migrated from w.r.t Economic Index).

Particulars	Value	df	Asymp. sig. (2-sided)
Pearson Chi-square	89.135	2	0
Likelihood ratio	69.023	2	0
Linear-by-linear association	15.691	1	0
N of valid cases	180		

The test was performed at 5% level of significance. The output of Chi-square test is as presented in Table 8.10. The Pearson Chi-square significance value is 0.000 and degree of freedom is 2. Therefore, null hypothesis is rejected, and alternative hypothesis is accepted. This reveals that there is a significant association between migrated from and economic index of slum people. This proves the hypothesis, that is, *there is a significant relationship existing migrated from and economic index of slum peoples.* In other words, these two factors are significantly associated. From the last row of the same table, it is also seen that Cramer's V value is significant with 0.000, and there is a degree of association between these two variables.

The following hypothesis can be formed to verify the test results of the tabulated values:

H_{02}: There is no significant relationship between migrated from and SSI of slum people

H_{a2}: There is significant relationship between migrated from and SSI of slum people

TABLE 8.11   Cross Tabulation between Migrated from and Social Status Index.

Particulars			Social status index			Total
			No change	Little change	Moderate change	
Migrated from	Rural area to urban area	Count	24	36	96	156
		%	15.4	23.1	61.5	100.0
	Urban area to urban	Count	12	0	12	24
		%	50.0	50.0	0.0	100.0
Total		Count	36	108	36	180
		%	20.0	20.0	61.50	100.0

Table 8.11 represents the association of migration of rural peoples and SSI. To measure the association, migration is subclassified into rural area to urban area and urban area to urban, whereas SSI was classified as no change, little change, and moderate change.

It can be observed that the sample populations that have migrated from rural area to urban area felt moderate change in their SSI having the highest percent (61.50%), whereas the sample population that moved from urban area to urban area has the highest percent (50%) who have felt no change in the SSI.

TABLE 8.12 Chi-Square Tests (Migrated from w.r.t Social Status Index).

Particulars	Value	df	Asymp. sig. (2-sided)
Pearson Chi-square	18.462	2	0.000
Likelihood ratio	20.186	2	0.000
Linear-by-linear association	6.885	1	0.009
N of valid cases	180		

The test was performed at 5% level of significance. The output of Chi-square test is as presented in Table 8.12. The Pearson Chi-square significance value is 0.000 and degree of freedom is 2. Therefore, null hypothesis is rejected, and alternative hypothesis is accepted. This reveals that there is a significant association between migrated from and SSI of slum people. This proves the hypothesis, that is, *there is a significant relationship existing migrated from and SSI of slum peoples.* In other words, these two factors are significantly associated. From the last row of the same table, it is also seen that Cramer's V value is significant with 0.000, and there is a degree of association between these two variables.

8.6 CONCLUSION

The fast development of population in urban focuses since the freedom has prompted the rise and development of urban slums in the nation. These low salary gatherings, without appropriate safe house, were settled in pockets of the slum territories described by congestion, haggard residences, absence of sanitation, and community enhancements. The formative exercises in urban focuses give work to the provincial vagrants just as the neighborhood urban population. Limit of country people groups relocating from provincial regions for the improvement of economic and social life is 73.90%. These people groups are remaining over 5 years (78.30%). Lion's share of slum people groups are getting work in development (43.50%) and afterward coming independent work identified with selling of vegetables, gupchup, and fish. Financial conditions assume significant job in the advancement of the individuals. Without more pay, nobody can live sound life. Salary improves wellbeing and living of standard of the slum occupants. Slum occupants have been contributing altogether to the economy of any city by giving moderate work to formal also casual segments of the economy. With the assistance of the aptitude upgrade programs, we can beat down the socioeconomic status of the slum tenants. They are contributing significantly to the financial development of the district. Income and health of the slum people are correlated. If the levels of income increase then no doubt the health standard of slum people also increases.

KEYWORDS

- **socioeconomic status**
- **living conditions**
- **measure**
- **index**
- **slum dwellers**

REFERENCES

Alamgir, M.; Jabbar, M.; Islam, M. Assessing the Livelihood of Slum Dwellers in Dhaka City. *J. Bangladesh Agri. Univ.* **2009,** *7* (2), 373–380.

Ameratunga, M. H.; Norton, R. Road-Traffic Injuries: Confronting Disparities to Address a Global-Health Problem. *Lancet* **2006,** *367* (9521), 1533–1540.

Dziuban, E. et al. Surveillance for Waterborne Disease and Outbreaks Associated with Recreational Water—United States 2003–2004. *MMWR Surveill Summ* **2010,** *55* (12), 1–30.

Fox, S. The Political Economy of Slums: Theory and Evidence from Sub-Saharan Africa. *World Dev.* **2014,** *54,* 191–203.

Hossain, S. Migration, Urbanization and Poverty in Dhaka. *J. Asiatic Soc. Bangladesh* **2013**, *58*(2), 369–382.

Joshi, S. M. Migration and Labor Market in Slum Areas. *Nagarlok* **2005**, *37* (3), 34–49.

Kamruzzaman, M.; Hakim, M. A. Livelihood Status of Fishing Community of Dhaleswari River in Central Bangladesh. *Int. J. Bioinform. Biomed. Eng.* **2016**, *2* (1), 25–29.

Kamruzzaman, M. Child Victimization at Working Places in Bangladesh. *J. Soc. Sci. Human.* **2015**, *1* (5), 516–520.

Kamruzzaman, M.; Hakim, M. A. Socio-economic Status of Child Beggars in Dhaka City. *J. Soc. Sci. Human.* **2015**, *1* (5), 516–520.

Karn, S. K.; Shikura, S.; Harada, H. Living Environment and Health of Urban Poor: A Study in Mumbai. *Econ. Polit. Week.* **2003**, *38* (34), 3575–3577+3579–3586.

Kumar, P. Declining Number of Slums: Nature of Urban Growth. *Econ. Polit. Week.* **2010**, *14* (41), 75–77.

Marx, B.; Stoker, T.; Suri, T. The Economics of Slums in the Developing World. *J. Econ. Perspect.* **2013**, *27* (4), 187–210.

Nautiyal, K. C.. Basic Education in Slums of Delhi: The Growing Menace of Urban Neglect. *J. Edu. Plan. Admin.* **1993**, *7* (3), 453–473.

Ompad, D.C.; Galea, S.; Caiaffa, W. T; Vlahov, D. . Social Determinants of the Health of Urban Populations: Methodological Considerations. *J. Urban Health* **2007**, *84* (1), 43–52.

Panda, A. et al. Health Status of Under-fives in a Ludhiana Slum. *Health Population-Perspectives Iss.* **1993**, *16* (3&4), 133–141.

Pillai, M. N.; Jayagovind, R. L. Socio Economic Status of the Slum Dwellers in Trivandrum. *Int. J. Inform. Futuristic Res.* **2017**, *4* (11), 8165–8178.

Siegel, C. et al. Geographic Analysis of Pertussis Infection in an Urban Area: A Tool for Health Services Planning. *Am. J. Public Health* **1997**, *87* (12), 2022–2026.

Singh, B. N. Socio-economic Conditions of Slums Dwellers: A Theoretical Study. *KAAV Int. J. Arts, Human. Soc. Sci.* **2016**, *3* (3), 77–91.

Stokes, C. J. A Theory of Slum. *Land Econ.* **1962**, *38* (3), 187–197.

Unger, A.; Riley, L. W. Slum Health: From Understanding to Action. *PLoS Med.* **2007**, *4* (10), 295.

UN-HABITAT. *The Challenge of the Slums: Global Report on Human Settlements*; United Nations: Nairobi, 2003.

WEBSITES

https://www.census2011.co.in/slums.php (accessed Aug. 23, 2018).
https://www.bmc.gov.in/programs/urban-poverty-alleviation (accessed Jan. 25, 2019).
http://cmccuttack.gov.in/poverty_alleviation.html (accessed Jan. 23, 2019).

CHAPTER 9

Sustainable Social Independence: Microfinance Experience

BISWAJIT PRASAD CHHATOI[1], PALLABI MISHRA[2], and
SHARADA PRASAD SAHOO[3*]

[1]Department of Economics and Management Khallikote, University, Odisha, India

[2]Department of Business Administration Utkal University, Bhubaneswar, Odisha, India

[3]Department of Economics and Management Khallikote, University, Odisha, India

*Corresponding author. E-mail: sharadaprasadsahoo@gmail.com

ABSTRACT

This chapter estimates the social sustainability of economically deprived households through microcredit. The respondents for the current research are 476 microcredit beneficiaries spread three blocks of three different districts of Odisha. Through a close-ended questionnaire following direct personal interview and group discussion, the perception of respondents was gathered. Descriptive and inferential statistics were used to manipulate the data to arrive at any conclusion considering the impact on members as a household. The estimated result predicts that sustainable social independence can be achieved through microfinance. But as regards the impact of microcredit, it does not have uniform impact on all the variables of social empowerment. The result of research is limited to its sample size and sample, that is, 476 respondents of geographical outreach, that is, three blocks. The result gives insights into the social enchainment of deprived women by estimating improvements in social mobility and financial decision-making.

9.1 INTRODUCTION

The state of Odisha is experiencing a rapid economy growth in India. As per the 2014–2015 economic survey, the gross domestic products of Odisha were anticipated to grow at 8.78 as compared to 2.21% in 2013–2014 whereas at 8.1% over the period of 2015–2020. The states have an agricultural base economy having more concentration of population in rural Odisha. Near about 61% of the population depends on agriculture whereas more than 84% reside in rural areas are characterized by poverty and backwardness. The overall development of the state is possible through the socioeconomic advancement of rural farmer families.

The sex ratio in Odisha was 978 (2011 census), which indicates that out of total population the female is near about 49%. The female literacy in Odisha has been lower than male and also has been consistently below the Indian level. The overall literacy of Odisha was 72.87% whereas particularly in female was only 64.01% as compared to 50.51% in 2001. As per the 2001 census, the percentage of women work in Odisha was 31.35% as compared to 10.75% in 1971. The change in rural work participation of women was at higher 34.5% (approximately) as compared to urban only 15.15%. Out of total women workforce, more than 75% of women work in the unorganized sector like agriculture. Most of the rural workforces primarily assist their spouse in the inherent profession of the spouse, which limits the financial and social freedom of the rural women. The families in rural Odisha are male-dominated families, where the women members of the family are dependent on the male members in the social and economic transaction and decision-making. The marginalized rural population have credit requirements for productive as well as nonproductive purpose. The productive purpose increases the income and capital asset but unproductive purpose enhances consumption and recurring expenses. The institutional source of rural credit has the limitation of collateral and free access to institutional credit agencies individually, which promote "Sahukars" in the rural area. To overcome the limitation of direct institutional credit, an alternative approach microcredit was developed. The broader objective of the study is to find the effect of microfinance on social enrichment of the women self-help group members in rural Odisha.

9.2   LITERATURE REVIEW

Hossain (1984, 1988) pointed out that the microcredit programs by the Grameen Bank have a positive impact on the alleviation of poverty and improvement of the social status of women by increasing the income. Rehman (1987) concluded that the participation in Grameen Banks in Bangladesh has a positive effect on domestic expenses and asset creation as well as significant impact on social aspects such as self-employment and children education (World Bank report). To support this, Khandker (1998) concluded increased participation of women in microcredit leads to increase day-to-day expenses. Pitt and Khandker (1998) concluded availing credit from Grameen Bank has a significant impact on economic condition as well as women empowerment of the household.

Wahid (1994) has identified through group liability system the improvement of the economic condition of women. He identified a higher recovery rate on noncollateral loans, that is, 95% of 2.4 million members are able to repay their loan, of which 95% was women. Nirantar (2007) examined the impact on women members joining self-help groups (SHGs) and identified the women self-help groups (WSHGs), which act as catalyst for social development and women empowerment. Chliova et al. (2014) identified a positive influence of microcredit on the development and sustainability of the client entrepreneurs. Crépon et al. (2015) suggested that the access to microcredit increases the asset base of beneficiaries and provides self-employment and financial independence. Islam (2015) recommended that the effects of microcredit are significant in the case of women, and the level of consumption is not uniform across different groups.

Lakew (1998) recommended that microfinance have positive impact on income and saving of the beneficiaries and also improved access to medical, education, and nutrition. and Hulme (1998) commented on the process of identifying the beneficiaries and estimation of poverty and concluded that the repayment of loan must not be considered as microfinance activity able to generate income.

Borchgrevink et al. (2005) ascertained microcredit participation. In estimating the impact of microfinance participation on socioeconomic condition of women beneficiaries researchers such as Hashemi et al. (1996), Hunt and Kasynathan (2002), Agha et al. (2004), Saraswathy and Panicker (2008), and Aruna (2011) concluded that in every aspect of life, the microfinance has some impact that leads to women empowerment in long run. Page and Czuba (1999) define that social empowerment is a multidimensional social process and assists in control over individual's life, a process that takes care empower people in their life, community, and society. Women empowerment has five components that are sense of self-worth; right to have and to determine choices; right to have access to opportunities and resources; right to have the power to control their own lives, both within and outside the home; ability to influence the direction of social change to create a more just social and economic order, nationally and internationally (UN, 1994 International Conference on Population and Development).

Leach and Sitaram (2002) pointed out that microfinance works as a catalyst for the social empowerment of women. Puhazhendhi and Satyasai (2001) pointed out that SHGs are actively contributing to reasonable economic, social, and cultural empowerment of the rural poor women.

Rural poor women have historically had less independence or rights and have less confidence to work outside their home due to restrictions from family members, conventional barriers. The participation in micro-credit programs has an identical impact on self-confidence and self-esteem of women (Anderson, 1996; Claridge, 1996; Kabeer, 2001). The impact of microcredit participation is unable to affect all the aspects of women empowerment (Beegle et al., 1998; Hashemi et al., 1996; Kishor, 2000; Malhotra and Mather, 1997). The development of microcredit has resulted in improving women participation in society, in governance, in awareness and knowledge base program, and in the political campaign that is considered as part of women empowerment (Bennett, 2002; Malhotra, 2002; Saraswathy and Panicker, 2008; Swain and Wallentin, 2007). Gibb (2008) identified the traditional role of women in the family as an hurdle to women empowerment and financial decision-making. In household, control over the economic decision and the monetary matter is a function of family structure (Malhotra and Mather, 1997), in nuclear family women has more autonomy. Identifying the impact on microcredit on women empowerment, Amin et al. (1998) concluded that it has significant and positive impact on autonomy of women.

Hashemi et al. (1996) identified a few indicators of women empowerment and improvement. The indicators include variables from political, economic, social, and legal aspects which affect the status of the women in family and society. Gaiha and Nandhi (2007) pointed out that access to microfinance has given significant effect on female autonomy in financial decisions, whereas Samanta (2009) concluded that microfinance participation has no impact on financial decision-making power of women even if no control over the loan amount.

Out of different perspectives of microcredit, the socioeconomic conditions of beneficiaries (Adjei et al., 2009; Yeboah, 2010) are considered to be a prominent field of research around the globe. A wide array of research revealed the fact that microfinance activities have improved the share of women on the various expenses such as "spending on" education of children (Agyapong et al., 2017; Hassan and Saleem, 2017; Hinrichsen, 2015; Joshi and Giri, 2016; Qamar et al., 2017; Viswanath, 2018), health care of own and family members (Agyapong et al., 2017; Jayashankar and Goedegebuure, 2011; Mafukata et al., 2014; The Pioneer, 2018), food and nutrition (Gumel, 2014; Moseson et al., 2014; Nawaz and McLaren, 2016; Onyekeni and Ihediwa, 2016; Sharif, 2005), and higher standard of living (Ariful et al., 2017; Onyekeni and Ihediwa, 2016). The microfinance activities have a positive effect on improving spending on household assets (Al-Mamun et al., 2013; Chhatoi and Mishra, 2017; Crépon et al., 2015). Microcredit is also aiming at social empowerment of rural women (Kumar et al. 2015; Nader, 2008) by enhancing financial responsibilities in the family (Kane, 2013).

9.3 RESEARCH GAP AND THE STATEMENT OF THE PROBLEM

Plenty of research on microcredit is there on identifying the impact of microcredit on the socioeconomic condition of participants across the globe. But, there is little research on the effect of microfinance on decision-making power and social mobility of clients (women the "real poor section" of the society). Studies conducted on impact of microcredit on economic decision like the use of income, control over loan, and savings but no study found "who takes decision" on the amount of savings, availing loan, and creation of business assets. Further, studies carried out in social empowerment are related to macro factors like participation in the political campaign, society, governance, awareness, and knowledge base programs. But micro factors like moving to natal home, take care of own health issues, moving with the group within the state have not been attempted by any researcher. Contextualizing the depiction of above narration, it is spellbound to make out the present study entitled "Social Independence of Marginalised WSHG Members: Microfinance Effect."

9.4   OBJECTIVE OF THE STUDY

The objective of the study is to measure the impact of microcredit on the socioeconomic decision-making power of WSHG members as an individual in the family.

9.5   HYPOTHESIS

$H_0 1$: Participation in MCP (micro credit participation) has no impact on the household's economic decisions.

$H_0 2$: Participation in MCP has no impact on mobility of microcredit participants.

$H_0 3$: Participation in MCP has no impact on change in financial contribution of microcredit participants.

9.6   RESEARCH METHODOLOGY

The literature section of the study discloses the earlier research on the current topic. Current section deals with the methodology adopted to conduct research. The current research is an exploratory and a nonexperimental research. The current research model tries to discover the impact of microcredit on the social condition of WSHG members as an individual in rural Odisha. The researcher has collected primary data for the current research.

The women microcredit borrowers of Odisha having more than 1-year experience in SHG activities are the universe of the study. Jagatsinghpur and Dhenkanal districts were selected for data collection. Purposively, one block selected from each district was covered under the study such as Pipili block from Puri district, Balikuda from Jagatsinghpur, and

Kamakhyanagar from Dhenkanal district. The respondents are the active women microcredit borrowers. The respondents are as an "individual" for the social impact whereas for economic impact as "household." The sample of 476 respondents is selected disproportionately from three clusters, that is, 176 respondents from Pipili block, 160 respondents from Balikuda block, and the rest 140 respondents from Kamakhyanagar block. The women microcredit borrowers having more than 1-year experience are considered as respondents. The social impact is measured considering the respondent as an individual.

The responses of the same respondents were collected in two rounds over a gap of 1 year through a close-ended questionnaire translating into the local language (Odia). A total of 176 questionnaires were distributed in every block over 44 WSHGs and four members from each WSHG were selected randomly. The first-round survey conducted over the period May 2017–July 2017 and 528 questionnaires are distributed, out of which only 496 questionnaires found complete. The second-round survey conducted over the period May 2018–August 2018. The researcher collected the response of 496 households in qualified the first round and only 476 are identified. Time taken to complete second- and first-round data collection were 4 months and 2 months, respectively. Descriptive and inferential statistics were used to analyze the data.

9.7 ANALYSIS AND DATA INTERPRETATION

TABLE 9.1   Respondents' Demographic Details.

Categories	Details	Number of respondents	%
Habitation	Rural	346	72.69
	Semi-urban	130	27.31
	Total	*476*	100.00
Age	<25 years	18	3.78
	25–35 years	326	68.49
	36–55 years	111	23.66732
	>55 years	21	4.41
	Total	*476*	100.00

TABLE 9.1 *(Continued)*

Categories	Details	Number of respondents	%
Caste	General	133	27.94
	SEBC/OBC	192	40.34
	ST	59	12.39
	SC	92	19.33
	Total	*476*	100.00
Education	Under metric	332	69.75
	Metric and intermediate	113	23.74
	Graduate and above	31	6.51
	Total	*476*	100.00

Table 9.1 contains the details of respondents' profile. It is evidenced that the respondents are uneducated (70% of respondents under metric), young (72% within the age of 40 years), general (together OBC and general is 68%), and rural women.

TABLE 9.2 Change in Decision Taker to Avail Loan in a Family Due to Microcredit.

	Details	Round 1		Round 2		Change (%)
		No. of respondents	%	No. of respondents	%	
	Self	314	65.97	332	69.75	5.73
	Spouse	15	3.15	12	2.52	−20.00
Availing loan	Self + spouse	147	30.88	132	27.73	−10.20
	Total	476	100.00	476	100.00	
	Self	332	69.75	365	76.68	9.94
Make savings	Spouse	0	–	0	–	–
	Self + spouse	144	30.25	111	23.32	−22.92
	Total	476	100.00	476	100.00	

TABLE 9.2 *(Continued)*

Details		Round 1		Round 2		Change (%)
		No. of respondents	%	No. of respondents	%	
Amount of savings	Self	213	44.75	233	48.95	9.39
	Spouse	75	15.76	72	15.13	−4.00
	Self + spouse	188	39.50	171	35.92	−9.04
	Total	476	100.00	476	100.00	
Utilizing loan/ savings	Self	62	13.03	73	15.34	17.74
	Spouse	289	60.71	271	56.93	−6.23
	Self + spouse	125	26.26	132	27.73	5.60
	Total	476	100.00	476	100	−
Expenditure out of own income	Self	259	54.41	293	61.55	13.13
	Spouse	38	7.98	35	7.35	−7.89
	Self + spouse	179	37.61	148	31.09	−17.32
	Total	476	100.00	476	100	−
Creation of household assets	Self	219	46.01	241	50.63	10.05
	Spouse	43	9.03	34	7.14	−20.93
	Self + spouse	214	44.96	201	42.23	−6.07
	Total	476	100.00	476	100	−
Creation of business assets	Self	129	27.10	140	29.41	8.53
	Spouse	201	42.23	182	38.24	−9.45
	Self + spouse	146	30.67	154	32.35	5.48
	Total	476	100.00	476	100	−

Source: Primary data.

WSHG members participate in the group loan. Availing loan is a financial decision in the family. The decision on "availing loan" is either taken by member herself or by spouse and or by both. The decision taken by the member to avail loan is increased by near about 6% in second round whereas decision is taken by spouse and both decreased by 20 and 10% as compared to the first round.

It is clear from Table 9.2 that "make savings" is either decided by the member or by the spouse and member together. Increased participation in microfinance increases decision taken individually on "make savings" by 9.94%.

"The decision for savings" and "decision on the amount of savings" differ from each other. The creation of savings is mandatory in a group activity for a minimum amount. But the creation of savings over and above minimum amount is not mandatory to the member. The change in the decision taken independently by the member is increased by 9.39% over the period of study.

The investigation result on decision maker of utilizing loan/savings from microcredit is summarized in the fourth section Table 9.2. It is cleared from the data that due to participation in microcredit, the women empowerment and participation are increasing. The shifting of decision-making from men to women is found in 18 families, out of which in 11 families, it is shifted from men to women.

By comparing the results of both the round it is observed that the decision-making power of women on household expenditure out of own income individually is increased by 13.13%, whereas the participative decision of women is decreased by 17.32% that indicates the empowerment of rural women. In the creation of household assets, the decision-making power of microfinance participants is assessed. The net change in decision-taking power of rural women independently is increased by 10% over the study period.

In the creation of business assets, the decision-making power of rural women is assessed. Independently, in the second round, more than 8% of the rural women decide to invest in business assets whereas jointly deciding to invest in business assets is increased by 5.48%.

Moving alone to manage own work is an indicator of empowerment and social independence. Over the study period, the change is measured and summarized in Table 9.3. The ability to move alone is increased by 4.3% in the second round as compared to the first round.

TABLE 9.3   Change in Mobility to Manage Own Work.

Overall ability to move alone

Details	Round 1		Round 2		Change
	No. of respondents	%	No. of respondents	%	
Yes	328	68.91	342	71.85	4.26829
No	148	31.09	134	28.15	−9.4595
Total	476	100.00	476	100	
Individual mobility for specific work					
Availing public transport	342	71.85	371	77.94	8.48
Government office	187	39.29	199	41.81	6.42
Solve own health issues	378	79.41	428	89.92	13.23
With group within state	103	21.64	129	27.10	25.24
Natal place	412	86.55	448	94.12	8.74
Outside state	29	6.09	33	6.93	13.79

Source: Primary data.

Change in mobility of microcredit participants to specific place is summarized in the second part of Table 9.3. The changes are positive over 1 year. The increased percentage of respondents are able to manage alone in "availing public transport," "government office," "solve own health issues," "with group within state," and "natal place" is, respectively, 8.48, 6.42, 13.23, 25.24, 8.74, and 13.79%.

TABLE 9.4   Change in Contribution Made by Respondents to the Family.

Details	Round 1		Round 2		Change
	No. of respondents	%	No. of respondents	%	
Contributing consumption expenses (food and small expenses)	313	65.76	321	67.44	2.56
Financial support for education of children	175	36.76	175	36.76	−

TABLE 9.4 *(Continued)*

Details	Round 1		Round 2		Change
	No. of respondents	%	No. of respondents	%	
Financial support for children's health care	317	66.60	342	71.85	7.89
Financial support for health care of spouse and other family members excluding children	130	27.31	134	28.15	3.08
Contributes for better standard of living	34	7.14	37	7.77	8.82
Contribute large share in creation of household assets	165	34.66	171	35.92	3.64
Provide financial support to spouse (for primary earning source of spouse)	179	37.61	185	38.87	3.35

Source: Estimated through primary data August 2018.

The financial responsibility bear by the WSHG member in the family is converted into the contribution of them to the family. No change in contribution is found in supporting the education of children over 1 year. The changes (increase in participation of a number of WSHG members) are 2.56, 7.89, 3.08, 8.82, 3.64, and 3.35% recorded for food and small expenses, health care of children, health care of other family members, contributes for better standard of living, creation of household assets, and assisting primary earning source, respectively.

9.8 HYPOTHESIS TESTING

$H_0 1$: Participation in MCP has no impact on the household's economic decisions.

The impact of microfinance on the household's economic decision is analyzed and some changes are identified over the study period. "Z" proportion test is applied to test the hypothesis.

TABLE 9.5 "Z" Proportion Test Summary on Change in Economic Decisions Ability.

Variables	Round 1	Round 2	Difference	Z-Value	P-Value
Avail loan	65.97	69.75	3.78	1.2	0.2118
Making savings	69.75	76.68	6.93	2.4	0.0158
Amount of savings	44.75	48.95	4.2	1.3	0.1941
Use of loan/savings	13.03	15.34	2.31	1	0.3071
Household expenses	54.51	61.55	7.04	2.2	0.0278*
Creation of household assets	46.01	50.63	4.62	1.4	0.1538
Creation of business assets	27.1	29.41	2.31	0.8	0.4286

Source: Compiled and computed data.

Out of seven economic decisions, the microcredit participation has significant influence on the changes in control over the decisions such as "making savings" and "household expenses" at 5% level, whereas the changes in the rest five decisions are not significant at 5%.

$H_0 2$: Participation in MCP has no impact on a woman's mobility.

TABLE 9.6 "Z" Proportion Test Summary on Change in Mobility Over Period of Study.

Variables	Round 1	Round 2	Difference	Z-value	P-value
Overall mobility	68.91	71.85	2.94	1	0.3205
Availing public transport	71.85	77.94	6.09	2.2	0.0303
Government office	39.29	41.81	2.52	0.8	0.4285
Solve own health issues	79.41	89.92	10.51	4.5	<0.0001
With group within state	21.64	27.10	5.71	2.0	0.0498
Natal place	86.55	94.12	7.57	4.0	<0.0001
Outside state	6.09	6.93	0.8	0.5	0.5994

Source: Compiled and computed data.

The changes in overall mobility and specific mobility of WSHG members tested applying Z proportion test. It is observed the change in overall mobility is insignificant and the hypothesis is accepted at 95% confidence level. Further, in specific mobility, out of six variables the changes in the variable "moving to government office" and "outside state" are not significant at 95% confidence level and the hypothesis is accepted. The changes in the rest four variables are significant and the hypothesis is rejected at 5% significance level.

$H_0 3$: Participation in MCP has no impact on change in economic contribution made by respondents to the family.

TABLE 9.7   "Z" Proportion Test Summary on Change Contribution to Family.

Details	Round 1	Round 2	Change	Z-value	P-value
Contributing day-to-day expenses (food and small expenses)	65.76	67.44	1.68	0.5	0.5826
Financial support for education of children	36.76	36.76	–	NA	NA
Financial support for children's health care	66.60	71.85	5.85	2.0	0.0512
Financial support for health care of spouse and other family members excluding children	27.31	28.15	0.84	0.3	0.7722
Contributes for better standard of living	7.14	7.77	0.63	0.4	0.7114
Contribute higher proportion in creation of household assets	34.66	35.92	1.26	0.4	0.6842
Provide financial support to spouse (for primary earning source of spouse)	37.61	38.87	3.35	0.4	0.6892

Source: Compiled and computed data.

Out of seven variables, there is no change observed for "financial support for education of children." The Z proportion test was applied at 95% confidence level and found that the changes are not significant.

9.9   FINDINGS, DISCUSSION, AND CONCLUSION

Microfinance institutions are present in most of the countries in the world and providing microcredit from underdeveloped to developed countries for different purposes. The popularity of microcredit becomes more common over the 1990s in developed countries (Counts, 1996; McDonnell, 1999; Pearson, 2000). The access to microcredit is the resultant of women empowerment through the world (Todd, 1996). Women themselves disclose about the increased self-reliance, self-esteem, self-confidence, and controlling own lives due to participation in microcredit. On the above background, the current study carried out to estimate the impact of microcredit on mobility and decision-making power of women in the family. In the economic decision, control over "avail loan," "make savings and amount of savings," "use of loan amount," "expenses on household," "household assets creation," and "business asset accumulation" is considered by the researcher as variables of economic empowerment. Out of the seven variables, Hashemi et al. (1996) pointed "ability to make small purchases on house hold expenses" and "ability to make larger purchases on household assets or business assets as components of economic empowerment of women." Further, control over the allocation of resources, savings, and investments as variables of economic empowerment was confirmed by Gaiha and Nandhi (2007) and control over credit as a component of women empowerment was confirmed by Samanta (2009). The changes on control over "availing loan," "making savings and amount of savings," "use of loan amount," "household expenses," "creation of household asset and business asset" individual WSHG member in the family are 5.73, 9.94, 17.74, 13.13, 10.05, and 8.53%, respectively. The changes are significant in the case of "making savings" and "household expenses." But changes on the rest components are not significant. Rural Odisha is characterized by male-dominated joint family where most of the economic decision is taken by senior-most member or male member of the family. The scope of economic empowerment is very limited as the decision-making power is under the control of the male members. The changes over make savings are group decision where the group members are decided a minimum amount of savings out of the income of activity they have undertaken. The changes are significant and supported by Hashemi et al. (1996) and Gaiha and Nandhi (2007) that access to microfinance has given significant effect on female autonomy in savings mobilization. The significant impact of microfinance on managing "expenses on household" is supported by the logic that the day-to-day expenses are very negligible in which the male members do not interfere and most of the male member let it to the spouses. Further, these findings are supported by the findings of Hossain (1984, 1988), Rehman (1987) and World Bank reported that the microcredit participation has positive impact on variables like household expenses, and findings of Hashemi et al. (1996) and Gaiha and Nandhi (2007) that microcredit programs are able to enhance the ability and decision-making power to make small purchases on household expenses. On rest variables such as control over "avail loan," "amount of savings," "use of loan amount," and "creation of household asset and business asset," the study identified an insignificant impact of microcredit. Rural poor women of Odisha have less independence or rights and have less confidence to take the financial decision because of family restrictions, social, and traditional barriers. Further, joint families are found in rural Odisha, where most of the financial decisions are taken by the senior member of the family. In joint family structure, the treasurer of the family is the senior-most female member of the family who assists the senior-most male member only keeping the money with her. Most of the WSHG member is the daughter-in-law (BOHU) of that family. The traditional role of daughter in law in a family is to take carry of all household work and family and with a limited exposure to participate in economic decisions that limit the impact of microcredit. These findings are supported by Gibb (2008) who concluded that microcredit was unable to empower microcredit beneficiaries (women) as she could not transform her traditional household role and also retain control over money decision, and Samanta (2009) pointed out that participations in microcredit women have no control over credit that limits the impact microfinance on empower women.

The second variable of the study is the mobility of WSHG members. Under mobility the variables of study are overall mobility, availing public transport service, access government office, taking care own health issues, move with group within the state, moving natal place, and move outside the state with the group. Out of the seven variables, the impact of microfinance is significant on availing public transport, solves minor own health issues, moving with the group within the state, moving alone to natal place. Increase in supply side and roads and other basic infrastructure facilities in rural Odisha makes it easy to avail the public transport at the doorstep of the rural villagers, which have a considerable impact on increasing in availing public transport among WHSH members that increase independence in moving to natal place alone. The awareness level of microcredit beneficiaries has been enhanced due to participation in SHG activity. The increase in health campaigns by government is one of the factors that motivated women to take care of their own health issues in serious and presence of health works in the rural Odisha is lead to significant increase in thinking independently the health issues. The production of different products through microenterprise has significantly increased due to SHG activity. One of the major ways of promoting sales of SHG products is arrangement different trade fares across the Odisha during different occasions. For the abovementioned purpose, the members of the WHSGs have to move different places inside the state to participate in trade fares organized by government, which aim at increasing the income of SHG and individual income. Due to pressure and exception of higher income generation, the changes in the variable are significant. On rest variables, the impact of microcredit is not significant.

As regard to the contribution of WHSGs members to different financial aspects of the family, the changes are not significant, because the changes were measured over a short period of time. Out of seven variables, no change was found for "financial support for education of children." Out of total respondents, more than 72% of respondents are of age less than 36 years where maximum children are in schooling. Since the Government of Odisha is taking care of all expenses up to completion of secondary level, the beneficiaries did not have to spend more on education.

For the rest six variables, an increased participation was observed from the WHSG members. The increase in spending for "contributing day-to-day expenses" was supported by Nawaz and McLaren (2016), Onyekeni and Ihediwa (2016), and Moseson et al. (2014); "financial support for health care of children," and "financial support for health care of spouse and other family members excluding children" were supported by The Pioneer (2018) and Agyapong et al. (2017); "contributes for better standard of living" was supported by Ariful et al. (2017), Onyekeni and Ihediwa (2016); "contribute large share in creation of household assets" was supported by Chhatoi and Mishra (2017), Crépon et al. (2015), and Al-Mamun et al. (2013); and "provide financial support to spouse" was supported by Kane (2013).

Microfinance is a fast-growing and dynamic part of the world financial sector. The need for microfinance is more in developing countries as compared to developed countries. But it is not yet very glowing as regards impact, approaches, and performance of microcredit organization. Microfinance activities generate additional income and employment to alleviate poverty in developing countries creating a positive social, economical, and cultural change at different levels of society. On the above backdrop, the current research tries to identify the impact of microfinance on women empowerment. The finds recommended that the microfinance is able to change the image of women in the family through participation in some of the economic decision and change in the social image through change in social mobility, confidence, and self-esteem. Further, the impact of microfinance is not significant in some areas. Consider microfinance participation as a magic bullet, which can achieve overall social, economical, and cultural empowerment over a short span of time is not true.

KEYWORDS

- microcredit
- women self-help group
- household

REFERENCES

Agha, S.; Balal, A.; Ogojo-Okello, F. The Impact of Microfinance Programs on Client Perceptions of Quality of Care Provided by Private Sector Midwives in Uganda. *Health Serv. Res.* **2004,** *39* (6pt2), 2081–2100.

Agyapong, D. A.; Adjei, P. O.; Boafo, J. Microfinance, Rural Non-farm Activities and Welfare Linkages in Ghana: Assessing Beneficiaries' Perspectives. *Global Soc. Welf.* **2017,** *4* (1), 11–19. DOI: http://dx.doi.org/10.1007/s40609-015-0037-x.

Amin, R.; Becker, S.; Byes A. NGO-Promoted Micro Credit Programs and Women's Empowerment in Rural Bangladesh: Quantitative and Qualitative Evidence. *J. Dev. Areas* **1998,** *32* (2), 221–236.

Anderson, J. Yes, But Is It Empowerment? Initiation, Implementation and Outcomes of Community Action. In *Critical Perspectives on Empowerment*; Humphries, B., Ed.; Venture Press: Birmingham, 1996; pp 69–83.

Ariful, C. H.; Das, A.; Rahman, A. The Effectiveness of Micro-Credit Programmes Focusing on Household Income, Expenditure and Savings: Evidence from Bangladesh. *J. Competitive* **2017,** *9* (2), 33–44. DOI: http://dx.doi.org/10.7441/joc.2017.02.03.

Aruna, M. The Role of Microfinance in Women Empowerment: A Study on the SHG Bank Linkage Program in Hyderabad. *Indian J. Commer. Manage. Stud.* **2011,** *II* (4), 77–95.

Beegle, K.; Frankenberg, E.; Thomas, D. Bargaining Power within Couples and Use of Prenatal and Delivery Care in Indonesia. *Stud. Fam. Plann.* **1998,** *32* (2), 130.

Bennett, L. *Using Empowerment and Social Inclusion for Pro-poor Growth: A Theory of Social Change;* Working Draft of Background Paper for the Social Development Strategy Paper, World Bank: Washington, DC, 2002.

Borchgrevink, A.; Tassew, W.; Gebrehiwot, A.; Woldeab, T. *Marginalized Groups, Credit and Empowerment: The Case of Debit Credit and Saving Institution (DECSI) of Tigray, Ethiopia*; Occasional Paper No. 14, Association of Microfinance Institutions: Addis Ababa, Ethiopia, 2005.

Brett, A. J. "We Sacrifice and Eat Less": The Structural Complexities of Microfinance Participation. *Hum. Organ.* **2006,** *65* (1), 8–19.

Chhatoi, B. P.; Mishra, P. Enhancing Economic Sustainability through Microcredit: An Analysis over Different Activity. In *Sustainability: Inspiration, Innovation and Inclusion*; IIM: Shillong, 2017, ISBN 978-1-78635-414-3; 177.

Chliova, M.; Brinckmann, J.; Rosenbusch, N. Is Microcredit a Blessing for the Poor? A Meta-analysis Examining Development Outcomes and Contextual Considerations. *J. Bus. Venturing* **2014**, *30* (1), 185.

Claridge, C. Women, Development and the Environment: A Method to Facilitate Women's Empowerment. Unpublished Ph.D. Thesis, Department of Agriculture, The University of Queensland: Brisbane, 1996.

Counts, A. *Give LIS Credit: How Small Loam Today Can Shape Our Tomorrow*; Times Books, Random House: Champaign, IL, 1996.

Crépon, B. Estimating the Impact of Microcredit on Those Who Take It Up: Evidence from a Randomized Experiment in Morocco. *Am. Econ. J. Appl. Econ.* **2015**, *7* (1), 123–150.

Crépon, B.; Devoto, F.; Duflo, E.; Parienté, W. Estimating the Impact of Microcredit on Those Who Take It Up: Evidence from a Randomized Experiment in Morocco. *Am. Econ. J. Appl. Econ.* **2015**, *7* (1), 123–150.

Gaiha, R.; Nandhi, M. A. *Microfinance, Self-Help Groups, and Empowerment in Maharashtra*; ASARC Working Papers 2007–15, Australian National University, South Asia Research Centre: Canberra, 2007.

Gibb, S. *Microfinance's Impact on Education, Poverty and Empowerment: A Case Study from Bolivian*; Altiplanio Development Research Working Paper Series, Institute for Advanced Development Studies, Humburg, Germany, 2008.

Gumel, G. B. Impact of Microfinance on Poverty Alleviation: A Case of North-western Nigeria. Paper presented at the **2014**, *5* (1), 304–311. Retrieved from: https://search.proquest.com/docview/1558853938?accountid=175698.

Hashemi, S.; Schuler, S.; Riley, A. Rural Credit Programs and Women's Empowerment in Bangladesh. *World Dev.* **1996**, *24* (4), 635–653.

Hassan, A.; Saleem, S. An Islamic Microfinance Business Model in Bangladesh. *Humanomics* **2017**, *33* (1), 15–37. Retrieved from: https://search.proquest.com/docvie w/1861096414?accountid=175698.

Hinrichsen, M. B. All Ways Are Roads: Everyday Survival and Microentrepreneurship among Men and Women at the Base of the Economic Pyramid in Urban Ecuador (Order No. 3705489), 2015. Available from ProQuest Central; ProQuest Dissertations & Theses Global. (1691327370). Retrieved from: https://search.proquest.com/docview/16913273 70?accountid=175698.

Hossain, M. *Credit for the Rural Poor: The Experience of Grameen Banks in Bangladesh*; BIDS Research Monograph No. 4, Bangladesh Institute of Development Studies: Dhaka, 1984.

Hunt, J.; Kasynathan, N. Reflections on Microfinance and Women's Empowerment. *Dev. Bull.* **2002**, *57*, 71–75.

Islam, A. Heterogeneous Effects of Microcredit: Evidence from Large-scale Programs in Bangladesh. *J. Asian Econ.* 2015, *37*, 48–58.

Jayashankar, P.; Goedegebuure, R. V. Marketing Strategies and Social Performance Outcomes: A Field Study on MFI Clients. *IUP J. Mark. Manage.* **2011**, *10* (2), 7–32. Retrieved from: https://search.proquest.com/docview/869507142?accountid=175698.

Joshi, P.; Giri, A. K. Economic and Social Impact of Micro Finance Programs: An Empirical Study of SHGs in Rajasthan, India. *IPE J. Manage.* **2016,** *6* (1), 131–150. Retrieved from: https://search.proquest.com/docview/1828144103?accountid=175698.

Kabeer, N. *Reflections on the Measurement of Women Empowerment, in Discussing Women Empowerment—Theory and Practice, Ida Studies No. 3*; Novum Grafiska AB: Stockholm, 2001.

Khandker, S. R. *Fighting Poverty with Microcredit: Experience in Bangladesh*; Oxford University Press: New York, 1998.

Kishor, S. In *Women Contraceptive Use in Egypt: What Do Direct Measures of Empowerment Tell Us?* Paper Prepared for Presentation at the Annual Meeting of the Population Association of America, March 23–25, Los Angeles, CA, 2000.

Lakew, B. Micro Enterprise Credit and Poverty Alleviation in Ethiopia: The Case the Project Office for the Creation of Small Scale Business Opportunities (POCSSBO) in Addis Ababa. Unpublished MSc. Thesis, Department of Economic, Addis Ababa University, 1998.

Leach, F.; Sitaram, S. Microfinance and Women's Empowerment: A Lesson from India. *Dev. Pract.* **2002,** *12* (5), 575–588.

Mafukata, M. A.; Kancheya, G.; Dhlandhara, W. Factors Influencing Poverty Alleviation amongst Microfinance Adopting Households in Zambia. *Int. J. Res. Bus. Soc. Sci.* **2014,** *3* (2), 1–19. Retrieved from: https://search.proquest.com/docview/1524709946?accountid=175698.

Malhotra, A. *Measuring Women's Empowerment as a Variable in International Development*; World Bank, Gender and Development Group: Washington, DC, 2002.

Malhotra, A.; Mather, M. Do Schooling and Work Empower Women in Developing Countries? Gender and Domestic Decisions in Sri Lanka. *Sociol. Forum* **1997,** *12* (4), 599–630.

McDonnell, S. *The Grameen Bank Micro-credit Model: Lessons for Australian Indigenous Economic Policy*; The Australian National University Centre for Aboriginal Economic Policy Research: Canberra, 1999.

Moseson, H.; Hamad, R.; Fernald, L. Microcredit Participation and Child Health: Results from a Cross-sectional Study in Peru. *J. Epidemiol. Commun. Health* **2014,** *68* (12), 1175. DOI: http://dx.doi.org/10.1136/jech-2014-204071.

Moslui, P.; Hulme, D. Microenterprise Finance: Is There a Conflict between Growth and Poverty Alleviation? *World Dev.* **1998,** *26* (5), 783–790.

Nawaz, F.; McLaren, H. J. Silencing the Hardship: Bangladeshi Women, Microfinance and Reproductive Work. *Soc. Altern.* **2016,** *35* (1), 19–25. Retrieved from: https://search.proquest.com/docview/1806212330?accountid=175698.

Nirantar. *Examining Literacy and Power within Self Help Groups: A Quantitative Study*; Nirantar, New Delhi, 2007.

Onyekeni, A. U.; Ihediwa, N. C. Mobilizing the Rural Poor in Nigeria through Microfinance. *Cogito* **2016,** *8* (3), 54–74. Retrieved from: https://search.proquest.com/docview/1869479049?accountid=175698.

Page, N.; Czuba, C. E. Empowerment: What Is It? *J. Ext.* **1999,** *37* (5).

Pearson, R. In *Gender, Globalization, arid Transitional Economies*, Gender Conference on Indochina: Women in SMEs and Working Women in Cambodia, Laos and Vietnam, Feb 26–28, 2000; WARI: Bangkok, 2000.

Pitt, M. M.; Khandker, S. R. The Impact of Group-based Credit Programs on Poor Households in Bangladesh: Does the Gender of Participation Matters? *J. Polit. Econ.* **1998**, *106* (6), 958–996.

Pokhriyal, A. K.; Ghildiyal, V. A Comparative Assessment of Banking and Microfinance Interventions in Uttrakhand. *Global J. Finance Manage.* **2011**, *3* (1), 111–121.

Puhazhendhi, V. Evaluation Study of Self Help Groups; NABARD: Tamilnadu, 2000. Retrieved from: www.nabard.org.

Puhazhendhi, V.; Satyasai, K. J. S. Economic and Social Empowerment of Rural Poor through Self Help Groups. *Indian J. Agric. Econ.* **2001**, *56* (3), 450–451.

Puhazhendhi, V.; Satyasai, K. J. S. Microfinance for Rural People –An Impact Study, NABARD, 2002. Retrieved from: see www.nabard.org.

Qamar, M. A.; Jibran, M. S.; Nasir, M. Impact of Microfinance on the Non-monetary Aspects of Poverty: Evidence from Pakistan. *Qual. Quantity* **2017**, *51* (2), 891–902. DOI: http://dx.doi.org/10.1007/s11135-016-0317-2.

Ravicz, L. Phenomenological Account of Peyote Use in the Religious Domain. Unpublished Thesis Paper, 1993.

Rehman, A. Alleviation of Rural Poverty, Replicability of Grameen Bank Model. *Agric. Rural Dev. Stud* **1987**, *1* (4), 457–486.

Samanta, G. Microfinance and Women: Gender Issues of Poverty Alleviation and Empowerment. *Microfinance Rev.* **2009**, *1* (1), 100–120.

Saraswathy, A. K. P.; Panicker, K. S. M. Microcredit and Women Empowerment: A Study in India. *Int. J. Global Bus.* **2008**, *1* (1), 184–213.

Sharif, I. A. Social Interactions, Election Goals and Poverty Reduction: Evidence from Anti-poverty Program in Sri Lanka (Order No. U206346). Available from ProQuest Dissertations & Theses Global. (301635231), 2005. Retrieved from: https://search.proquest.com/docview/301635231?accountid=175698.

Swain, R. B.; Wallentin, F. Y. *Does Microfinance Empower Women? Evidence from Self-help Groups in India*; Working Paper No. 2007: 24, Department of Economics, Uppsala University: Sweden, 2007.

The Pioneer. Microfinance, Its Contribution to Healthcare. *The Pioneer*, Sept 5, 2018. Retrieved from https://search.proquest.com/docview/2099126038?accountid=175698.

Todd, H. *Women at the Centre: Grameen Bank Borrowers after One Decade*; West View Press: Boulder, CO, 1996.

USAID. *Assessing the Impacts of Microenterprise Interventions: A Framework for Analysis*; Microenterprise Development Brief No. 9, Washington, DC, 1995. Retrieved from: aims@msiinc.com.

Viswanath, P. V. Microfinance and the Decision to Invest in Children's education. *Int. J. Financi. Stud.* **2018**, *6* (1), 16. DOI: http://dx.doi.org/10.3390/ijfs6010016.

Wahid, A. N. M. The Grameen Bank and Poverty Alleviation in Bangladesh: Theory, Evidence and Limitations. *Am. J. Sociol.* **1994**, *53* (1): 1–15.

Yeboah, E. Microfinance in Rural Ghana: A View from Below. A Thesis Submitted to the University of Birmingham for the Degree of Doctor of Philosophy, e-theses Repository, 2010; pp 1–178. Retrieved from: http://etheses.bham.ac.uk. Accessed Jan 26, 2019.

CHAPTER 10

Health Programs Analogy for Sustainable Amelioration of the Women Community in Chennai

BANDITA KUMARI PANDA[1*] and P. REKHA[2]

[1]Department of Mass Communication and Media Technology, Khallikote University, Berhampur, India

[2]Department of Media Sciences, Anna University, Chennai, India

*Corresponding author. E-mail: bandita.p@gmail.com

ABSTRACT

Promoting health education via media literacy is the strategy that has been adopted by the Anna FM radio, Chennai and broadcasted through its health programs that are targeted at women health care. These programs are providing health knowledge to women and simultaneously empowering them to embrace vigor. The researchers have used qualitative study of content analysis, focus group discussion from the Anna FM program *"Magalir Neram"* (women's time). The study supported with the theory of planned behavior mediates to improvise women's lives by promoting health literacy through Anna FM programs. The researchers have analyzed how the content is useful for the women community and they attempted to find out that the vernacular talk used in the program educates them. This study tries to research about the health promotion via media literacy education among women, including theoretical foundations that subjugate good health and longer sustainability of life.

10.1 INTRODUCTION

Good health and well-being, the goal three of the United Nations Sustainable Development Goals (SDGs) objective was to achieve universal health coverage, and provide access to safe and affordable health for all (www.undp.org). The rational and cultural imperative skills that determine the enthusiasm and ability of individuals to understand and make use of information in ways which promotes and maintains good health are the challenge (WHO, 2013). Traditional information strategies are not enough to prevent unhealthy behaviors among the mankind. In India, apart from the public and private radio broadcasting, community radios (CRs) are also magnanimously contributing. Anna University is the first in the country to commission the campus CR on February 1, 2004. It is impressive that it is run for and by the community with cooperation from the students, staffs, social welfare groups. It bestows to serve the needs and promotes interest and aspirants of the community (Nirmala, 2015). The listeners of Anna FM radio are urban low and middle class from the nearby urban clusters in a 5–10-km range of Anna University.

Mass media echelons are among the most important social agents in influencing the health behaviors especially among women. In CR, the people voluntarily participate and produce programs that are usually designed for their self-benefit. It tries to play an important role in the lives of women as it creates awareness, provides information, and educates to improve their skills.

10.2 LITERATURE REVIEW

Over the past 30 years, a small body of research on the effectiveness of health-promoting media literacy education has emerged, although the studies have been conducted with less rigor, achieved differing results and many questions about effectiveness remain to be answered (Bergsma and Carney, 2008).

CR, like all media, it can be used to serve both positive and negative causes to promote or to distort truth. However, whilst all media is susceptible to manipulation, the structure of CR can make it more vulnerable to appropriation by negative forces (Myers, 2008).

UNESCO defines CR as a broadcast station that "is operated in the community, for the community, about the community and by the community." While the term "community media" refers to a diverse range of mediated forms of communication, electronic media such as radio and television, print media, and electronic network initiatives encompass characteristics of both traditional print and electronic media.

Empowerment is a process where women, individually and collectively, become aware of how power relations operate in their lives. With this awareness, they gain self-confidence and strength to challenge gender inequalities at the household, community, national, regional, and international levels (Kumar and Varghese, 2005).

10.3 OBJECTIVES

- To find out the awareness of the women health literacy among the community.
- To promote the health literacy among women community through the Anna FM programs.
- To find the effectiveness of the Anna FM health programs among women groups.

10.4 METHODLOGY

The present research study uses qualitative content analysis and focus group discussions from the Anna FM program *Magalir Neram* (Women's Time). The women commune who listened to *Magalir Neram* were incorporated in this research study. The programs are compilation of a mixed format of skit and interview by an expert. Three health-oriented audio programs were randomly chosen based on the titles and were played to each of the women groups separately. After completion of the audio, one of the researchers became the moderator and initiated the discussion and the other collected the feedback and answers.

The Anna FM health-oriented programs that are considered for the analysis are as follows:

- Diet for women
- Diet and food regime for pregnant women
- Feeding your baby

10.5 THEORETICAL FRAMEWORK

The theory of planned behavior was proposed by Icek Ajzen in the year of 1985. It has been applied to studies of the relations among beliefs, attitudes, and behavioral intentions in the various fields such as advertising, public relations, and health care. The theory states that attitude toward behavior, subjective norms, and perceived behavioral control together shape an individual's behavioral intentions and behaviors (Ajzen, 1991).

The theory of planned behavior is applied in this research to study the following parameters in the Anna FM program about women's health literacy:

- Behavioral beliefs
- Normative beliefs
- Control beliefs

10.6 FOCUS GROUP DISCUSSION

Focus group discussion was the methodology adopted for the present study. It is the form of methodology that is used to qualitatively interpret the results from the respondents. In this research, this methodology is implemented to acquire the knowledge of the women in a community. Electronic medium was involved in conveying the message to the community women. Through the electronic medium, an audio program was played to the women folks representing in groups about the importance of women's health. This was presented to the community women in Saidapet in Chennai region.

A total of three focus group discussions with six members in each group were conducted. Each discussion consists of homemakers of women from the Saidapet community. The prime objective of focus group discussions was to identify the awareness of their self-health and the effectiveness of the CR programs among the women folks.

Through the discussions held with the three different ladies groups, the researchers were able to gather information regarding various CR programs that they had already listened beforehand. The discussions started after playing the three CR programs to women of three different groups and the topics that were covered in the audio programs were on general diet for women, diet and food regime for women during pregnancy and feeding your baby. All the three topics shared here have been translated from Tamil to English.

The first focus group discussion was involved with diet for women. In this discussion, the researchers were able to get information about how the women concentrate on their personal health. They said and agreed that they all are aware about taking self-health care but they are not spending enough time to take care of themselves because of their workload at home. They concentrate on paying more attention and care to their family. They usually eat their food when they feel need for it like breakfast, lunch, and dinner but only after when the family members finish and leave. The main thing they learnt from this program is that if women are healthy, then only they can take care of their family better. The content that was used in the audio was easily understandable to them and they said that they will try to follow it since it is very difficult to follow it in their daily life.

The second focus group discussion was involved with a program about diet and food regime for women during pregnancy. This group discussion had involved the expectant women group as well as senior old ladies as the program lays on the importance of diet for the pregnancy women. From this discussion, it was found out that almost all the women were not even aware of the separate diet that should be followed during pregnancy period. The discussion helped them to concentrate on their diet and also, they were able to know about the importance of fruits and vegetables that need to be included in their daily diet. As they got to know that how important the diet plays a vital role in their health, they assured to include some of the possible food and vegetables hereafter. The content used for the discussion was clear and easily understandable for them as it was expressed by all.

The third focus group discussion was about the program about feeding your baby. This group involved ladies who were lactating. The program emphasized on the importance of breastfeeding to an infant right from newborn up to 6 months and additionally to include other food substitutes after 6 months for a baby. From this discussion, the researchers were able to get information that the mothers had given to their infant's only breast-feeding up to almost a year and they were not aware of the substitute foods available for a child. They even added that they were also scared to give the other food supplements to their children. From this program, they were able to know about the availability of other supplements of food for their babies. As an expert has spoken in the program, so they believed they can start including those in their kids menu here onwards.

10.7 CONTENT ANALYSIS—GIST OF THE ANNA FM PROGRAMS

10.7.1 PROGRAM NAME: DIET FOR WOMEN

This program is a mixed format with skit and interview with Mr. John Kendey, a food nutritionist. He explains in the program how food is important for women to lead a healthy life.

In the skit, the talk happens between a mother and a daughter about the household chores. The mother shouts at her daughter for always playing with the mobile phone and then the mother asks her daughter to put to dry the washed clothes in the terrace. When she goes to the terrace, she notices her neighborhood aunt has got fainted in the common terrace. She calls her mother and tells that her aunty has lost consciousness. The mother reaches hurriedly and enables to wake up the aunt, she asks her "whether you had your breakfast?" The aunt replies that she generally eats breakfast late, hence for that reason she used to take only coffee. The mother character says to the aunt, "that's why your body is like this, come we will go to our home." Then the mother provides her a glass of carrot juice. Then she advises her, "consuming only coffee/tea is not good for the health. You should eat fruits, vegetables and should consume your food on time." Then, the mother-in-law of the aunt while searching for her at home arrives. She mentions, "I was sure, you must have been here to chit chat." Then the first mother character says "she got fainted and my daughter noticed her. Then, I brought her home and gave some refreshment." She added, "As your daughter-in-law always take care of your family, she should have proper diet that too on time." The Mother-in-law realizes it and agrees to take care of her henceforth.

10.7.1.1 INTERVIEW

1. Importance of breakfast for women.
    Mr. John says, "Breakfast is a must. Often, it's observed that women never eat the food on time. Usually, they will finish all the household works on time and then they will eat. Some will be taking lunch directly by skipping breakfast and rely only on tea or coffee. Due to this they will have problems like digestion, headache, fatigue, etc. They should not only eat on time but also try to consume more fruits and vegetables to keep themselves fit."

2. When women should consume food?

   Mr. John: "As per tradition in our culture, women should serve first for the members of the family and only at the last she can consume the food. By the time she intakes her food, her hunger temptation in her stomach will slow down. For this reason, she could consume the food whenever she feels hungry then only she can have proper ingesting of food."

   They should also avoid taking all the stale and leftover foods which had been made a day before as it causes serious problems to their health later. So they have to always eat fresh foods.

3. Timings should be maintained while having food, is it good or bad?

   Mr. John replies, "Humans are not machines to follow a time to eat. Eat the food whenever you feel hungry, then you can notice that you will have proper digestion and you will feel fresh. One can even have buttermilk and juices in between."

10.7.2 PROGRAM NAME: DIET AND FOOD REGIME FOR PREGNANT WOMEN

This program has interview with Dr. Sartha Bharathi. She explains about the food consumption and also the problems faced by women during the pregnancy period.

In this skit, two senior ladies are having a conversation in a hospital. They never knew each other before and start chatting about their pregnant daughters. One from them says that it had been a long time that her daughter had gone inside the room for checkup. She also expresses her worriedness that "I don't know how she is going to deliver a baby." Then the other person asks her the one who went inside the room is she your daughter? She nods her head and confirms. The mother tells about her daughter, "she had completed her degree and she wanted to do job but it was me who refused and got her married. After marriage her husband is not taking care of her. My husband is the only working member in our family." The lady tells the mother you had made her to get married in such a young age. The mother says, "Yes it was a big mistake, now in her pregnancy time, am facing difficulty to take care of her. She is vomiting, has leg pain and now after check-up they say, she has high sugar level (diabetic) and now I don't know what to do." The other lady says, "Yes, I had noticed your daughter's legs are swollen." The mother says not only that she is complaining of having pain, she hardly moves from one place to another and keeps eating so many unwanted things. Then the daughter comes out and the skit is over.

10.7.2.1   *INTERVIEW*

1. What type of food can the pregnant women consume daily?
    Dr. Saratha says, "pregnant women can eat normal food as they wish to eat as per their tastebuds and one more important thing is they need to eat more healthy foods which has more protein and their bones have to be strong for the mother to give birth to a child. They should eat green leafy vegetables for iron and whatever they eat they need to increase their weight."
2. What type of food comes under iron?
    As Dr. Saratha opines, "it comes from greens and milk. It's my advice that they need to eat salads made of cucumber, carrot, drumsticks, an egg in a day and daily night before sleep need to drink milk."
3. During pregnancy period women get diabetics, why is it so?
    Dr. Saratha answers, "Diabetes can be caused due to many reasons. One of the main reason for getting it, is hereditary. It is caused because of the pregnancy stress. It will not happen to all the women only to person who have less immune. After confirmation, hence women should frequently visit their doctors and keep monitoring on their sugar level."
4. During pregnancy, the women's legs and hands get swollen. What is the reason?
    The Doctor replies, "It will not happen for all the women. Only 10 percent of women whose legs are swollen heavily, their child is taken out in emergency case."

10.7.3   *PROGRAM NAME: FEEDING YOUR BABY*

This program is mixed with interview by community people and then it is followed by a skit that uses a folk song that tells us what all foods should be given for the babies who are between 4 and 6 months. Then it is followed by an interview by a food expert Ms. Aruna Shyam. She explains about what type of food will help the baby to lead a healthy life.

10.7.3.1   INTERVIEW WITH COMMUNITY PEOPLE VIEWS

What type of food and how to feed them for the 4–6-month baby?

Person 1: Breastfeeding is important for baby and ragi malt can be given. A variety of vegetables soups can be given.

Person 2: Green leafy, vegetables, ragi malt, dal rice can be given.

Person 3: Ragi and millets, add milk or water, no lumps and feed a spoon occasionally.

Person 4: Boiled potato, tomato, soups.

Person 5: Softened rice mashed with milk, small spoons with a time gap. Start only once a day and later increased to two times a day.

A folk song has been sung narrating about the essential foods and their importance in providing strength to the baby. From the song, it is clearly understood that "ragi and millets" are very important for the lactating mothers and infants. Also a few varieties of vegetables, including boiled mashed potato, tomato puree, cooked dal water, and fruits, should be given to the baby.

The skit involves a talk between two sisters-in-law about the 1-month baby's health. The elder one advises the younger lady, "from now onwards you need to take care of yours and your baby properly." The younger sister-in-law asks, "Please tell the steps to follow to take care of my baby up to next 3-4 months?" She replies, "one of the most important thing is breast feeding. It helps the baby to fight from diseases. We need to give the baby sufficient water and after 4 months we need to give them juices and ragi malt can be included in their diet 6 months onwards. I will keep you informed through phone." "Thanks, you are a sweet sister and I am so lucky" says the younger one. The skit gets over.

10.7.3.2   INTERVIEW

1.   We are substituting breastfeeding with other food, your advice on this?

Ms. Aruna says, "This period is known as weaning period. That's why we are asking the mothers to substitute with other foods because at this time period for the baby, the milk itself will not be sufficient and they need to get more proteins, calories."

2. Does this substituting will suit every baby?

Ms. Aruna replies, "There is allotment of food varieties at what time period it can be given and the amount of food which the lactating mothers need to feed them. One needs to follow the pattern. There is a diet chart and visit to a doctor and taking advice and following as per doctor's prescription is advisable as some babies may get allergies to certain foods."

3. When does one need to start with the food substitutes?

As Ms. Aruna adds, "For the healthy growth, babies should continue to have milk from breastfeeding from the birth to 4 months as they will get smaller amount of vitamin C. For iron, we need to get it from other food stuffs. Hence fifth month onwards other alternates needs to be practised by the mother."

10.8 PARAMETERS TO ANALYZE WITH THE ANNA FM PROGRAMS

(a) *Behavioral beliefs*

- In the program "Diet and food for pregnant women," the parameters to analyze were as the pregnant lady consumes food whatever she feels to take that is considered as an improper diet and also, she is not able to walk from one place to another place. For this reason as she had a gestational diabetes was her mother's perception.

- In the program "Diet for women," the practice of having food at a particular timing is raised by the interviewer. Even the lady who falls unconscious in the terrace, including her mother, thinks that having tea or coffee and having late breakfast is quite normal and enough for the body to provide strength.

- In the program "feeding your baby," the awareness about mothers having failed to acknowledge about other varieties of food stuff already available to feed their children has not been included in daily norms as generally only milk feeding was the only accepted practice.

(b) *Normative beliefs*
- The program named with "Diet and food regime for pregnant women" in the skit, the lady tells that by a social normative pressure, she made her daughter to get married instead of sending her to job to enhance her skills.
- In "feeding your baby" program, usually breast milk or skimmed milk powder is prepared and given to the baby up to 1 year as other food substitutes are not encouraged.
- In the program, "Diet for Women" tradition wise, the ladies of the family serve first to their family members like men and kids and eat their food at the end. Someone consuming the breakfast, lunch, or dinner with family at same time is given less regard and respect.

(c) *Control beliefs*
- The program "diet for women," the theoretical perspective, it is comprehended that the aunt character believes that if she has early breakfast, she will not be able to do any household work, and she will feel tired for that reason she used to drink only coffee in the morning and she skipped her breakfast as that was her individual perception.
- In "feeding your baby" program, the community people give a wide variety of opinions and that gets acceptable by the listeners easily. But the food nutritionist advises to be checked with their doctors as there might be sign of reactions from some food.

10.8.1   OBSERVATIONS FROM THE ABOVEMENTIONED PARAMETERS

- Theory of planned behavior has been clearly proved with the parameters for promoting health literacy for women
- The program "food for pregnancy women" has been analyzed with both the parameters that are behavioral belief and normative beliefs.
- The program named "diet for women" has been analyzed with all the three parameters of control beliefs, behavioral, and normative in theoretical perspective of theory of planned behavior.

10.8.2   MAJOR FINDINGS FROM THE GROUP DISCUSSIONS

- Before the discussions, the respondents of various group members were asked about the three topics, that is, diet for women, diet for women during pregnancy, and feeding your baby. Few members were not aware of these topics and they were not exposed to the society.

- The programs were useful to them and they said that they will try to implement in their diet, though they are also aware about the importance of diet in their life, but it is difficult for them to implement in their daily routine.

- The contents used for these discussions were easily understandable and the language used for the discussion is local language (Tamil).

- From the three group's discussion, the researchers found that the women folks are not aware about giving the importance to their personal health. Even, if they are aware also as expressed by few ladies, they are not paying any extra efforts or attention in taking care of their health.

- Out of three discussions, the two topics diet for pregnant women and importance of feeding the child played a significant role among the women community. The respondents showed more interest to know about the information and they said that this information was useful for them to implement in their life.

- The skits were informative as expressed by the women community in the group discussions. As the characters sketched and portrayed in the audio programs were drawn from common backgrounds, it was easy on their part to identify and correlate as one of the persons among them. They could easily connect, visualize, and understand what the characters were trying to convey to them through the programs.

- When asked about the interview part, all the ladies expressed that it was additionally helpful as the doctors and food experts have narrated it in simple language and clear description of what needs to be done is described.

- The majority of ladies even said they have tuned to the programs of Anna FM, but such group listening and discussion have cleared lots of doubts and they look forward for such quality conversation.

- The researchers have analyzed how the program content is useful for the womanhood. It was derived that spoken word language and simple terms were used for the easy understanding of the community people. The researcher got feedback from the listening community how the programs are essential and suit aptly with the taste of the listeners.

10.9 CONCLUSION

Through this research study, it was found out that the CR has put efforts as a medium of social responsibility by broadcasting information regarding health programs for women. The study revealed that the importance of health for women, diet for pregnancy women, and feeding your baby plays an important role in the lives of women in today's society. CR can change the lives of women and it gives voice and it creates awareness about various issues from the beginning of health, maternity, and nutrition. It increases their general knowledge and enables them to showcase their talent and motivate them on various issues, including health and education. Anna University for its part played an important role in social, economic, and political empowerment of women in its area. CR has given voice to the women of the community and health programs are informative and educating the mass to take proper care of themselves and the community as a whole. If one group or community is able to have a good regime and develops longer life sustainability, the message spreads through voice of mouth and encourages others to adapt similar sustainable developed strategies in long run. CR plays an imperative role in creating awareness, provides information, and tries to improve the vigor skills through its programs. This in longer run leads toward achieving pink health milestones in balanced and harmonized way.

KEYWORDS

- community radio
- health programs
- women health
- sustainability
- health literacy
- health education

REFERENCES

Ajzen, I. 1991. https://www.researchgate.net/publication/272790646_The_Theory_of_ Planned_Behavior.

Al-hassan, S.; et al. *The Role of Community Radio in Livelihood Improvement*, 2011.

http://www.undp.org/content/undp/en/home/sustainable-development-goals/goal-3-good-health-and-well-being.html.

Randolph, W.; Viswanath, K. *Ann. Rev. Public Health* **2004**, *25*, 419–437.

Bergsma, L. *J. Media Lit. Educ.* **2011**, *3*(1), 25–28.

Bergsma, L. J.; Carney, M. E. The Effectiveness of Health Promoting Media Literacy Education: A Systematic Review. *Health Educ. Res.* **2008**, *23*, 522–542.

Binod, C. A.; et al. Ahmedabad: Project in Radio Education for Adult Literacy (PREAL) by Social Research Group, Development and Educational Communication Unit, ISRO, 1993.

Chapman, R.; Blench, R.; Kranjac-Berisavljevic', G.; Zakariah, A. B. T. Rural Radio in Agricultural Extension: The Example of Vernacular Radio Programmes on Soil and Water Conservation in Northern Ghana; Agricultural Research & Extension Network; Network Paper No. 127, January 2003.

http://www.tandfonline.com/action/journalInformation?journalCode=rmea20.

http://www.who.int/healthpromotion/conferences/7gchp/track2/en/.

Girard, B. *The One to Watch: Radio*; New ICTs and Interactivity, 2003.

Kumar, H.; Varghese, J. *Women's Empowerment, Issues, Challenges, and Strategies: A Source Book*; Regency Publications: New Delhi, 2005.

Myers, M. *Radio and Development in Africa—A Concept Paper*; The International Development Research Centre (IDRC): Canada, 2008.

Nirmala, Y. The Role of Community Radio in Empowering Women in India. *Media Asia* **2015**, *42* (1–2), 41–46. DOI: 10.1080/01296612.2015.1072335.

World Bank Institution. Empowering Radio. Good Practices in Development & Operation of Community Radio: Issues Important to Its Effectiveness. Program on Civic Engagement, Empowerment & Respect for Diversity [Online], 2007. Retrieved July 14, 2019 from: http://siteresources.worldbank.org/INTCEERD/Resources/WBI5--CountryStudy.pdf.

CHAPTER 11

In-Stream Flows: The Need for Ecological Considerations in Integrated Water Resources Management to Ensure Crucial Environmental Flows

B. ANJAN KUMAR PRUSTY*

Department of Natural Resources Management and Geo-informatics, Khallikote University, GMax Building on NH 16, Konisi, Berhampur 761008, India

E-mail: bakprusty@khallikoteuniversity.ac.in; anjaneia@gmail.com

ABSTRACT

The concept of integrated water resource management (IWRM) though aims maximizing social equity, economic efficiency, and ecological sustainability in water resource use, the third one relating to fulfilling minimum water requirements for ecosystem needs to sustain ecosystem services (ES) has been largely neglected while executing the water management policies. There are always unceasing conflicts for water among various competing water users, including the silent water users, biodiversity, and ecosystem. This chapter examines the existing issues of in-stream flows and highlights the need for ecological considerations in IWRM since that is the fundamental feature of this resource management that could help ensure the social and economic aspects. This is to ensure the environmental flow, crucial for ecosystem sustenance. This chapter discusses, inter alia, e-flow and its importance from the viewpoint of optimizing ES, community dependence on ecosystems, river valley project regulations, and the need for inclusion of e-flow in the same in the Indian context.

11.1   INTRODUCTION

Water is a prime concern in the 21st century, since not only the gross requirement, but also the apportionment among different stakeholders becomes a difficult task for policy makers and for execution of the identified strategy. Major water conflicts in India are centered on resource sharing of rivers among interest groups and stakeholders spread across various administrative and geographic boundaries in the country. As conflicts over apportioning water resources among upstream and downstream users, among states, and even among countries are well known, in recent years, conflicts are also arising among water users over issues of water quality. Given the earlier statement, and especially in view of the importance of the problems, it is important to understand the conflicts from scientific, legal, political, and socioeconomic terms to find ways to address the issues, for sustainable utilization of the resources and to understand and estimate the requirements of water for ecosystem sustenance. In fact, conventional water management was largely focusing on apportioning the total water resource among different stakeholders, broadening access to it, and spreading its distribution to newer stakeholders just like new irrigation channels taking water across river basins. The in-stream flow as a part of natural ecosystem functioning, as an integral of the natural material flow, and as a basic requirement to sustain ecosystem services (ES) from a surface water body was largely neglected by water resource managers until the later quarters of the 20th century.

In fact, water resource management was revolving around flood control, irrigation, drinking water, and power generation. Water as the crucial medium for lesser explicit, but crucial, ecological functions remained largely subdued. However, this had several repercussions, both tangible and intangible, such as crash in downstream ecological diversity, environmental security, local extinction of several life forms, drying up of aquifers, social deprivations and resultant conflicts, and so on. Several rivers lost their downstream flows and the ecosystems and ecological process supported by these flows in the country as well as elsewhere due to water harvesting/diversion structures that disregarded required in-stream flows. Some of the inland water bodies became saline or dried up. Such consequences were indicative of serious conflicts among the stakeholders. The issues seized the attention of concerned, public, political groups, decision makers, states, intellectuals, and researchers. This provided required impetus for integrated water resource management (IWRM) in the field of water management, wherein the understanding on in-stream flows and thereby determining the environmental flow (EF) is a prerequisite.

11.2 DEVELOPMENT OF INTEGRATED WATER RESOURCES MANAGEMENT

The central dogma of IWRM is the consideration of water as a natural resource, which is a social and economic good to be accessible to all the stakeholders. The nature of its utilization is a function of its quantity and quality, thereby making it an integral part of the ecosystem. Recognizing water as social and economic good, also IWRM accredits it as a crucial component of ecosystem. In contrast with the conventional water resource management that focuses on anthropocentric utility of the resources, this implies the sustainable management of the aquatic ecosystems to preserve them and retain the ES as vital. The United Nations call for rivers worldwide is based on the earlier considerations, and thus, it needs to be managed accordingly. Although the developed nations seemed to manage their water resources and/or river systems in that line, the situation is different in other countries. As an initial step to manage rivers in this line, the United States has promulgated acts such as the SECURE Water Act that however is yet to fully achieve the goal.

In order to address the ecosystem needs, researchers are working toward establishing realistic in-stream flows, factoring in various conflicting interests, which ensure EFs (e-flows) within river basins. As noted earlier, water being most crucial for human survival and development, most uses, such as that for industrial and irrigation purposes, are apparently competing and exclusive. Joy et al. (2011) categorize these uses under four categories: (1) basic needs, (2) ecosystem needs, (3) livelihood needs, and (4) sociocultural needs. Several are the decisions from governments allocating water for basic needs, livelihood needs, and socioeconomic needs (though largely motivated by political interests), but the EFs that essentially ensure environmental security for a larger section of the lesser privileged social segments as well other living beings are neglected. The issue of meeting the water requirements of ecosystems is always ignored, compelling to lament "*ecosystems don't have voice and vote.*"

One vital issue while allocating water resources is to protect optimal flows in the river course, the required flow being determined considering the ensuing ecological conditions in the river basin. This also involves informed decision-making on the resultant ecological condition after apportioning water for various uses. Sufficient flows are vital to provide water for in-stream uses such as river channel processes, habitat for aquatic species, life-sustaining water for wildlife and plants, and for human uses such as recreation, hydropower, recharging aquifer, or wastewater assimilation. In-stream flow level is the volume of water in a river or stream channel at any given time (Dimmitt, 2009). This amount may not be adequate to provide for any or all the functions mentioned earlier, but any of the given needs and fulfilling them is highly site-specific. A designated minimum in-stream flow is one that recognizes and sets aside the minimum quantity of water needed for one, some, or all of the desired in-stream uses for a particular reach, so that this water cannot be withdrawn for other uses outside the stream channel. Even the designated in-stream flows, for problems concerning its estimations, can be insufficient to conserve the natural ecological structure and processes. In general, estimating the desirable water levels in a riverine ecosystem for its long-term sustenance and for sustaining ecosystem goods and services remains inconclusive. Therefore, it requires an informed decision-making and trade-offs.

11.3   CONCEPT OF E-FLOWS AND IN-STREAM FLOWS

In the context of in-stream situation, taking water as the medium for most of the flows, EFs, also known as ecological or e-flows, is defined as *"the quantity, quality and timing of water flows required for sustaining freshwater and estuarine ecosystems and the human livelihoods and wellbeing that depend on these ecosystems"* (GEFN <www.eflownet.org>). It is essential that this definition needs to be explicated to include the flows required for sustaining the ES. In the case of rivers that are under active intervention by formal institutions/authorities for apportioning the water resource, estimates of these flows are usually the result of a formal process of negotiated settlement considering human and ecological needs, prominence virtually given to the former as water management of reservoirs, diversions, and other human works is protected or administered under a permit, water right, or other legally recognized means. As noted earlier, the ecological needs for a required flow gets lesser or no importance in conventional water management. It is appropriate to take note that in general the ecological condition in a river system is a function of the water flow more or less positively associated, that is, lesser flow means lower ecological diversity. The recognition of flow as a key driver of aquatic ecosystems has led to the development of EF concept (Dyson et al., 2003). For routine management of a particular river, Smakhtin and Anputhas (2006) describe environmental requirements as "*a suite of flow discharges of certain magnitude, timing, frequency and duration.*" These flows are referred to as "environmental flows" (Knights, 2002; Dyson et al., 2003), "environmental water requirements" (Lankford, 2002), "environmental flow requirements" and "environmental water demand" (Smakhtin et al., 2004a,b), etc. They facilitate maintaining a sustained flow regime, thereby supporting functioning of a complex set of aquatic habitats and ecosystem processes.

The e-flows, a pattern resembling the natural hydrograph, imply a minimum flow or flow regime and facilitate maintaining and/or promoting ecosystem diversity, its integrity, and its functioning with its seasonal dynamics. It implies to an ecologically acceptable flow regime designed to maintain a river in an agreed upon or predetermined state. Tharme (2003) defined e-flow as "*an assessment of how much of the original flow regime of a river should continue to flow down it and onto its floodplains in order to maintain specified, valued features of the ecosystem, hydrological regimes for the rivers, the environmental flow requirements, each linked to a predetermined objective in terms of the ecosystem's future condition.*" However, this involves addressing complex issues. Thus, to meet e-flows, consistently, in the future, it is essential that the basin-wide water resources management programs integrate e-flows into the models. However, such an integration involves several technical issues. Furthermore, due to the ever-increasing demands coupled with increasing human populations, water resources are becoming scarcer, and the situation will be aggravated by climatic uncertainties (Vorosmarty et al., 2000). These often result in increasing conflicts, that is, human versus human and human versus environmental uses of water (Poff et al., 2003). This necessitates meticulous and long-term planning, which will optimize several competing demands on the resources, without sacrificing the unseen (by the market or economy) but valuable ES.

Ecosystem functions/services are essential for maintaining the ecological, structural, and functional integrity as well as the livelihood support base of that ecosystem and humankind. Compared to other ecosystems, riverine ecosystems are prone to drastic changes due to developmental activities and human interventions and thereby the ES getting severely undermined. Inability to maintain in-stream flow requirement, the e-flows, is the reason for the shrinking of ES. Water diversion and abstraction for various purposes through impoundments and structures for navigation and flood control thereby curtailing the flow in the rivers have been a common issue across the globe. As a consequence of such modification and interventions, the flow regimes are significantly altered in terms of reduction in total flow, thereby affecting the natural variability and seasonality. It is estimated that hydrological alterations result in habitat fragmentation of around 60% of the world's rivers, causing degradation of aquatic ecosystems (MEA, 2005), and thereby experiencing reduced associated aquatic biodiversity. This degradation could have been mitigated to a great extent for provision of minimal water flow, which would maintain the riverine ecosystem integrity.

11.4   ECOSYSTEM SERVICES AND E-FLOWS

The term EFs comprehends all components of the river taking cognizance of the need for natural flow variability over a spatiotemporal gradient, addressing social, economic, and biophysical issues, and is dynamic over time. EF is essential, since each ecosystem performs a wide array of functions specific to each ecosystem and these functions result in services that are beneficial and at times essential for human beings and crucial for numerous other species. Such functions or services of a wide range are offered by riverine ecosystems, some of which are directly dependent on natural flow of energy or material. Babu and Kumara (2009) and Babu (2010) synthesize four major categories of ES provided by rivers, namely, production, regulation, information, and life support. Each of these categories ES specifies as what type of particular service is provided, its associated key flow–related functions, and the specific EF components as indicators. For example, provisioning of vegetables and fruits is one of the major ES provided by river ecosystems which falls under the "Production" category, for which the supply of nutrients, organic matter, and seasonal variation in soil moisture conditions are the "key flow related functions." Thus, for the present case, "floodplain inundation" and "flows sustaining riparian vegetation" are indictors or key EF components. The said synthesis considers various ES under production (eight ES—water for people; fish/shrimp/crabs: nonrecreational; fertile land; wildlife; vegetables and fruits; fiber/organic raw materials; medicinal plants; inorganic raw materials), regulation (11 ES—water quality; water quantity; flood mitigation; groundwater replenishment; health control; pest control; erosion control; salinity control; prevention of acid sulfate soil development; carbon sequestration; microclimate stabilization), information (three ES—recreation and tourism; biodiversity conservation; cultural/religious/ historical/symbolic activities), and life support (one ES—prior existence of healthy ecosystems) categories pertaining to river ecosystems. Hence, EF being vital to ensure these ES, its understanding serves well to make informed, equitable and effective decisions for managing water resources sustainably. The degradation or loss of those services would have ecological, economical, and cultural–religious implications. Declining profits, remedial measures, damage repairs, and lost opportunities are some of the factors representing economic costs of loss of ES. Typically, these losses/ costs are mainly borne largely by people from the poorer segment of the society, that is, those dependent on the ES directly. Thus, the sustainable development goals can be achieved with an in-depth understanding of the ES and recognizing their full value, and appropriately investing in securing them, thereby safeguarding the livelihoods for a larger proportion of the population, which will save considerable costs (Dyson et al., 2003). Thus, failing to do so can seriously jeopardize any such efforts. While powerful (economically and/or politically) users can manage their requirements relatively well, the ecosystem people, the silent water users, and other life forms often face challenging situations, often deprived of access to water resources (quality and quantity). This leads to ecosystems getting frequently neglected while formal water allocation decisions are made.

Historically, the only consideration for EFs, specific to in-stream flows, was in terms of a minimum quantity flow. However, various researchers (Richter et al., 1996; Poff et al., 1997: Poff and Zimmerman, 2010) suggest the ecological importance of all aspects of a river's flow regime, including low flows, peak flows, and inter and intra-annual variability. Thus, Acreman and Dunbar (2004) suggest that the closer the flows are to natural flows, the more pristine the ecosystem will remain. However, human interventions have been causing rapid decline in the flows in rivers, and for this reason, Kingsford (2011) opines flow alteration as one of the most *"pervasive and deleterious"* factors degrading rivers today.

11.5 RIVER VALLEY PROJECT REGULATIONS AND E-FLOW IN THE COUNTRY

The issue of environmental water demand has remained neglected so far in many developing countries including India. In contrast, largely the Western countries have carried out considerable research on response of ecosystems to flow alterations, developing tools for quantifying the flow alterations and addressing proper management of rivers for ecosystem benefits. An extensive review of studies on ecosystem responses to flow alterations was carried out by Poff and Zimmerman (2010) compiling 165 studies, of which a majority of the case studies were from North America, Europe, South America, Africa, and Oceania. The said review and synthesis included the aspects as how do macroinvertebrates, fishes, riparian vegetation, aquatic primary producers, birds, and amphibians respond to changes in flow magnitude, duration, timing, frequency, and rate of change.

India witnessed the first national level brainstorming on e-flows in New Delhi during March 2005 where over 60 participants from different agencies and research institutions participated. While the workshop generated considerable interest on the concept of e-flows in the country, it also revealed the conceptual obscurity. Furthermore, the debate on environmental water demand in India was kept alive by various researchers. Smakhtin and Anputhas (2006) suggested a simple desktop assessment method and applied it in some of the major river basins. However, the methods had its own limitations. One of the major problems is that the existing knowledge on some of the aquatic ecosystem components (e.g., fish) has never been interpreted in the context of EF assessments (EFAs) and never used in decision-making and execution. Thus, there is lack of clarity as how different ecosystem components over a wide biogeographical gradient respond to flow regime influenced by land use changes and developments. For example, the impacts of flow alterations or change in flow regime on sediment, riparian vegetation, invertebrates, fish, birds, or mammals are not quantified and never for less tangible ES.

Several researchers (Postel and Carpenter, 1997; Revenga et al., 2000) describe a range of services provided by freshwater and freshwater-dependent ecosystems for humans, including flood protection, fish, and wildlife. Thus, maintaining these services require water allocation to ecosystems, as it is being done to other uses like agriculture, power generation, domestic, and industry. Since there has been an increase in human population and associated water demands, it is critical that the requirements of the aquatic environment and other uses are balanced in many of the world's river basins including those in India. Moreover, assessing water to meet freshwater-ecosystem requirements is challenging for the complexity of physical processes and interactions between the components of the ecosystems (Smakhtin and Anputhas, 2006). Presently, the issue of EFA and management is a focal point of deliberation in many of the international forums and is high on the world agenda; nevertheless, it remains a less-explored field of research. Many countries, including India, have not even made a crude assessment of water requirements of riverine and associated aquatic ecosystems; thus, it is necessitated that such issues are addressed in the country. Smakhtin and Anputhas (2006) and Smakhtin et al. (2007) made earliest modest initiative in this regard; however, these works have not considered the water requirement of principal ecosystem level process or the key indicator species of the system. While examining wider concept of environmental water requirements, Mohile and Gupta (2005) suggested inclusion of both terrestrial and aquatic ecosystems requirements.

River valley projects, aimed at the developmental and societal needs such as agriculture, irrigation, and flood control, fall under the projects that require environmental clearance from the Ministry of Environment, Forests and Climate Change, Government of India. They require comprehensive environmental impact assessment (EIA) examining the tangible and nontangible impacts. The guidelines for EIA of river valley projects are also framed by IELRC (1985). The ecological consideration in the case of river valley projects covers several environmental aspects: location, topography, demography, ecological features, human settlements, catchment, command area, etc., although in most of the cases emphasis is given only to the area under submergence and the associated displacements and relocations of people/habitations. However, the issues related with flow regime in the downstream stretch of the river are often excluded, similar to the associated impact on the dependent aquatic species and depletion of ground water in the area. Interventions such as water harvesting and distributional networks reduce the in-stream flow to a large extent and the flow of material and energy to downstream locations. Organic matter (autochthonous and allochthonous) and nutrients, both integral components of a fluvial ecosystems, and their flow from the upstream to the downstream are very much essential to sustain the different trophic levels in the riverine ecosystem. Environmental assessment of river valley projects not only need to consider the socioeconomic needs but also the long-term and sustainable availability of water for the needy, that is, the poor as well as the organisms inhabiting the river.

Indicators of Hydrologic Alteration method is used for determining the degree of flow alteration due to dams or other abstractions. This method uses 32 parameters indicating the degree, duration, timing, and frequency of alteration on a temporal scale, that is, from days to years (Richter et al., 1996). Flow alteration can help monitoring or assessing conditions over large spatial areas. Döll et al. (2009) assessed the global impacts of diversions and reservoirs to river flows by applying the flow alteration metric worldwide. The flow alteration metric is meaningful at temporal scales from hours to years. Furthermore, Holden (1999) and Muth et al. (2000) identified specific flow targets, which will benefit the ecosystem for particular reaches. Thus, appropriate correction strategy can be adopted after finding the ecosystem response and determining an acceptable degree of alteration. Bureau of Reclamation (2005, 2006) suggests modification of existing general methods, for operating reservoirs to benefit the environment and reservoir operations, to meet the required e-flows, and one such general methods is offered by Watts et al. (2011). E-flow requirements usually vary temporally in order to mimic the natural variability of the system.

Climate change is known to be another major factor impacting river systems. Palmer et al. (2008) estimate the projected change in discharge is anywhere from 90% increase to 90% decrease globally. Both increases and decreases in flow negatively impact the ecosystem (Poff and Zimmerman, 2010). Gibson et al. (2005) and Döll and Zhang (2010) projected that as a factor to cause flow alterations climate change will outweigh all other factors together. Booth et al. (2006) opine that frequency and durations of floods and pulse flows can be altered due to climate change. Due to such inordinate changes, the ability of ecosystems for adapting to the hydrologic variability could be impacted. Since, historically, species evolved and adapted under local conditions, such rapid changes in variability could have adverse effect on the species. Since the "natural" state is continuously changing in a dynamic climatic regime, the baseline for flow alterations is not clearly defined. In such prevailing situations, a global analysis of relevant e-flow metrics was performed by Döll and Zhang (2010), though a future projection of demands due to the scale of the required assessment was not incorporated.

11.6 FLOW REGIME AND TECHNIQUES FOR E-FLOW ESTIMATION

Flow, being a key driver of fluvial geomorphologic processes, exerts significant control on stream channel morphology (Arthington and Zalucki, 1998) and the structure and functions of the ecosystem. Earlier researchers (Ward and Tockner, 2001; Ward et al., 2001; Knights, 2002) suggest that the maintenance of spatiotemporal patterns of river flow and variability, which affect the structural and functional diversity of rivers and their floodplains, and which in turn influence the species diversity of the river, should be considered as a major criterion for determining EF. On the whole, EF should encompass the amount of water needed and duration and pattern of flow in the river. One of the integral parts of the ecosystem sustenance is geomorphologic processes and associated hydrological changes and vice versa and hence need to be considered while making EFAs. Furthermore, channel morphology is also known to have vital ecological implications (Arthington and Zalucki, 1998). Nevertheless, hydraulic, geomorphologic, and ecological responses to hydrological changes are interdependent.

Although relatively new in scientific research, various methods, models, approaches, and frameworks, for estimating EFs, have been developed by researchers across the globe to address the issue of EFs. Whereas specific assessments of the ecological requirements are done using *methods, approaches* are the ways of deriving such assessments, for example, through expert teams, and a broader strategy for EFA is provided by *frameworks* for flow management, whereas *Models* help in predicting flow regime and estimating corresponding in-stream flow and e-flow for different situations (rivers with varied geomorphological and ecological condition). Each one of these are suitable in specific cases and has its own advantages and disadvantages, which are described by Acreman and

Dunbar (2004), Korsgaard (2006), Babu and Kumara (2009), Babu (2010), and Zeefat (2010).

In recent years, many methods have emerged to determine these requirements, which are known as EFAs. In this context, total annual water volume that could be allocated for environmental purposes indicate nothing but the mean annual sum of estimated EFs. Presently, a diversity of opinions on this subject ranging from comprehensive expert panel approach to arbitrarily selected hydrological indices (e.g., Tharme, 2003) are reproduced as EFA methods. Two commonly used methods, for determining the ecologically acceptable flow regime, are as follows:

(1) Detailed assessment, mostly using field assessments and holistic methods (e.g., habitat modeling). These methods adopt a whole ecosystem view in assessing EF. In such case, a multidisciplinary panel of experts identify the ecologically and/or socially important flow events and define an ecologically acceptable flow regime. Such an exercise involves substantial amounts of field work and consumes considerable amount of time for collecting ecological data, preferably round the year, considering the flow variability.

(2) Desktop assessment methods, using hydrological indices largely, which are ecologically relevant or analysis of hydrological time series. Desktop EFAs are more diverse and desirable for initial, reconnaissance, or planning-level assessments.

Till date, four different methods are in practice for estimating the EF for a particular river system, namely, (1) Lookup Tables, (2) Desktop Analysis, (3) Functional Analysis, and (4) Habitat Modeling. A comparative assessment of these methods can be precisely made by synthesizing the advantages and disadvantages as suggested by Tennant (1976), Matthews and Bao (1991), Richter et al. (1997), Hughes and Hannart (2003), Acreman and Dunbar (2004), Korsgaard (2006), Babu and Kumara (2009), Babu (2010), and Zeefat (2010). Lookup tables (see Tennant, 1976; Matthews and Bao, 1991 for detailed description) or detailed analysis of hydrological time series (see Richter et al., 1997; Hughes and Hannart, 2003 for further details) are useable in Desktop EFAs. It takes a considerable amount of time for developing lookup tables before they can be used. On the contrary, the methods based on the time series require observed and/or simulated discharge time series. However, in the cases that need EFs to be defined in greater details, habitat modeling is suitable.

Several methods are available for estimating the water availability and requirements in rivers. The selection of the method depends upon the river and site characteristics and the dimension of the issue. A summary of the selection approach for the abovementioned four methods is given in Table 11.1. However, its utility varies with the expert group's involvement, etc. The resource assessment and management (RAM) framework considers the potential abstractors, other water users, and local wildlife groups. The allowable abstractions at different points (flow percentiles) of the curve for each weighting band are specified under this RAM. The Q_{95} and Q_{90} flows are most often used as low flow indices, while Q_{75}, Q_{84}, Q_{96}, Q_{97}, Q_{98}, and Q_{99} flows are also occasionally noticed. Some less conventional indices include the percentage of time that 25% average flow is exceeded (Jha et al., 2008). Similarly, the ratio Q_{20}/Q_{90} may be interpreted as a measure of stream flow variability and the ratio Q_{50}/Q_{90} the variability of low-flow discharges. The reverse ratio Q_{90}/Q_{50} may be interpreted as an index representing the proportion of stream flow originating from ground-water stores, excluding the effects of catchment area. Jha et al. (2008) have found the Q_{95} value corresponding to the probability of exceedance of 95% to be most suitable "environmental design flow" for Brahmani and Baitarani rivers and is used for the duration curve drawn for daily, 7-day mean, and 30-day mean values. The Q_{95} flow index has been used globally by researchers for different uses as shown in the Table 11.2. Acreman and Dunbar (2004) suggested different percentages of natural Q_{95} flow that can be abstracted and their corresponding environmental weighting band (Table 11.3), although these are not well supported by hydro-ecological studies and are intended only as a default method.

TABLE 11.1 Suitability and Choice of Environmental Flow Assessment Methods.

Dimension/Scope	Site details	Lookup tables	Desktop analysis	Functional analysis	Habitat modeling
Scoping study or national audit	–	–	–	–	–
Basin-scale planning	–	×	×	–	–
Impact assessment	Single-site	–	–	×	×
	Multisite	–	–	×	×
River restoration	Single-site	–	–	×	×
	Multisite	–	–	×	×

TABLE 11.2   Uses of Q_{95} for Low Flow Studies.

Flow index	Use	Studies undertaken/References
Q_{95}	Commonly used low-flow index or indicator of extreme low-flow conditions	Riggs et al. (1980), Brilly et al. (1997), Smakhtin (2001), Wallace and Cox (2002), Tharme (2003), Smakhtin et al. (2007), Jha et al. (2008)
	Minimum flow to protect the river	Petts (1996)
	Minimum monthly condition for point discharges	MDEQ (2002)
	Licensing of surface water extractions and effluent discharge limits assessment	Higgs and Petts (1988), Smakhtin and Toulouse (1998)
	Biological index for mean monthly flow	Dakova et al. (2000)
	Used to maintain the natural monthly seasonal variation used to optimize environmental flow rules	Stewardson and Gippel (2003)

Q_{95}, allowable water abstractions at 95 percentile of the annual flow curve.

TABLE 11.3   Percentages of Natural Q_{95} Flow and Environmental Weighting Bands.

Percentage of Q_{95} that can be abstracted	Environmental weighting band
0–5	A
5–10	B
10–15	C
15–25	D
25–30	E
Special treatment	Others

Source: Acreman and Dunbar (2004), Dunbar et al. (2004).

As described earlier about four different methods used in estimating EFs, each of them considers certain indicators while estimating the water requirement. Smakhtin et al. (2007) attempted to develop procedures to assess the ecological status of Indian river basins in the context of e-flow. The study, first of its kind in the country, not only initiated the thought process among the researchers but also listed out the probable indicators and/or parameters to be considered. Though many of the river valley projects in India are multipurpose ones, aimed at irrigation, flood control, and hydropower, the water requirement for the aquatic organisms or ES were seldom considered. Smakhtin et al. (2007) have enumerated several indicators and grouped them under two categories based on their relation with (1) ecological value (importance and sensitivity) and (2) ecological condition of aquatic ecosystems in the basin. The indicators falling under the first category are (1) aquatic biota (unique, rare, and endangered), (2) diversity of the habitat, that is, aquatic habitat, (3) presence of pristine areas and areas of natural heritage, that is, protected areas those are crossed by the main watercourse in the basin, and (4) sensitivity of the ecosystem (aquatic) to flow alteration (reduction). The indicators falling under the second category are (1) percentage of watershed and floodplain remaining under natural vegetation cover types, (2) anthropogenic structures causing restrictions of moment of aquatic biota in a watershed (percentage of watershed impacted/closed), (3) extent of flow regulation and fragmenta-tion, (4) fish species richness (relative richness), (5) exotics: percentage of aquatic biota, (6) human population density (entire basin as percentage of those in the main floodplain), and (7) overall water quality in the basin.

Though the earlier listed indicators can be considered on a macroscale, the relevance of each of the indicators will vary in the individual river basin level due to (1) topographical and geographical spread of basins, (2) varying degrees of data availability, (3) availability of aquatic organisms due to climatic conditions, and (4) climatic variability and seasonal effect. Even each of the indicators will respond to intrariver variability; in most of the river systems, significant habitat heterogeneity is seen from the head waters to downstream locations. This very often gets reflected in the aquatic community and species diversity. The earlier study, that is, the study by Smakhtin et al. (2007), included some of the major river basis in India, namely, Narmada, Krishna, Cauvery, Periyar, and part of Ganga, and was based on data and expertise available for each basin. Similarly, Jha et al. (2008) assessed the flow pattern and EF in Brahmani and Baitarani River systems in Odisha, facing more or less similar competing users of water: farmers, industries, and urban agglomerations. Since, the available data, specifics of basins and professional judgment vary among the river basins, the utility of each of the individual indicators may also vary, and thus, the indicators could be considered as a set of general indicators. Additional indicators could be considered for specific situations such as for rivers with different degrees of fragmentation (e.g., Krishna and Cauvery).

11.7   E-FLOWS AND THE COMMUNITY

Aquatic ecosystems, both fresh water and marine, are known to provide a wide variety of benefits to people. Prusty et al. (2017) enumerate such benefits as per the Millennium Ecosystem Assessment. These include "goods" (e.g., clean drinking water, fish, and fiber) and "services" (e.g., climate regulation, water purification, flood mitigation, ground water recharge, local weather control, and recreational opportunities). Furthermore, the cultural significance (particularly for indigenous cultures) of healthy rivers and associated ecosystems cannot be ruled out, which are an intrinsic value to people (IUCN, 2003), and due to the difficulty in identifying and quantifying, this intrinsic value is often overlooked.

Water and other allochthonous inputs such as detritus and sediment are essential in keeping rivers and other aquatic ecosystems healthy and providing sustained benefits to native denizens and dependent communities. Thus, EFs are a critical contributor in such cases, as they define the "recharge" or "discharge" nature of river ecosystems. Lack of such flows is known to damage the entire aquatic ecosystem, thereby threatening the populace and dependent communities. Thus, in extreme cases, the very existence of dependent ecosystems including lives and livelihood and security of downstream communities and industries are jeopardized due to the long-term absence of EFs. Hence, notwithstanding the realization on the need for EFs, it is essential to know that whether and for how long a society can afford not to provide EFs, and if so, what alternatives are to be in place for maintaining the ecological integrity of aquatic ecosystems.

As described in earlier sections, anthropogenic influences on flow regulations have been a major issue for degradation of riverine ecosystems. Berkamp et al. (2000) describe how the impacts of such long-term regulations on aquatic ecosystems are evident increasingly. Furthermore, a growing concern over these impacts in association with an increased political awareness and action has made the issue of EF more relevant while planning for water resource development programs, as communities are a driving force in determining and maintaining the EFs. One such case was reported from California, United States, where managing Mono Lake, proactive fishing groups (series of actions) and a court decision forced the government for making EF releases. It is encouraging to note that various international instruments and statements on water resources are increasingly recognizing that environmental requirements need to be an integral part of water resource management. For example, WCD (2000) identified different priorities w.r.t. environmental requirements, that is, "sustaining rivers and livelihoods, and recognising entitlements and sharing benefits as priorities." Thus, it is essential that dams provide for releases for EFs, and are designed, modified, and operated accordingly. Similarly, IUCN (2000) under its the "Vision for Water and Nature" program calls for *"leaving water in the system to provide environmental services such as flood mitigation and water cleansing."* This program aims at protecting and managing water resources including *"caring for and managing fresh-water resources in river or drainage basins"* through a six-part framework action plan.

In the history of a river or drainage basin, EFs are a relevant consideration at every stage. However, during the first allocations of water for consumptive uses, or while carrying out EIAs for water storage infrastructures, such issues are not considered seriously. Thus, addressing EFs is also an opportunity while developing water allocation plans or river rehabilitation programs. Therefore, "the sooner the better" approach needs to be followed in the case of EFs, though the progress is apprehended to be delayed for the lack of political attention/will and relevant information. However, uncaring approach in addressing EFs will have serious economic, environmental, and social repercussions and the solutions, if any, will be challenging and cost-prohibitive.

11.8 NEED FOR INCORPORATING E-FLOW ESTIMATES IN WATER DIVERSION PROGRAMS AND POLICIES

Taking care of EFs requires (1) drastic changes in the execution and operation of water harvesting/diversion infrastructures such as dams, and (2) active flow management or restrictive management through reducing the abstractions for other uses. The entire flow regime including low flows and floods can be generated through proper active flow management action plans, thereby assuring required e-flows and its variability. Furthermore, the allocation policies for restrictive flow management will control abstractions and diversions to ensure appropriate flow in the river during the lean periods. Such interventions require a broad societal support based on informed decision, which, however, would be dependent on the behavior/attitude of people, that is, changing attitude is a prerequisite. This also requires acceptance of such an operational protocol on ground by the operators. Revisit to our water policies and water management strategy giving due attention to the specificities of river systems, our diversified and rising needs, and ensuring the flows of materials and energy along the river course to sustain seen and unseen ecosystem components and services provided by the rivers would take us a long way in ensuring our environmental and livelihood securities for times to come.

ACKNOWLEDGMENT

The inputs provided and comments made by Dr. P. A. Azeez, former Director, Sálim Ali Centre for Ornithology and Natural History (SACON), on a draft version of this chapter is gratefully acknowledged.

KEYWORDS

- desktop analysis
- ecosystem services
- environmental flow
- flow regime
- habitat modeling
- in-stream flow
- river valley projects

REFERENCES

Acreman, M. C.; Dunbar, M. J. Defining Environmental River Flow Requirements a Review. *Hydrol. Earth Syst. Sci.* **2004**, *8* (5), 861–876.
Arthington, A. H.; Zalucki, J. M. Comparative *Evaluation of Environmental Flow Assessment Techniques: Review of Methods*; Land and Water Resources Research and Development Corporation: Canberra, ACT, 1998; 141 pp.
Babu, K. L. In *Livelihood Support Base and Ecosystem Services: State of Affairs in Tungabhadra*, Proceedings of National Seminar on Ecological Economics: An Approach Towards Socioeconomic and Environmental Sustainability; Nautiyal, S., Nayak, B. P.,

Eds.; Centre for Ecological Economics and Natural Resources, Institute for Social and Economic Change: Bangalore, 2010; pp 103–111.

Babu, K. L.; Kumara, H. Environmental Flows in River Basins: A Case Study of River Bhadra. *Curr. Sci.* **2009**, *96* (4), 475–479.

Berkamp, G.; McCartney, M.; Dugan, P.; McNeely, J.; Acreman, M. *Dams, Ecosystem Functions and Environmental Restoration Thematic Review II*; World Commission on Dams: Cape Town, 2000. www.dams.org.

Booth, E.; Mount, J.; Viers, J. H. Hydrologic Variability of the Cosumnes River Floodplain. *San. Franc. Estuary Watershed Sci.* **2006**, *4* (2), 1–19.

Brilly, M.; Kobold, M.; Vidmar, A. In *Water Information Management System and Low Flow Analysis in Slovenia*, FRIEND' 97—Regional Hydrology: Concepts and Models for Sustainable Water Resource Management, Proceedings of the International Conference, 1997; Vol. 246, 117–124.

Bureau of Reclamation. *Operation of Flaming Gorge Dam Final Environmental Impact Statement*; Bureau of Reclamation, 2005.

Bureau of Reclamation. *Final Environmental Impact Statement Navajo Reservoir Operations*; Bureau of Reclamation, 2006.

Döll, P.; Zhang, J. Impact of Climate Change on Freshwater Ecosystems: A Global-Scale Analysis of Ecologically Relevant River Flow Alterations. *Hydrol. Earth Syst. Sci.* **2010**, *14* (5), 783–799.

Döll, P.; Fiedler, K.; Zhang, J. Global-Scale Analysis of River Flow Alterations Due to Water Withdrawals and Reservoirs. *Hydrol. Earth Syst. Sci.* **2009**, *6* (4), 2413–2432.

Dakova, S.; Uzunov, Y.; Mandadjiev, D. Low Flow—The River's Ecosystem Limiting Factor. *Ecol. Eng.* **2000**, *16*, 167–174.

Dimmitt, M. L. Sustainable River Flows for North Carolina. MSc Dissertation, Nicholas School of the Environment, Duke University, 2009; 36 pp.

Dunbar, M. J.; Acreman, M. C.; Kirk, S. Environmental Flow Setting in England and Wales—Current Practice: Future Challenges. *J. Water Environ. Manage.* **2004**, *18*, 5–10.

Dyson, M.; Bergkamp, G.; Scanlon, J. *The Essentials of Environmental Flows*; IUCN: Gland: Switzerland and Cambridge, 2003; Xiv + 118 pp.

GEFN. *Terminology and Definitions Adopted by eFlowNet*; Global Environmental Flow Network. http://www.eflownet.org/viewinfo.cfm?linkcategoryid=4&linkid=13&siteid=1&FuseAction=display.

Gibson, C. A.; Meyer, J. L.; Poff, N. L.; Hay, L. E.; Georgakakos, A. Flow Regime Alterations under Changing Climate in Two River Basins: Implications for Freshwater Ecosystems. *River Res. Appl.* **2005**, *21* (8), 849–864.

Higgs, G.; Petts, G. Hydrological Changes and River Regulation in the UK. *Regul. Rivers: Res. Manage.* **1988**, *2*, 349–368.

Holden, P. B., Ed. *Flow Recommendations for the San Juan River*; San Juan River Basin Recovery Implementation Program, USFWS: Albuquerque, NM, 1999.

Hughes, D. A.; Hannart, P. A Desktop Model Used to Provide an Initial Estimate of the Ecological In-stream Flow Requirements of Rivers in South Africa. *J. Hydrol.* **2003**, *270*, 167–181.

IELRC. *Guidelines for Environmental Impact Assessment of River Valley Projects*; Department of Environment, Ministry of Environment and Forests; International Environmental Law Research Centre: Geneva, Switzerland, January, 1985; 11 pp.

IUCN. *Vision for Water and Nature: A World Strategy for Conservation and Sustainable Management of Water Resources in the 21st Century*; IUCN: Gland, Switzerland and Cambridge, 2000.

IUCN. *The Essentials of Environmental Flows*; Dyson, M., Bergkamp, G., Scanlon, J. Eds.; IUCN: Gland, Switzerland and Cambridge, 2003; 118 pp.

Jha, R.; Sharma, K. D.; Singh, V. P. Critical Appraisal of Methods for the Assessment of Environmental Flows and their Application in Two River Systems of India. *KSCE J. Civ. Eng.* **2008,** *12* (3), 213–219.

Joy, K. J.; Sangameswaran, P.; Latha, A.; Dharmadhikary, S.; Prasad, M. K.; Soma, K. P. *Life, Livelihoods, Ecosystems, Culture: Entitlements and Allocation of Water for Competing Uses*; Forum for Policy Dialogue on Water Conflicts in India: Pune, India, 2011; 88 pp.

Kingsford, R. T. Conservation Management of Rivers and Wetlands under Climate Change—A Synthesis. *Mar. Freshwater Res.* **2011,** *62* (3), 217–222.

Knights, P. In *Environmental Flows: Lessons from an Australian Experience*, Proceedings of International Conference: Dialog on Water, Food and Environment, Hanoi, Vietnam, 2002; 18 pp.

Korsgaard, L. Environmental Flows in Integrated Water Resources Management: Linking Flows, Services and Values. Ph.D. Thesis, Institute of Environmental & Resources, Technical University of Denmark, 2006; 60 pp.

Lankford, B. A. Environmental Water Requirements: A Demand Management Perspective. *J. Chart. Inst. Water Environ. Manage.* **2002,** *17* (1), 19–22.

Matthews, R. C.; Bao, Y. The Texas Method of Preliminary in Stream Flow Determination. *Rivers* **1991,** *2* (4), 295–310.

MEA. *Ecosystems and Human Wellbeing, Volume 1: Current State and Trends. Millennium Ecosystem Assessment*; Island Press: Washington, DC, 2005; 917 pp.

MDEQ. *Total Maximum Daily Load for Mercury for Hammell Creek, Houghton County, Michigan*; Michigan Department of Environmental Quality, Surface Water Quality Division, 2002. http://www.deq.state.mi.us/documents/deq-wd-water-tmd/-hammellcreek.pdf; p 7.

Mohile, A. D.; Gupta, L. N. In *Environmental Water Requirement—Concept and Coverage*, Abstracts of the NIE/IWMI Workshop on Environmental Flows, New Delhi, March 2005; pp 3–4.

Muth, R. T.; Crist, L. W.; LaGory, K. E.; Hayes, J. W.; Bestgen, K. R.; Ryan, T. P.; Lyons, J. K.; Valdez, R. A. *Flow and Temperature Recommendations for Endangered Fishes in the Green River, Downstream of Flaming Gorge Dam*; Final Report, Project FG-53, Upper Colorado Endangered Fish Restoration Program, 2000.

Palmer, M. A.; Reidy Liermann, C. A.; Nilsson, C.; Flörke, M.; Alcamo, J.; Lake, P. S.; Bond, N. Climate Change and the World's River Basins: Anticipating Management Options. *Front. Ecol. Environ.* **2008,** *6* (2), 81–89.

Petts, G. E. Water Allocation to Protect River Ecosystems. *Regul. Rivers: Res. Manage.* **1996,** *12*, 353–365.

Poff, N. L.; Zimmerman, J. K. H. Ecological Responses to Altered Flow Regimes: A Literature Review to Inform the Science and Management of Environmental Flows. *Freshwater Biol.* **2010,** *55* (1), 194–205.

Poff, N. L.; Allan, J. D.; Palmer, M. A.; Hart, D. D.; Richter, B. D.; Arthington, A. H.; Rogers, K. H.; Meyer, J. L.; Stanford, J. A. River Flows and Water Wars: Emerging Science for Environmental Decision Making. *Front. Ecol. Environ.* **2003**, *1* (6), 298–306.

Poff, N. L.; Allan, J. D.; Bain, M. B.; Karr, J. R.; Prestegaard, K. L.; Richter, B. D.; Sparks, R. E.; Stromberg, J. C. The Natural Flow Regime: A Paradigm for River Conservation and Restoration. *BioScience* **1997**, *47* (11), 769–784.

Postel, S.; Carpenter, S. Freshwater Ecosystem Services. In *Nature's Services: Societal Dependence on Natural Ecosystems*; Daily, G. C., Ed.; Island Press: Washington, DC, 1997; pp 195–214.

Prusty, B. A. K.; Chandra, R.; Azeez, P. A. *Wetland Science: Perspectives from South Asia*; Springer: New Delhi, 2017. DOI: https://doi.org/10.1007/978-81-322-3715-0.

Revenga, C.; Brunner, J.; Henninger, N.; Kassem, K.; Payne, R. *Pilot Analysis of Global Ecosystems: Freshwater Systems*; World Resources Institute: Washington, DC, 2000; 65 pp.

Richter, B. D.; Baumgartner, J. V.; Wigington, R.; Braun, D. P. How Much Water Does a River Need? *Freshwater Biol.* **1997**, *37*, 231–249.

Richter, B. D.; Baumgartner, J. V.; Powell, J.; Braun, D. P. A Method for Assessing Hydrologic Alteration within Ecosystems. *Conserv. Biol.* **1996**, *10* (4), 1163–1174.

Riggs, H. C.; Caffey, J. E.; Orsborn, J. F.; Schaake, J. C.; Singh, K. P.; Wallace, J. R. Task Committee of Low-Flow Evaluation, Methods, and Needs of the Committee on Surface-water Hydrology of the Hydraulics Division. Characteristics of Low Flows. *J. Hydraul. Div.: Proc. Am. Soc. Civ. Eng.* **1980**, *106*, 717–731.

Smakhtin, V.; Anputhas, M. *An Assessment of Environmental Flow Requirements of Indian River Basins*; IWMI Research Report 107, International Water Management Institute: Colombo, Sri Lanka, 2006; 42 pp.

Smakhtin, V.; Arunachalam, M.; Behera, S.; Chatterjee, A.; Das, S.; Gautam, P.; Joshi, G. D.; Sivaramakrishnan, K. G.; Unni, K. S. *Developing Procedures for Assessment of Ecological Status of Indian River Basins in the Context of Environmental Water Requirements*; IWMI Research Report 114, International Water Management Institute: Colombo, Sri Lanka, 2007; 40 pp.

Smakhtin, V. U. Low Flow Hydrology: A Review. *J. Hydrol.* **2001**, *240*, 147–186.

Smakhtin, V. U.; Revenga, C.; Döll, P. *Taking Into Account Environmental Water Requirements in Globalscale Water Resources Assessments*; IWMI Comprehensive Assessment Research Report 2, Research Report of the CGIAR Comprehensive Assessment Programme of Water Use in Agriculture, International Water Management Institute: Colombo, Sri Lanka, 2004a; 24 pp.

Smakhtin, V. U.; Revenga, C.; Döll, P. A Pilot Global Assessment of Environmental Water Requirements and Scarcity. *Water Int.* **2004b**, 29, 307–317.

Smakhtin, V. U.; Toulouse, M. Relationships between Lowflow Characteristics of South African Streams. *Water SA* **1998**, *24*, 107–112.

Stewardson, M. J.; Gippel, C. J. Incorporating Flow Variability into Environmental Flow Regimes Using the Flow Events Method. *River Res. Appl.* **2003**, *19*, 459–472.

Tennant, D. L. In-Stream Flow Regimens for Fish, Wildlife, Recreation and Related Environmental Resources. *Fisheries* **1976**, *1*, 6–10.

Tharme, R. E. A Global Perspective on Environmental Flow Assessment: Emerging Trends in the Development and Application of Environmental Flow Methodologies for Rivers. *River Res. Appl.* **2003**, *19*, 397–441.

Vorosmarty, C. J.; Green, P.; Salisbury, J.; Lammers, R. Global Water Resources: Vulnerability from Climate Change and Population Growth. *Science* **2000**, *289* (5477), 284–288.

Wallace, T. B.; Cox, W. E. *Locating Information on Surface Water Availability in Virginia*, 2002; 24 pp. http://www.rappriverbasin.state.va.us/studies.

Ward, J. V.; Tockner, K. Biodiversity: Towards a Unifying Theme for River Ecology. *Freshwater Biol.* **2001**, *46*, 807–819.

Ward, J. V.; Tockner, K.; Uehlinger, U.; Mallard, F. Understanding Natural Patterns and Processes in River Corridors as the Basis for Effective River Restoration. *Regul. Rivers: Res. Manage.* **2001**, *17*, 311–323.

Watts, R. J.; Richter, B. D.; Opperman, J. J.; Bowmer, K. H. Dam Reoperation in an Era of Climate Change. *Mar. Freshwater Res.* **2011**, *62* (3), 321–327.

WCD. *Dams and Development: A New Framework for Decision-Making*; The Report of the World Commission on Dams, Earthscan: London, 2000; 404 pp.

Zeefat, P. Validation & Improving Smakhtin Environmental Flow Requirements Method. Master in Civil Engineering & Management Thesis, University Twente: Enschede, 2010; 43 pp.

CHAPTER 12

Role of Pressurized Irrigation Network Systems (PINS) in Enhancing Irrigation Coverage and Water-Use Efficiency: Evidence from Gujarat, India

MRUTYUNJAY SWAIN[1*], S. S. KALAMKAR[2], and KALPANA KAPADIA[2]

[1]*Department of Economics and Management, Khallikote University, Berhampur, Odisha, India*

[2]*Agro-Economic Research Centre, Sardar Patel University, Vallabh Vidyanagar, India*

Corresponding author. E-mail: mrutyunjay77@gmail.com

ABSTRACT

Water scarcity for agriculture has been growing year after year due to various reasons, for which the government has been very keen to increase the water-use efficiency with its new slogan "more crops per drop." The government has envisaged promoting micro-irrigation system (MIS) and increasing the area under these water-saving technologies. The pressurized irrigation network system (PINS) is one such new innovative concept that acts as interface between water source and MIS in farm plots and increases the area under irrigation through adoption of MIS. However, there is a dearth of studies on its performance and management by water user associations (WUAs). Thus, the present study assesses the extent of adoption and performance of PINS in Gujarat, India. The study also analyzes the role of PINS in enhancing irrigation coverage and water-use efficiency in the selected states of the country. The study is based on both secondary and primary data. PINS were selected from both surface irrigation command (mainly canal) and groundwater irrigation command areas (mainly tube well). A total of 200 beneficiary and 100 nonbeneficiary households (hhs) were surveyed in the state. The study finds that tube well PINS are performing well whereas all the canal PINS are defunct in the state. The water savings due to judicious use of water, increase in agricultural income, and electricity saving were the major common benefits accrued by the beneficiary water users/farmers in the state. The results of the probit model indicated that more area under PINS–MIS, uninterrupted regular power supply, more depth of tube well, sufficiency of water in PINS, and group membership helped in realizing the benefits like increase in yield and income, water saving, and energy saving by the beneficiary farmers. The study suggests to discourage more water-consuming cropping pattern through incentives/disincentives, checking water theft, revising water rates, and relocating the canal PINS at far-off places from minors/subminors for better adoption of canal PINS for enhancing irrigation coverage and water-use efficiency, which will reduce the level of instability in agricultural production in these water-scarce states.

12.1   INTRODUCTION

Irrigation has been a high-priority area in economic development of India with more than 50% of all public expenditure on agriculture having been spent on irrigation alone. The land area under irrigation has expanded from 22.6 million ha in 1950 to about 89.4 million ha in 2010–2011, with 52% area being irrigated by surface water through canal network. Most of the irrigation networks are unlined and the huge amount of the irrigation water is lost in the main canal, distributaries, minors, and field channels (FCs). About 71% of the irrigation water is lost in the whole process of its conveyance from headworks and application in the field (Navalwala, 1991). The overall efficiency of canal irrigation system worldwide is very low that leads to poor utilization of irrigation potential, created at huge cost. Recognizing the fast decline of irrigation water potential and increasing demand for water from different sectors, a number of demand management strategies and programs have been introduced to save water and increase the existing water-use efficiency in Indian agriculture (Narayanamoorthy, 1997; Rosegrant, 1997; Vaidyanathan 1998; Dhawan 2002; Narayanamoorthy, 2010).

The need of the hour is to increase irrigation efficiency of existing projects and use saved water for irrigating new areas or reducing the gap between potential and actual irrigated areas (Dhawan and Datta, 1992; Sivanappan, 1994; Shah et al, 2000). Shifting to pressurized irrigation can be an option for increasing this irrigation coverage and efficiency. Pressurized irrigation network systems (PINS) with micro-irrigation system (MIS) have the potential to avoid the water loss compared to surface irrigation, increasing the irrigation efficiency from 45 to 60% in open canal to the range of 75–95% with pressurized irrigation. While open canal systems have high labor requirement for maintenance, the pressurized systems require skilled labor. The benefits of micro-irrigation in terms of water savings and productivity gains are substantial in comparison to the same crops cultivated under flood method of irrigation. MIS is also found to be reducing energy (electricity) requirement, weed problems, fertilizer and pesticides requirement, and cost of cultivation (Shah et al., 1994, 2009; Sahu and Rao, 2005; Jiterwal, 2008; Devasirvatham, 2009; Siag et al., 2009; Postal et al., 2001; Narayanamoorthy, 2015; Viswanathan and Bahinipati, 2015). Srivastava et al. (2010) evaluated the feasibility of pressurized irrigation system on one outlet of a minor irrigation command at Water Technology Centre for Eastern Region, Bhubaneswar. They reported that the system can be used with the canal irrigation system because it reduced the turbidity of the water and provided continuous supply of water. The system is also capable of providing irrigation through drip to part of a command during summer, by using water stored in service reservoir after the canal is closed in first week of April. To take care of sediment in the canal water, there are three stages of filtration: first, hydrocyclone filter that filters heavy suspended materials, namely sand and silt; second, the sand filter; and, finally, the screen filter. The three-stage filtration reduces the turbidity to the desired level. The benefit–cost ratio of the system was found to be 1.126.

Adoption of new irrigation scheduling practices is a dynamic process that is potentially determined by various factors, including farmers' perceptions of the relative advantage and disadvantage of new technology vis-à-vis that of existing technologies and the efforts made by extension and changed agents to disseminate these technologies. Other factors, which influence in respect of new irrigation practices, are resource endowments, socioeconomic status, nature of crop production and from their profitability, etc. Due to scarcity of irrigation water and improved agronomical practices recommended for scheduling irrigation for commercial crops, farmers showed reasonable attraction and awareness of irrigation technologies that could help them irrigate crop more accurately with water-saving technique.

In this context, the present chapter intended to assess functioning of PINS command area and the experiences of beneficiary farmers in the command area using MIS in their lands compared with nonbeneficiary farmers around the PINS command area. It is sought to assess the performance of PINS project with MIS such as sprinkler and drip in terms of their functioning, costs and benefits, adoptability, and constraints.

12.2 IMPORTANCE OF PRESSURIZED IRRIGATION NETWORK SYSTEMS (PINS) IN INDIA

A pressurized irrigation system is a network installation consisting of pipes, fittings, and other devices properly designed and installed to supply water under pressure from the source of the water to the irrigable area (FAO, 2007). In this system of irrigation, water is pressurized, supplied to farm plots that use MIS such as drip and sprinkler and thus precisely applied to the plants under pressure through a system of pipes. The PINS is an innovative concept that comprises pipe network with controls, pumping installations, power supply, filtration, and intake well/diggy (Fig. 12.1). It is a common and shared infrastructure (by group of farmers) facilitating individual beneficiary for installing and operating MIS.

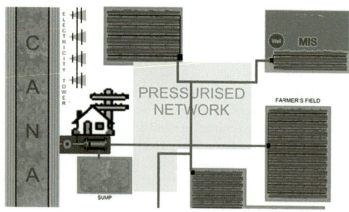

FIGURE 12.1   Concept of PINS—network bridge between canal and MIS in the field.

As per the requirement, the pressure is given at different levels depending on the size of PINS. As stated in Table 12.1, the pressure can be exerted at village service area (VSA) level (300–500 ha), Chak level (40–60 ha), and sub-Chak level (5–8 ha). Obviously, pressurization at terminal point, that is sub-Chak level, would be the most economical option but would also require a more number of power connections. Evidently to take the advantage of cost and feasibility aspects of power connections, sub-Chaks are reoriented radially from the center of a Chak and pressurized flow is only resorted to the head of sub-Chaks.

TABLE 12.1 Levels of Pressurization (Canal Command).

Sr. no	Level of pressurization (command block)	Capital and operational cost	Power connections per VSA
1	VSA (300–500 ha)	Very high	1 connection
2	Chak (40–60 ha)	High	5–6 connections
3	Sub-Chak (5–8 ha)	Low	About 50 connections

Source: Ganpatye (2011).

The PINS–MIS enjoys many advantages over conventional flow irrigation as presented in Table 12.2. The PINS–MIS helps in ensuring more crops per drop of water by enhancing water-use efficiency and covering more area under irrigation with saved water from switching over from flow irrigation.

TABLE 12.2 Advantages of PINS–MIS over Conventional Flow Irrigation.

Sr. no.	Particulars	Flow	PINS+MIS
1	Distribution	Gravity	Pressure
2	Water losses		Nil
	1. Conveyance losses	7–9%	Drip 2–3%
	2. Application losses	25%	Sprinkler 10–15%
3	Water availability	Not enough for optimum irrigation and yield	Availability can be increased
4	Water productivity	Low	High
5	Conjunctive use necessity	More	Less

TABLE 12.2   *(Continued)*

Sr. no.	Particulars	Flow	PINS+MIS
6	Poor quality of water	Use will deteriorate soil and crop productivities	Reasonably poor quality of water can be used without affecting soil productivity
7	Land requirement (ha)	170 m^2 required for subminor and FC	24 m^2 required for storage (8 h supply)
8	Land topography restriction	Restriction	No restriction
9	Maintenance of water courses	Recurring maintenance expenditure	No maintenance problems
10	Drainage	Is a must. In long run, problems may arise	Drainage related problems minimal
11	Soil health	Prone to deteriorate	Health maintained
12	Poor irrigable soils	Cannot be irrigated	Can be irrigated
13	Other than command areas	Cannot be irrigated	Can be brought under irrigation
14	Incidences of pests, diseases, weeds	More	Less
15	Cost of cultivation	More	About 20% lesser than flow
16	Watch and ward	More	Less
17	Ground water pollution	Highly prone	Nil
18	Double cropping	Not possible	Enough scope
19	Crop quality	Normal	Improved
20	Employment generation	Labor/unskilled	Skilled manpower
21	Energy requirement	No	Yes

Source: Ganpatye (2011).

12.3   DATA AND METHOD

The present study has used both secondary and primary data. The primary data were collected from three selected districts of Gujarat state, viz., Mehsana, Patan, and Gandhinagar. PINS were selected from both surface irrigation command areas (mainly canal) and groundwater irrigation command areas (mainly tube well). The data were collected from sample households and PINS–water user associations (WUAs) as per the distribution stated in Table 12.3. 2015–2016 were the reference years of the study.

TABLE 12.3   PINS Sample Size Distribution for Gujarat (Beneficiary and Nonbeneficiary Farmers).

Districts	Govt.-PINS with MIS		Underground pipeline (UGPL)		Pvt. PINS with MIS*(BH)	Govt. PINS without any irrigation (defunct/not used)*(NBH)	Total no. of households	
	BH	NBH	BH	NBH			BH	NBH
Mehsana	57	15	14	04	09	–	80	19
Patan	76	50	–	–	05	10	81	60
Gandhinagar	17	10	–	–	06	–	23	10
Ahmedabad	–	–	16	11	–	–	16	11
State total	150	75	30	15	20	10	200	100

Notes: BH, beneficiary households; NBH, nonbeneficiary households.

Out of 200 beneficiary hhs, 150 hhs were having access to government PINS with MIS. Remaining 50 were drawn from private PINS with MIS and underground pipeline (UGPL) program. Out of 100 nonbeneficiary hhs, about 10 samples were drawn from peripheral regions of defunct government PINS failing to provide any irrigation facility.

Four kinds of survey schedules were administered on the major stake-holders: (1) implementing agencies/ promoting companies, (2) PINS–WUAs, (3) beneficiary households, and (4) nonbeneficiary households. In addition to survey method, the focused group discussion and key informant interviews were conducted to capture institutional dynamics in operation and maintenance in various command areas of the country. PINS operators, WUA management committee members, and farmers were interviewed for understanding the effectiveness of institutional arrangements for operation and management of irrigation systems and distribution of irrigation water and the difficulties they face.

Simple statistical tools, case studies, and probit models were used for data analysis and interpretation of results. The performance of PINS–MIS was evaluated with respect to water savings, irrigation productivity, costs, and benefits of the systems. The probit model was fitted so as to ascertain the significance of various determinants of benefits accrued from tube well PINS. The benefits such as increase in agricultural yield and income, water saving, energy saving, and reduction in fertilizer and pesticide use were considered as the binary response variables, whereas the determinants of benefits such as age of HH head, years of schooling of HH head, years of farming experiences, amount of loan taken for investment on PINS–MIS, group membership, land location in the command area of the PINS, sufficiency of water in PINS project, area under PINS–MIS, total operational area, horsepower of pump set, total area under Rabi, total area under horticultural crops, depth of tube well, no interruption in regular supply of power, and better water management by WUA were considered as the explanatory variables in the probit model. The model was administered on the members of tube well users association (TUA) in the state.

12.4   OVERVIEW OF PINS PROGRAMS IN GUJARAT

The land area under irrigation in India has expanded from 22.6 million ha in 1950 to about 91.53 million ha in 2011–2012, with 52% area being irrigated by surface irrigation through canal network. Unfortunately, the overall efficiency of canal irrigation system is very low that leads to poor utilization of irrigation potential, created at huge cost. On the other hand, the demand for increasing irrigation coverage has been growing. For enhancing the irrigation efficiency, the MIS is being promoted through many programs. The concept of PINS is one such program that was developed at Design Office of Sardar Sarovar Narmada Nigam Limited (SSNNL) as a necessity step to introduce MIS in the command area of Sardar Sarovar Narmada Project (SSP). Later on, the concept was used in various other states. Since it is a new concept popularized in the last 10 years, the literature and statistics on the same are mostly unavailable. Therefore, only aforesaid four front runner states were included in the study for the detailed study.

The Government of Gujarat has put in lots of efforts to replace conventional irrigation by micro-irrigation so as to improve water-use efficiency and to increase area under irrigation in the state. The pilot project on PINS is one such effort started in 2007–2008 in the command area of SSP. Accordingly, about 25 pilot projects were initiated in the state covering 1029 farmers with 1491.6 ha of CCA and estimated budget of Rs. 1306.3 lakh. The average spending incurred per PINS was Rs. 35.4 lakhs against the estimated Rs. 52.3 lakhs. The estimated per hectare expenditure on PINS at Chak level was Rs. 20,340. Because of PINS, the per hectare of water savings was estimated to be to the tune of Rs. 15,000 for *Bhal* and *Bara* areas (mainly saline areas) and Rs. 19,560 for other zones, respectively. The project work was carried out by various companies, for example Jain Irrigation Ltd (56%), Parikhit Industries (32.0%), and EPC Industries (8.0%).

The idea was to promote micro-irrigation through WUA by providing the basic irrigation infrastructure at the farmers' field. With the PINS program, a common facility was provided to draw water from the canal and distribute it at farmers' field by imparting necessary pressure required for operating MIS. For encouraging the adoption of MIS, about 75% subsidy was provided to the farmers and necessary credit facilities were also provided to the farmers for purchasing the MIS.

12.4.1 ESTIMATED EXPENDITURE AND PAYBACK PERIOD ON PINS

It may be noted from Table 12.4 that the estimated per hectare expenditure on PINS at Chak level was Rs. 20,340. It may be noted that the case of 24-h electric, high voltage distribution system (HVDS)/express feeder is very cost-effective and attractive option. However, 24-h electricity supply is to be made available at Chak level, that is six connections per VSA. This can be made possible through HVDS and express feeders. However, the option two with power availability of 8 h through agrifeeder is highly desirable and cost-effective alternative as it is in tune with GOG's policy of power distribution for agriculture in the state and the estimated per hectare expenditure on PINS as per the option two was Rs. 28,740. Taking Rs. 20,340, being the lower, as the average capital cost per hectare on PINS, the payback period on investments made by the farmers on cotton cultivation with adoption of PINS and drip systems varies from 1.7 to 2.8 years depending on location-specific factors in the state (Table 12.5). Both farmers and government were expected to be benefited in terms of lower expenses on land and construction and energy consumption. Suppose that the PINS is not constructed, the government and farmers had to spend more amount on minor, subminors, and FCs to the tune of Rs. 13,565 and Rs. 6220 per ha, respectively. Because of PINS, the per hectare of water savings was estimated to be to the tune of Rs. 15,000 for *Bhal* and *Bara* areas (mainly saline areas) and Rs. 19,560 for other

TABLE 12.4 Cost-Effective and Feasible Estimates on PINS at Chak Level.

Options	Power availability	Water sources	Storage with lining	Pipes		Pump house	Pumps electric	Total capital cost (Rs/ha)	
				PVC	HDPE			PVC	HDPE
1	24-h electric, HVDS/express feeder	Minors operated at half design discharge for all days	0	10,275	14,700	3240	2400	15,915	20,340
2	8 h through agrifeeder	Direct lifting from perennial canal (MC/BC/rtd) all along both the banks	0	10,275	14,700	2000	4800	17,075	21,500
3	8 h through agrifeeder	Pond of 1 day storage and minors operated at half design discharge	6000	10,275	14,700	3240	4800	24,315	28,740

Source: Ganapatye (2011).

zones, respectively. Similarly, considering the wheat crop cultivation, the per hectare of water savings was estimated to be Rs. 8000 for *Bhal* and *Bara* areas and Rs. 10,480 for other zones, respectively. The estimates for the irrigation department have been more than that for farmers because of larger coverage by the department.

TABLE 12.5 Estimates on Expenditure and Payback Period on Canal PINS in Gujarat. (Case of Cotton with Drip System)

Particulars	Government		Farmers	
	Bhal and Bara	Other zones	Bhal and Bara	Other zones
PINS cost	20,340	20,340	0	0
Land and construction	−13,565	−13,565	−6220	−6220
Net PINS cost	6775	6775	−6220	−6220
MIS system cost	42,000	42,000	42,000	42,000
Energy cost	1659	1659	387	387
Total cost	57,209	57,209	29,947	29,947
Water savings	15,000	19,560	1700	1700
Yield increase	–	–	10,000	18,000
Fertilizer savings			1080	1080
Total savings	15,000	19,560	12,780	20,780
Payback period (crop seasons)	3.3	2.7	2.8	1.7

Source: Ganapatye (2011).

Though the Government of Gujarat followed a proactive approach to increase the adoption of PINS by the water users, the existing practices of farmers such as relying more on conventional flow method for irrigation did not change much due to various reasons. The farmers did not want to change the cropping pattern that was highly water intensive. They did not want to spend anything on installation of MIS since canal water was available to them plentifully, almost free of cost. There are no much strict rules and regulations enforced to check the illegal use of canal water and water theft.

Looking at the unsatisfactory experience of canal PINS in the state, an attempt was made by the irrigation department in devising a suitable solution to address various issues. The main features included promotion of underground pipeline system (UGPL) network for micro canals such as minors, which have been discussed in the next section. The combination of UGPLs and PINS replacing minors, subminors, and FCs has also been put in some places in the state. The major benefits of UGPL system are the land saving and water saving (up to 10–20%), less implementation period, feasibility even in flood zone/undulating area, avoidance of land fragmentation, integrating FCs with the subminors, and less operation and maintenance (O&M) expenditure. However, it has some limitations. It requires energy for lifting operation in some patches. It is suitable mainly for falling topography. It may save the water to the desirable extent since the majority of farmers still use flood irrigation. Moreover, there are some issues in implementation of UGPL in subminors. Farmers were not willing to pay 10%, their contribution, which was later reduced to 2.5%. Farmers are continuously growing some crops and hence not willing to allow the laying of UGPL.

Among three types of water sources, tube well is the major source of water for successful PINS operation in the Gujarat state. The tube well PINS have been operating for a long time as a viable method of irrigation in the state. The Government of Gujarat introduced the policy of pressurized irrigation system in the command area of public tube wells under Gujarat Water Resources Development Corporation (GWRDC). As per the government norms, MIS provided in the command area of 309 tube wells covering 1452 ha in five districts of the state, that is, Banaskantha, Mehsana, Patan, Gandhinagar, and Sabarkantha. The State Government had decided in March 2013 to provide MIS in government tube wells at 100% government cost in total nine districts. Accordingly, the State Government provided MIS system in 162 tube wells in 2013–2014 covering 1531 ha and 1037 farmers. The MIS works covering 2984 ha of 3780 farmers were in progress in 208 tube wells, which was likely to be completed in 2014–2015. Till January 2016, a total of 674 tube wells have been covered by GWRDC, of which 54.0% was through government subsidy and remaining 44% was given partial assistance.

12.5   PERFORMANCE OF PINS IN GUJARAT

The progress in various PINS programs and adoption of certain types of PINS depend on various factors such as suitability to farmers' preference on cropping pattern and methods of irrigation, nature of existing access to available water resources, and existing policy regimes. This section particularly examines the perceptions and experiences of the farmers/water users in terms of the adoption, benefits, and costs of accessing irrigation water from available PINS systems. Among the sample farmers in Gujarat, the majority (68.7%) had less than 1 ha area under tube well PINS. About 95.3% of sample beneficiary farmers adopted drip, whereas the 10% of them adopted sprinkler in the state (Table 12.6). The total cost of drip and sprinkler systems was Rs. 42,950 and Rs. 30,133 per hh in the study areas. About 68.7% of beneficiary farmers were from marginal farmer category who received subsidy of Rs. 1842 per hh (Table 12.7). On the other hand, only 1.3% of large farmers received the subsidy with an average of Rs. 21,230 per hh. The average subsidy received by the large farmers was higher due to more land covered under MIS by them.

The major motivating factors for the beneficiary farmers for adoption of PINS–MIS were to get assured amount of water for irrigation (79.3%), better and stable crop yield and farm income (78.0%), saving more water and to cover more area under irrigation (67.3%), facilitating judicious or efficient distribution of water among the water users (54.7%), and avoiding unnecessary conflicts with other farmers (28.7%).

The water savings due to judicious use of water (94.0%), increase in agricultural income (86.7%), getting water in right time (88.0%), proper distribution of water among farmers (62.7%), getting more information on how to use water judiciously (56.7%), electricity saving (54.0%), and improved maintenance of the system (26.7%) were the major benefits accrued by the beneficiary water users/farmers. The proportion of area under more remunerative Rabi crops was also found to be higher (28.7% of GCA) in the case of beneficiary farmers as compared to nonbeneficiary farmers. It was observed that, except a few crops like groundnut, mung, and cumin, beneficiary farmers had enjoyed better crop yields as compared to nonbeneficiary farmers. The percentage change in yield under drip over flood and change in yield under sprinkler over flood has been spectacular with respect to some crops like castor (117.6% and 102.1%, respectively) and cotton (83.1%). Among Rabi crops, major benefits were observed in

TABLE 12.6 Adoption of Micro-irrigation Systems (MIS) under PINS Programs.

Type of MIS used	No. of farmers used	%.of farmers used	Average area under MIS (ha/hh)	Total cost of the system (Rs./hh)	Amount paid the farmers (Rs./hh)	Subsidy (%)	Received subsidy from the State Government (%)	Agency for the subsidy program
Drip	143	95.33	0.73	42,950	3153.2	92.77	95.3	GGRC
Sprinkler	15	10.00	0.46	30,133	2233.3	91.33	10	GGRC

Source: Field survey.

the case of wheat (by 83.3% and 108.4%, respectively), fennel (55.1%), rapeseed-mustard (59.9%), and tobacco (by 84.6%).

TABLE 12.7 Distribution of Farmers According to Subsidy Received on MIS.

Subsidy received on MIS	Amount paid by farmers (Rs.)	No. of farmers	% farmers
Marginal (Up to 1.0 ha)	1842	103	68.7
Small (1.01–2.0 ha)	3924	35	23.3
Medium (2.01–4.0 ha)	6875	10	6.7
Large (4.0 to more)	21,250	2	1.3
Total	2922	150	100.0

Source: Field survey.

Some of the factors those helped in generating some benefits were better water management by WUA members (58.0%), better education and awareness of the farmer (43.3%), more area under PINS–MIS (34.0%), and more area during Rabi (37.3%) were the major ones. The results of the probit model indicated that more area under PINS–MIS, uninterrupted power regular supply, more depth of tube well, sufficiency of water in PINS, and group membership helped in realizing the benefits like increase in yield and income, water saving, and energy saving by the beneficiary farmers. Among the major activities undertaken by different types of PINS TUAs, operation and maintenance of PINS project, deciding the timing of water release, judicious water distribution, collection of water rates, and collection of per capita operation and maintenance cost were the major activities of government TUAs. The main source of income for these TUAs was annual maintenance fees collected whereas the major heads of expenditures were the expenditure on electricity bill, repairing expenses, and salary expenses. Besides, in case of PINS, the charges to Irrigation Department as miscellaneous expenses were incurred by the WUA/TUAs.

12.6 DETERMINANTS OF BENEFITS FROM PINS IN GUJARAT

Some of the major factors those helped in generating some benefits as discussed in preceding section were better water management by WUA members (58.0%), better education and awareness of the farmers (43.3%), more area under PINS–MIS (34.0%), and more area during Rabi (37.3%) (Table 12.8).

TABLE 12.8   Determinants of the Benefits Accrued by Participating in WUA

Benefits accrued	% farmers benefited
Better education and awareness of the farmer	43.33
More area under PINS–MIS	34.00
More area during Rabi	37.33
More area during summer	21.33
More depth of tube well	24.00
More horsepower of pump	23.33
No interruption in regular supply of power/electricity	18.67
Better water management by WUA members	58.00
Any other (in-time water arrival and lower labor cost)	1.33

Source: Field survey.

Among the PINS program covered in Gujarat, the majority were from command areas of tube well PINS from about 10 districts of the state. The beneficiary farmers have reported that the tube well PINS has been very useful for them on various aspects such as water saving, increase in yield and farmers income, energy saving, and reduction in application of fertilizer and pesticides Thus, an attempt has been made in this section so as to ascertain the significance of various determinants of benefits accrued from tube well PINS using the probit model. Table 12.9 presents the marginal effects of accessing benefits of PINS–MIS. The Wald Chi-Square Test was found to be significant in all models, which indicates that the independent variables taken as a group are quite significant in explaining the benefits accrued from PINS–MIS.

The major benefits provided by the WUAs to its members were arrival of water in time, proper distribution of water among farmers, more information on how to use water judiciously, saving of water, electricity and labor cost, improved maintenance of the system, and less conflicts around water. The results of the probit model indicated that more area under PINS–MIS, uninterrupted power regular supply, more depth of tube well, sufficiency of water in PINS, and group membership helped in realizing the benefits like increase in yield and income, water saving, and energy saving by the beneficiary farmers (Table 12.9).

TABLE 12.9 Probit Odds Ratio of Determinants of Benefits of PINS with MIS.

Explanatory variables	Dependent variables			
	Increase in agri-cultural yield and income	Water saving	Energy saving	Reduction in fertilizer and pesticide use
Intercept	−5.89*** (1.935)	−0.741 (1799.000)	0.651 (1.218)	1.147 (1.301)
Age of HH head (years)	0.034 (0.022)	0.094* (0.049)	−0.010 (0.016)	−0.002 (0.017)
Years of schooling of HH head (years)	0.049 (0.050)	0.144 (0.107)	0.015 (0.038)	−0.005 (0.042)
HH Head's experience in farming (years)	0.006 (0.019)	0.057* (0.034)	0.002 (0.014)	−0.010 (0.015)
Amount of loan taken (in Rs.)	0.000 (0.000)	0.000 (0.000)	0.000 (0.000)	0.000 (0.000)
Group membership other than TUA/WUA	0.070 (0.403)	0.654 (0.899)	0.699** (0.277)	0.578* (0.327)
Land location in the command area of the PINS	−0.292 (0.369)	0.102 (0.647)	0.386 (0.271)	−0.623** (0.296)
Sufficiency of water	0.668 (0.598)	−6.813 (1799.000)	−0.886* (0.533)	0.673 (0.495)
Operational area (ha)	0.526* (0.284)	0.320 (0.598)	0.131 (0.091)	−0.079 (0.104)
Area under PINS–MIS (ha)	0.552 (0.403)	0.175** (1.088)	0.199 (0.194)	0.174 (0.222)
Horsepower of pump set	0.029** (0.013)	−0.018 (0.030)	−0.007 (0.008)	−0.003 (0.009)
Total area under Rabi (ha)	0.590* (0.316)	−1.95** (0.881)	−0.056 (0.209)	0.211 (0.266)

TABLE 12.9 *(Continued)*

Explanatory variables	Dependent variables							
	Increase in agricultural yield and income		Water saving		Energy saving		Reduction in fertilizer and pesticide use	
Total area under horticultural crops (ha)	−0.351	(0.600)	5.973	(3.733)	−0.517	(0.377)	0.093	(0.427)
More depth of tube well	0.207	(0.495)	0.502	(1.379)	−0.815**	(0.362)	0.433	(0.403)
No interruption in regular supply of power	1.346***	(0.379)	11.690	(505.900)	1.523***	(0.267)	−0.299	(0.291)
Better water management by WUA	0.203	(0.448)	0.075	(1.415)	−0.363	(0.316)	0.288	(0.331)
Number of observations	150		150		150		150	
Pseudo R^2	0.107		0.145		0.0833		0.064	

Note: Figures in the parentheses indicate standard errors; significance codes: $*p < 0.1$, $**p < 0.5$, $***p < 0.01$.

Source: Computed from primary data.

The major suggestions provided by the farmers were to (1) impart training to farmers on need, importance, and use of MIS with PINS; (2) provide better quality components of MIS so as to reduce the damages caused by rodents (squirrels, rats, etc.), insects, etc.; (3) promote of fertigation and chemigation; (4) take measures to regulate agencies supplying MIS to the farmers and adhering to standard norms on maintaining quality; (5) provide proper and regular services for the repairing of the MIS subsystem within reasonable time limits; (6) establish more testing facilities for quality checking of equipment; and (7) provide the required extension advisory services to the farmers, especially on maintenance and applicability of PINS–MIS for different crops. WUAs/TUAs in Gujarat also faced some constraints in management of their associations. Among these constraints, the funds constraints, unavailability of required quantity of water, unavailability of proper maintenance and repairing services, and electricity problems were the major ones.

12.7 CONCLUSIONS

The water resources for irrigating more area have been a challenge for the country. It is desirable to utilize the available water resources more judiciously, so that the "more crops per drop" slogan of the government can be realized and farmers' income can be doubled within the stipulated time period. Thus, PINS infrastructure with MIS is inevitable for the farmers since it saves the water and the collected water can be used for further increase in area under irrigation. The present study has examined some aspects of working on PINS at different levels. During the survey, the sample farmers have also given some useful feedbacks that have been discussed earlier. Besides, some additional suggestions on different types of PINS—those are drawn from the study—are presented next.

12.7.1 SUGGESTIONS ON CANAL PINS

- Though the State Government has followed an innovative approach by developing and implementing the concept of PINS, the existing practices of farmers such as relying more on conventional flow method for irrigation did not change much due to some specific reasons. The farmers did not want to change the cropping pattern which was highly water intensive. Thus, it is necessary to discourage more water-consuming cropping pattern, by encouraging suitable cropping pattern through some incentive structure.

- It was found that the farmers did not want to spend any amount on MIS since canal water was available to them almost free of cost. Thus, it is suggested to revise the water rates that are very less, and strict rules and regulations should be enforced to check the illegal use of canal water and water theft.

- Farmers having land at favorable locations (canal vicinity) do not find it to be a lucrative proposition. One of the major factors that contributed to less adoption of canal PINS in the state was that PINS projects were located very close to minors or subminors, where farmers are able to get water in alternative ways. Thus, it is suggested to relaunch this canal PINS program with required amendments by locating these projects at far-off places where farmers are struggling to get irrigation water. Though it involves little more investments in terms of infrastructure expenditure, the adaptation and long-term sustainability would be surely achieved just like the success of PINS projects in Sanchore region in Rajasthan.

- The areas where PINS+MIS are techno-economically not feasible, normal/conventional flow irrigation as per present SSNNL policy may be allowed to continue.

- The majority of sample farmers were marginal with small land holdings who faced difficulties in getting bank loans due to incomplete land documents and other outstanding debts. The measures may be taken to provide affordable credit facilities to small and marginal farmers.

12.7.2   SUGGESTIONS ON TUBE WELL PINS

- The study finds that maintenance and electricity cost for beneficiaries of tube well PINS is a major part of their expenses that is reasonably high, and thus the subsidy may be given on electricity provided to farm plots.

- Drip system is damaged at some cases due to animal attack (pig, rat, squirrel, rabbit, and blue bulls), and sometimes due to poor awareness of agricultural workers. Thus, better quality systems should be provided. The fencing subsidy may be provided to encourage fencing by farmers.

- Services provided by some companies were unsatisfactory; frequency of their visits was insufficient. Thus, there is a need to take measures to regulate the agencies supplying MIS to the farmers and adhering to standard norms on maintaining quality and providing proper and regular services for the repairing of the PINS–MIS within reasonable time limits. There is also a need to have more testing facilities for quality checking of equipment.
- Farmers are unaware, uneducated about the use of PINS and MIS. So the required extension advisory services should be provided to the farmers, especially on maintenance and applicability of PINS–MIS for different crops. The training and awareness program should be regularly conducted to impart training to farmers on need, importance, and use of MIS with PINS and also to promote fertigation and chemigation.

12.7.3   SUGGESTIONS ON UGPL WITH PINS

- Since the UGPL system pipeline infrastructure is used as PINS as well as for conventional irrigation, the new scheme has been well adopted by some farmers in Gujarat. However, there are some issues in implementation of UGPL in subminors. Farmers were not willing to pay 10%, their contribution, which was later reduced to 2.5%. Farmers are continuously growing some crops and hence not willing to allow the laying of UGPL. There is a need of strict adherence of government guidelines so as to complete the implementation work in a time-bound manner. Provisions should be made to pay required compensation for crop loss for the laying of UGPL.
- Due to poor maintenance of FCs, the nearby lands are affected by water logging. Thus, it is suggested to arrange regular repairing and maintenance of minors and FCs, which are used by UGPL.
- Due to poor management culture in WUAs, the maintenance and distribution of water were badly affected in some cases. In many cases, WUAs were not formed that affected to regulate the proper supply of water among water users. Thus, there is need to strengthen

existing WUAs and to form WUAs in a time-bound manner, where they are not available.

• The combination of UGPLs and PINS replacing minors, subminors, and FCs needs to be systematically promoted to help saving land as well as water. The UGPL system with PINS should gradually focus on more adoption of MIS with appropriate financial incentives for effective management of irrigation water while taking care of farmers' preferences for different cropping pattern. The services of NGOs and model WUAs may be taken as motivators for more adoption of water-saving technologies under UGPL with PINS.

KEYWORDS

- pressurized irrigation network system
- MIS
- irrigation water-use efficiency
- WUAs

REFERENCES

Devasirvatham, V. A Review of Subsurface Drip Irrigation in Vegetable Production. CRC for Irrigation Futures Irrigation Matters. Series No. 03/09, 2009.

Dhawan, B. D.; Datta, H S. Impact of Irrigation on Multiple Cropping. *Econ. Polit. Week.* 1992, *28*, 15–18.

FAO. *Technical Handbook on Pressurized Irrigation Techniques*; Food and Agriculture Organization of the United Nations: Rome, 2007.

Ganpatye, A. P. Concept and Design of PINS. Seminar on Pressurised Irrigation Network System, SSNNL, Gandhinagar, March 07, 2011.

GWRDC. The Gujarat Water Resources Development Corporation Limited (GWRDC), 2016.

Jiterwal, R. C. Impact of Drip Irrigation Technology among Farmers in Jaipur Region of Rajasthan. Ph.D. Thesis submitted to Rajasthan Agricultural University, Bikaner; Campus: Jobner, 2008.

Narayanamoorthy A. Potential for Drip and Sprinkler Irrigation in India. Research Report Submitted to Gokhale Institute of Politics and Economics (Deemed University), Pune, 2010.

Narayanamoorthy, A. *Drip and Sprinkler Irrigation India: Benefits, Potential and Future Directions*; Alagappa University: Karaikudi, Tamil Nadu, India, 2015; pp 253–266.

http://www.iwmi.cgiar.org/Publications/Other/PDF/Paper%2015% 20of% 20NRLP%20 series%201.pdf, Accessed on 15 Oct 2015.

Narayanamoorthy, A. Economic Viability of Drip Irrigation: An Empirical Analysis from Maharashtra. *Indian J. Agric. Econ.* 1997, *52* (4), Oct–Dec, 728–739.

Navalwala, B. N. Waterlogging and Its Related Issues in India. *J. Irrig. Power* 1991, 55–64.

Postal, S.; Polak, P.; Gonzales, F.; Keller, J. Drip Irrigation for Small Farmers: A New Initiative to Alleviate Hunger and Poverty. *Water Int.* 2001, *26* (1).

Rosegrant, W. M. *Water Resources in the Twenty-First Century: Challenges and Implications for Action*; Food and Agriculture, and the Environment Discussion Paper 20, International Food Policy Research Institute: Washington, DC, 1997.

Sahu, R. K.; Rao, V. N. Development and Evaluating of Micro Drip Irrigation System in Farmer's Field. *Drain. Irrig. Water Manage.* 2005, 118–135.

Sanmuganathan, K.; Bolton, P. Water Management in Third World Irrigation Schemes-Lessons from the Field. ODI Bull. No. 11, Hydraulics Research, Wallingford, 1988.

Shah, T.; Alam, M.; Kumar, D.; Nagar, R. K. N.; Singh, M. Pedaling Out of Poverty: Social Impact of a Manual Irrigation Technology in South Asia. IWMI Research No. 45. International Water Management Institute: Colombo, Sri Lanka, 2000.

Shah, T.; Ballabh, V.; Dobrial, K.; Talati, J. Turnover of State Tubewells to Farmers Cooperatives, Assessment of Gujarat's Experience, India. Paper presented at the International Conference on Irrigation Management Transfer, Wuhan, China, 20–24 September, 1994.

Shah, T.; Ashok, G.; Hemant, P.; Ganga, S.; Jain, R.C. Secret of Gujarat's Agrarian Miracle after 2000. *Econ. Polit. Week.* 2009, *XLIV* (52),45–55.

Siag, M.; Chawla, J. K.; Vashist, A.; Bhushan, I. Efficient Use of Canal Water through Drip Irrigation in Cotton (*Gossypium hirsutum*). *Indian J. Agric. Sci.* 2009, *79* (10), 794–797.

Sivanappan, R. Prospects of Micro-Irrigation in India. *Irrig. Drain. Syst.* 1994, *8* (1), 49–58.

Srivastava, R. C.; Mohanty, S.; Singandhuppe, R. B.; Mohanty, R. K.; Behera, M. S.; Ray, L. I.; Sahoo, D. Feasibility Evaluation of Pressurized Irrigation in Canal Commands. *Water Resour. Manage.* 2010, *24* (12), 3017–3032.

Vaidyanathan, A. *Water Resource Management: Institutions and Irrigation Development in India*; Oxford University Press: New Delhi, India, 1998.

Viswanathan, P. K.;Bahinipati, C. Exploring the Socio-Economic Impacts of Micro-Irrigation System (MIS): A Case Study of Public Tube Wells in Gujarat, Western India. *SAWAS J.* 2015, *1* (1), 1–25.

CHAPTER 13

Indo-EU Relations: A Paradigm Shift Toward Economic and Sustainable Development

PRADIP KUMAR PRADHAN

G. M. Jr. College, Sambalpur, Odisha, India

E-mail: kumarpradip80@gmail.com

ABSTRACT

The trends of economy development between India and European Union (EU) have widen from the enduring multifaceted cross-border relationship, owing to the globalization of the Indian economy, which has been developed substantially since the adoption of 1993 declaration and transformed to strategic partnership, from The Hague summit in 2004. Keeping in view the ongoing relationship, it is essential to anatomize the impact of this strategic partnership on the economic development and sustainability. This chapter focuses on the comparative analysis of the gross domestic product (GDP), foreign direct investment (FDI) and other economic indicators between India and EU as well as their impact on the environment and sustainable development by comparing per capita carbon dioxide (CO_2) emission. The data for this research are collected from the secondary sources and analyzed by using statistical techniques such as descriptive statistics, correlations, and regression model. It is established from the analysis of GDP, FDI, gross fixed capital formation (GFCF), and CO_2 emission that there exists a positive relation between these economic indicators and CO_2 emission in India and a negative relation in EU, which shows that EU has given more importance on the sustainability by reducing its CO_2 emission in comparison to India. This study has set a direction toward escalating the relationship between the duos for sustainable economic development. Although this study uses limited economic indicators and for a short time period, more study may be conducted for improved analysis by using additional indicators and extended time period.

13.1   INTRODUCTION

The Indo-EU relation is a prolonged relationship, started 55 years ago, and has efforts toward reducing poverty, expanding trades, preventing disasters, climate change, and enhancing security measures. Furthermore, they are also promoting joint research in health, energy, agriculture, and several other fields of mutual interest. The trends of economic development between India and European Union (EU) have widen from the enduring multifaceted cross-border relationship, owing to the globalization of the Indian economy, which has been developed substantially since the adoption of 1993 declaration and transformed to strategic partnership, from The Hague summit in 2004. Subsequently, a number of new agreements are signed between them to intensify their relationship toward modernization, trade and investments, and innovation and climate change.

India is one of the fastest growing economies in the world. Being a developing economy, it develops its trade and investment partnership with many developed economies. EU is one of them, which is the largest trading partner with €85 billion trade in goods during 2017. India is also EU's ninth largest trading partner with 2.3% of EU's trade, even if the comprehensive free trade agreement (FTA) is suspended in the year 2013 owing to a gap in the aspiration between them, which was commenced on 2007. Still they are committed toward signing different agreements toward a flourishing economic growth. This chapter studies the sustainable economic development among them in recent times.

13.2   REVIEW OF LITERATURE

The available past literature on this issue have so far been conducted to evaluate various economic indicators in the economy of India and EU. A study on the FTA between EU and India (Woolcock, 2007) considered that EU's objectives for shifting to a more active use of FTAs lie behind the motivations and forces and EU has no model FTA like the United States.

Zakarya et al. (2015) analyzes the relations that may exist among the total energy consumption, economic growth, FDI, and the emission of carbon dioxide (CO_2) in the BRICS countries, and there exists a cointegration relationship between CO_2 emissions and economic variables, which indicates unidirectional causality from CO_2 to the independent variables. In another research, Mohapatra (2015) observed that India needs for value addition to amplify the market share, which has been underutilized. He is further suggested that the trade summits and negotiations are reducing the discomforts in trade and investment obstruction between two trading partners, which needs FTA and other supportive trade policies. Pazienza (2015) has suggested that an increase of the considered type of FDI has reduces the CO_2 level, hence FDI assumed to be playing a favorable role in the environment. Jain (2005) has examined "how recognition of India's growing stature and influence regionally and globally has led to a strategic partnership between India and the European Union." This chapter evaluates the economic, political, and security aspects of the strategic partnership and claims that the United States is closer than EU whereas China would remain to be more vital than India in the Asia strategy of EU.

In a study of whether FDI leads to lower CO_2 emission, Zhang and Zhou (2016) recommend that FDI has contributed to the diminution of CO_2 emission in China, which is evident from different regions in support of the claims that through FDI greener technologies are transferred to developing countries from developed countries for conducting environmentally friendly business. Again, Zhu et al. (2016) studied the impact of FDI, energy consumption, and economic growth on carbon emissions and found that independent variables are heterogeneous, whereas FDI has negative impact and energy consumption has higher impact on CO_2 emission but the economic growth and population size seem to lessen emissions. To study the future greenhouse gas (GHG) emission by different countries, Liu et al. (2017) developed GHG emission model on economic and energy sector development at the national level of EU, US, China, and India from 2016 to 2060. They found that both EU's and United States' emissions will fall from the year 2020, China's emission will be at peak in 2044, whereas India's emission will grow until 2060. In a study on sustainable development goals in international trade pattern, Xiao et al. (2017) compared producer (domestic) social risk and consumer social risk footprints resulting from international trade patterns. They found that the developed countries show higher social risk footprints except United

Kingdom and Ireland, while developing countries show higher domestic social risks in the developed world except China and India. This study would help UN in developing partnerships to address the Sustainable Development Goals.

In a review paper of biofuel policy in India, Saravanan et al. (2018) opined that many policies lack easy outreach among public and industries, which needs marketing by the government that secures a clean energy future in India. However, it might be quite difficult to enact a dedicative legislation to deal with the challenges of biofuel marketing for sustainable development. To establish the barriers of sustainable development, Kirchherr et al. (2018) found that cultural barriers such as consumer interest, awareness, and a hesitant company culture are considered the main barriers of circular economy, which in turn, are induced by a lack of synergistic governmental interventions to accelerate the transition toward a circular economy and sustainable development. To find out the correlation between financial development and economic growth, Asteriou and Spanos (2019) studied the impact of financial development on economic growth during financial crisis of EU from 1990 to 2016 and established that prior to financial crisis, financial development encourages economic growth, whereas after the crisis financial development hindered economic activities. Again, Sachdeva (2019) illustrated that historically Europe has been important for India, both for trade and investment. He opined that Europe has emerged as an important destination for cross-border investments and overseas acquisitions for Indian companies and made a realistic assessment of the possibility for a trade and investment agreement between Europe and India during the next few years.

Most of the past literatures have given importance on sustainable development and economic growth in international level. They considered various micro and macrolevel elements to substantiate their studies. Furthermore, it is evident that most of the studies were conducted upon the impact of various indicators on economic growth and sustainability. This chapter strives to outline the impact of the strategic relationship between India and EU in the economic development with sustainability.

13.3   OBJECTIVES OF THE STUDY

The following objectives are set forth for this study.

1. To study the trends of trade and economic development in both India and EU.
2. To analyze the impact of various economic indicators on sustainable development.
3. To suggest some measures to maximize economic development from the strategic partnership.

To achieve the above stated objectives, the available data are analyzed by using statistical techniques.

13.4 HYPOTHESIS

To substantiate the above objectives, the hypotheses formulated for this study are hypothesis-I, H_o—there is no significant difference between the economic indicators between India and EU and hypothesis-II, H_o—there is no significant impact of various economic indicators on CO_2 emission in India and EU. The alternative hypotheses are hypothesis-I, H_a—there is a significant difference between the economic indicators between India and EU, and hypothesis-II, H_a—there exists a significant impact of various economic indicators on CO_2 emission in India and EU. These hypotheses are tested by using suitable technique in the analysis section to draw inferences.

13.5 MATERIAL AND METHODOLOGY

This research is a descriptive and correlational research, which utilizes the secondary data from secondary sources for analysis and interpretation. Data for this study are collected from the published and unpublished statistical reports at national and international level from both online and offline mode. Online data are collected from different websites of Organisations for Economic Co-operation and Development, European Commission, Eurostat database, Government of India database, etc., and offline data are collected from published reports of Government of India and international bodies. This study analyzes the trends of gross fixed capital formation (GFCF), exports, imports, foreign direct investment (FDI), gross domestic product (GDP), and CO_2 emission of both India and EU to substantiate the stated research objectives.

Data for this study are collected for 13 years from 2005 to 2017 and presented in different tables and figures for better visibility. Furthermore, available data are analyzed by using different statistical techniques and tools such as trends, ratios, correlations, regressions, and descriptive statistics to study the phenomena. Hypotheses set for this study are tested by using t-test, ANOVA, and regression models to draw necessary inferences and to test the reliability of the data—Levene's test, Durbin–Watson, and P–P plots are used. SPSS and MS Excel software programs are also used for improved analysis.

13.6 DATA ANALYSIS AND INTERPRETATION

The trends and magnitude of various economic indicators of both India and EU are illustrated under this section. Various economic indicators as well as their impact upon sustainability coefficient of CO_2 emission are studied with the help of the descriptive statistics. Available data are categorized as per their homogeneity and analyzed scientifically. Specifically, the variables related to India are analyzed, followed by EU and again a comparative study is also undertaken for extensive research. The variables considered for this study are GFCF (gross domestic investment), FDI inflows, exports and imports, GDP, CO_2 emission, etc. To begin with, the data related to India are presented in Table 13.1, which shows the data related to the study period with its mean and standard deviation.

TABLE 13.1 Trends and Magnitudes of Various Economic Indicators of India.

Year	GFCF in US$ bn.	FDI inflow total in US$ bn.	Export in US$ bn.	Import in US$ bn.	GDP (total) in US$ bn.	GDP (per capita) US$	CO_2 emission total/ million tons	CO_2 emission tons per capita
2005	1061.39	7.26	720.48	774.58	3238.31	2906.31	1072.10	.9
2006	1233.04	20.02	867.14	940.97	3647.02	3226.43	1143.90	1.0
2007	1462.31	25.22	918.52	1036.88	4111.05	3585.82	1257.00	1.1
2008	1522.07	43.40	1052.60	1272.39	4354.79	3745.75	1334.80	1.1
2009	1632.28	35.58	1003.28	1245.21	4759.94	4038.25	1498.00	1.2
2010	1775.08	27.39	1200.09	1439.58	5312.41	4414.06	1580.60	1.3

TABLE 13.1   *(Continued)*

Year	GFCF in US$ bn.	FDI inflow total in US$ bn.	Export in US$ bn.	Import in US$ bn.	GDP (total) in US$ bn.	GDP (per capita) US$	CO_2 emission total/ million tons	CO_2 emission tons per capita
2011	1984.01	36.49	1387.01	1742.74	5782.03	4739.37	1665.00	1.3
2012	2076.38	23.99	1481.41	1847.68	6209.84	5028.21	1801.00	1.4
2013	2100.92	28.15	1596.84	1697.17	6713.10	5366.19	1851.90	1.4
2014	2207.88	34.57	1625.23	1711.96	7339.96	5793.19	2015.30	1.6
2015	2284.37	44.00	1534.33	1611.37	8024.58	6254.55	2026.10	1.5
2016	2483.89	44.45	1610.31	1676.04	8705.01	6701.32	2076.80	1.6
2017	2695.49	39.96	1700.13	1883.49	9460.76	7170.00		
Mean	1886.09	31.58	1284.41	1452.31	5973.75	4843.80	1610.21	1.3
S. D.	488.37	10.92	337.95	364.93	1983.86	1355.93	353.38	.23

Source: Compiled by author from the data available in https://data.oecd.org.

Above table shows the data for 13 years period from 2005 to 2017 starting from the GFCF. The GFCF of India has been increased from 1061.39 bn. US$ to 2695.49 bn. US$, with an increase in 154% during the study period but the FDI inflow has increased from 7.26 bn. US$ in 2005 to a maximum of 44.45 bn. US$ in the year 2016 reflecting 512% increase during that period, indicating that the FDI inflow has increased more than three times of GFCF. Again, the average GFCF is around 60 times of average FDI inflow during the study period, which shows a very negligible FDI inflow to India. The exports and imports show a similar trend with trade deficit during the period. The total GDP of India has been increased from 3238.31 bn. US$ to 8705.01 bn. US$, that is, 169% whereas GDP per capita was increased from 2906.31 US$ to 7170.00 US$, that is, 147% from 2005 to 2017. The CO_2 emission in India also shows an increasing trend from 1072.10 million tons in 2005 to 2076.8 million tons in 2016 with an increase in 93.7% during 12 years, whereas the per capita emission increased by 77.7% in same time period.

Further, the data of EU are presented in the Table 13.2 likewise the previous table. It shows the GFCF, FDI, export, and import in billion US$;

beside these, the GDP and CO_2 emission are shown in both total and per capita basis.

TABLE 13.2 Trends and Magnitudes of Various Economic Indicators of European Union.

Year	GFCF in US$ bn.	FDI inflow total in US$ bn.	Export in US$ bn.	Import in US$ bn.	GDP (total) in US$ bn.	GDP (per capita) US$	CO_2 emission total million tons	CO_2 emission tons per capita
2005	2897.72	457.54	5626.58	5539.38	13,654.99	27,591.00	3921.70	7.9
2006	3245.66	526.28	6160.73	6053.56	14,826.14	29,849.63	3927.80	7.9
2007	3560.00	827.30	6542.66	6436.04	15,779.59	31,639.99	3872.80	7.8
2008	3713.18	317.18	6623.50	6485.59	16,558.82	33,072.09	3789.00	7.6
2009	3323.91	378.73	5857.08	5751.27	16,210.33	32,259.62	3508.40	7.0
2010	3362.83	358.30	6474.31	6305.12	16,780.02	33,311.69	3612.40	7.2
2011	3530.55	424.87	6908.00	6575.37	17,519.68	34,703.36	3466.40	6.9
2012	3513.99	336.46	7062.31	6540.88	17,841.85	35,257.91	3432.20	6.8
2013	3563.91	343.57	7223.28	6657.96	18,508.52	36,499.32	3347.20	6.6
2014	3697.51	248.08	7562.35	7002.26	19,090.24	37,557.55	3162.60	6.2
2015	3892.89	626.83	8033.75	7502.20	19,734.72	38,714.56	3206.60	6.3
2016	4103.64	553.11	8291.70	7824.47	20,560.39	40,209.21	3192.30	6.2
2017	4394.81	290.48	8734.66	8155.17	21,778.77	42,493.58	–	–
Mean	3600.05	437.59	7007.76	6679.17	17,603.39	34,858.42	3536.62	7.0
S.D.	382.95	160.81	941.98	768.68	2312.16	4208.69	286.62	.65

Source: Compiled by author from the data available in https://data.oecd.org.

Various economic indicators of EU are presented in Table 13.2 for 13 years from 2005 to 2017. The GFCF shows an increasing trend from 2897.72 bn. US$ to 4394.81 bn. US$, with an increase in 51.67% during the study period but the FDI inflow shows a seesaw trend during this period with a minimum inflow of 248.08 bn. US$ in the year 2014 to a maximum of 827.30 bn. US$ in the year 2007, which proves that EU has no steady policy for FDI inflow. Again, the average GFCF is around 8.23 times of average FDI inflow during the study period, which shows a very significant FDI inflow to EU in comparison to India. The exports and imports show a similar trend with trade surplus during the period. The total GDP of EU has been increased from 13,654.99 bn. US$ to 21,778.77 bn. US$, that is, 59.49% whereas GDP per capita is increased from 27,591.00 US$ to 42,493.58 US$, that is, 54.01% from 2005 to 2017. The CO_2 emission in EU shows a decreasing trend from 3921.70 mil. tons in 2005 to 3192.30 mil. tons in 2016 with a negative growth of −18.6% during 12 years, and the per capita emission is also decreased by −21.52% during the same time period.

Beside these, a comparative data of GFCF and FDI of both India and EU is presented in the Figure 13.1 for better understanding.

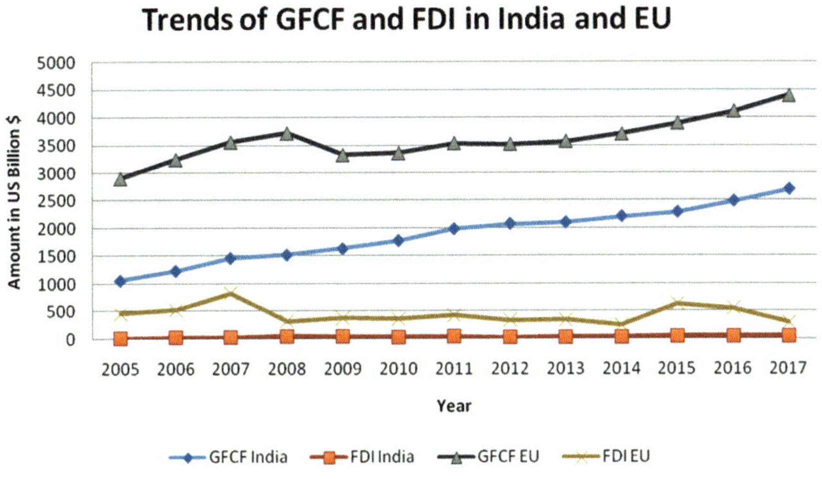

FIGURE 13.1   Trends of GFCF and FDI in India and EU.
Source: Prepared by author in MS Excel from the data available in https://data.oecd.org.

It is found that there is a symmetrical trend of both GFCF and FDI inflow in India. However, in EU, both show asymmetrical trends. In addition to this, the figure shows that the GFCF and FDI inflow of EU are much higher than that of India, which is witnessed that EU has a larger economy than India but India has a steady economy.

Again, the growth rate of per capita GDP and CO_2 emission is depicted in the Table 13.3, which shows the annual growth rate of the variables during the study period.

TABLE 13.3   Growth Rate of Per Capita GDP and CO_2 Emission of India and EU.

Year	India				European Union			
	GDP (per capita) US$	GDP growth rate	CO_2 emission tons per capita	CO_2 growth rate	GDP (per capita) US$	GDP growth rate	CO_2 emission tons per capita	CO_2 growth rate
2005	2906.31		.90		27,591.00		7.90	
2006	3226.43	11.01	1.00	11.11	29,849.63	8.19	7.90	.00
2007	3585.82	11.14	1.10	10.00	31,639.99	6.00	7.80	−1.27
2008	3745.75	4.46	1.10	.00	33,072.09	4.53	7.60	2.56
2009	4038.25	7.81	1.20	9.09	32,259.62	−2.46	7.00	−7.89
2010	4414.06	9.31	1.30	8.33	33,311.69	3.26	7.20	2.86
2011	4739.37	7.37	1.30	.00	34,703.36	4.18	6.90	4.17
2012	5028.21	6.09	1.40	7.69	35,257.91	1.60	6.80	1.45
2013	5366.19	6.72	1.40	.00	36,499.32	3.52	6.60	2.94
2014	5793.19	7.96	1.60	14.29	37,557.55	2.90	6.20	−6.06
2015	6254.55	7.96	1.50	−6.25	38,714.56	3.08	6.30	1.61
2016	6701.32	7.14	1.60	6.67	40,209.21	3.86	6.20	1.59
Mean	**4649.95**	**7.91**	**1.28**	5.54	34,222.16	3.51	7.03	**−2.13**

Source: Compiled by author from the data available in https://data.oecd.org.

It is observed from the table that the average growth rate of GDP of India is 7.91% during the study period in comparison to the 3.51% of EU, whereas the per capita GDP of EU is around 7.36 times higher than that of India. The correlation between GDP of India and EU shows a highly positive correlation with $r = .983$ and its growth rate shows low positive correlation of $r = .420$. Again, the average growth rate of CO_2 emission of India is positive with 5.54% in comparison to a negative growth of −2.13% in EU with a negative correlation of $r = -.252$ and the correlation of the CO_2 emission is −.969. It witnessed that EU has used advanced technology to condense the deteriorated impact of CO_2 emission as well as for sustainable development but still it is 5.49 time higher than India.

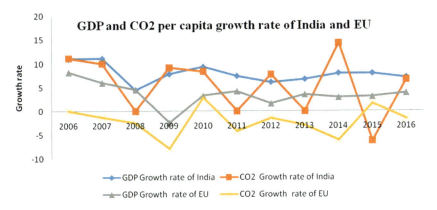

FIGURE 13.2   GDP and CO$_2$ per capita growth rate of India and EU.
Source: Compiled by author from the data available in https://data.oecd.org.

Figure 13.2 shows the growth rate of GDP and CO$_2$ from 2006 to 2016 of both India and EU. It is found that the line chart shows zigzag line of different variables, among which the GDP growth shows a constant growth and CO$_2$ emission by EU shows a negative growth.

From the analysis of the trade flows between India and EU countries, it is observed that the India has a positive trade balance during the later stage of the strategic partnership as depicted in Table 13.4.

TABLE 13.4   India's Trade Flows and Balances with EU.

Year	Exports		Imports		Balance	Total trade
	Amount in Million (€)	Growth (%)	Amount in Million (€)	Growth (%)	Amount in Mio (€)	Amount in Mio (€)
2007	26,666		29,181		−2515	55,847
2008	29,632	11.12	31,356	7.45	−1724	60,988
2009	25,503	−13.93	27,499	−12.3	−1996	53,002
2010	33,464	31.22	34,985	27.22	−1521	68,449
2011	39,927	19.31	40,648	16.19	−721	80,575
2012	37,528	−6.01	38,595	−5.05	−1067	76,123
2013	36,842	−1.83	35,959	−6.83	883	72,801
2014	37,170	.89	35,655	−.85	1515	72,825
2015	39,492	6.25	38,125	6.93	1367	77,617

TABLE 13.4   *(Continued)*

	Exports		Imports		Balance	Total trade
Year	Amount in Million (€)	Growth (%)	Amount in Million (€)	Growth (%)	Amount in Mio (€)	Amount in Mio (€)
2016	39,372	−.3	37,792	−.87	1580	77,164
2017	44,215	12.3	41,719	10.39	2496	85,934
Mean	35,437.36	5.90	35,592.18	4.23	−154.82	71,029.55

Source: Compiled by author from the data available in https://ec.europa.eu/eurostat/ statistics, India-EU—international trade in goods statistics.

It has been established that Indian total trade with EU reached to € 85,934 million in the year 2017 from € 55,847 million with an average total trade of € 71,029.55 million. Furthermore, the growth percentage of exports by India to EU shows a minimum of −13.93% to maximum of 31.22%, with an average of 5.9% during the study period. The import growth rate are also varies from −12.3% to 27.22% with an average growth of 4.23%, which witnessed that India has significantly increases its export trade with EU. Hence, it may be concluded that the strategic relationship between India and EU has directed toward a positive impact on Indian trade.

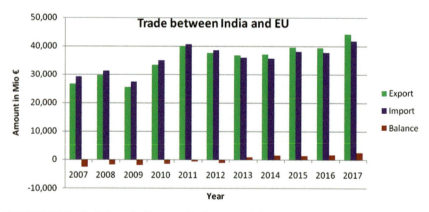

FIGURE 13.3   India's trade flows and balances with EU.
Source: Compiled by author from the available data in https://ec.europa.eu/eurostat/ statistics.

It is apparent from Figure 13.3 that the bilateral trade between India and EU till 2012 experienced a negative trade balance and later it showed a positive trade balance. On the contrary, it is found that the strategic partnership between India and EU is ended in the year 2017 is a setback for India. Hence, it is essential to continue or to begin a new era of relation, which may boost the Indian economy.

13.7   TEST OF HYPOTHESES

The available data are analyzed by using various statistical techniques in this section to test the hypothesis. The hypothesis-I is tested to draw the inference. The null hypothesis set for this test is, H_o—there is no significant difference between the economic indicators between India and EU and the alternative hypothesis is H_a—there is a significant difference between the economic indicators between India and EU. To test this hypothesis, independent t-test is applied, where the variables are GFCF, FDI inflow, GDP per capita, and CO_2 emission between India and EU. The t-test result of this hypothesis processed through SPSS is presented in Table 13.5.

The t-test result processed by SPSS software is depicted in the table, which shows the t value of GFCF, FDI inflow, GDP per capita, and CO_2 emission between India and EU and their P value. The Levene's test is conducted to test the homogeneity of the variances among the variables. The GFCF of India and EU shows the t-value of -9.96 with P-value of .00, which is significant at .05% significance level. This test rejects the null hypothesis and accepts the alternative hypothesis. The homogeneity of variance of this variable shows insignificant, which shows that the variables are not homogenous. Again, the test result of FDI inflow shows the t-value of -9.08 and P-value of .00 rejects the null hypothesis and the Levene's test shows the homogeneity of the variances.

From the test of per capita GDP between India and EU, the t-value shows that 24.47 is highly significant, which rejects the null hypothesis and accepts the alternative hypothesis with P-value of .00. Furthermore, the per capita CO_2 emission between the two shows that the t-value of 28.96 and P-value of .00, rejects the null hypothesis and accepts the alternative. Hence, the first hypothesis is rejected and the alternative hypothesis is accepted that there exists a significant difference between the economic indicators between India and EU.

TABLE 13.5 Independent t-Test of GFCF, FDI Inflow, GDP Per Capita, and CO_2 Per Capita Emission Between EU and India.

Independent samples test

		Levene's test for equality of variances		t-Test for equality of means					95% Confidence interval of the difference	
		F	Sig.	t	df	Sig. (2-tailed)	Mean difference	Std. error difference	Lower	Upper
GFCF	Equal variances assumed	1.70	.21	−9.96	24	.00	−1713.96	172.13	−2069.21	−1358.71
	Equal variances not assumed			−9.96	22.71	.00	−1713.96	172.13	−2070.28	−1357.64
FDI_Inflow	Equal variances assumed	18.28	.00	−9.08	24	.00	−406.02	44.70	−498.28	−313.75
	Equal variances not assumed			−9.08	12.11	.00	406.02	44.70	−503.32	−308.72
GDP_Per capita	Equal variances assumed	10.09	.00	−24.47	24	.00	−30,014.62	1226.36	−32,545.71	−27,483.53
	Equal variances not assumed			−24.47	14.47	.00	30,014.62	1226.36	−32,637.01	−27,392.23
CO_2_Emi_ Per capita	Equal variances assumed	12.61	.00	−28.96	22	.00	−5.75	.20	−6.16	−5.34
	Equal variances not assumed			−28.96	13.70	.00	5.75	.20	−6.18	−5.32

Source: Data processed through SPSS software.

The second hypothesis of this study is tested by applying multiple regression models in both India and EU. The null hypothesis is set for the second hypothesis test is H_o—there is no significant impact of various economic indicators on CO_2 emission in India and EU. The regression model is run for the variables of India and presented in Table 13.6.

TABLE 13.6 Multiple Regression Model Showing the Impact of Different Economic Indicators of India on CO_2 Emission.

Variables entered/removed[a]			
Model	Variables entered	Variables removed	Method
1	GDP, FDI_Inflow, GFCF[b]		Enter
[a]Dependent variable: CO_2_Emission.			
[b]All requested variables entered.			

Model summary[b]					
Model	R	R square	Adjusted R square	Std. error of the estimate	Durbin–Watson
1	.991[a]	.983	.976	54.39508	1.508
[a]Predictors: (Constant), GDP, FDI_Inflow, GFCF.					
[b]Dependent variable: CO_2_Emission.					

ANOVA[a]						
Model		Sum of squares	df	Mean square	F	Sig.
1	Regression	1,349,998.055	3	449,999.352	152.087	.000[b]
	Residual	23,670.594	8	2958.824		
	Total	1,373,668.649	11			
[a]Dependent variable: CO_2_Emission.						
[b]Predictors: (Constant), GDP, FDI_Inflow, GFCF.						

Coefficients[a]								
Model		Unstandardized coefficients		Standardized coefficients	t	Sig.	95.0% Confidence interval for B	
		B	Std. error	Beta			Lower bound	Upper bound
1	(Constant)	267.229	93.354		2.863	.021	51.954	482.505
	GFCF	.563	.184	.704	3.056	.016	.138	.987
	FDI_Inflow	−1.886	2.022	−.059	−.933	.378	−6.549	2.776
	GDP	.066	.045	.331	1.479	.177	−.037	.170
[a]Dependent variable: CO_2_Emission.								

TABLE 13.6 *(Continued)*

Residuals statistics[a]

	Minimum	Maximum	Mean	Std. deviation	N
Predicted value	1066.0983	2159.8418	1610.2083	350.32427	12
Residual	−83.04173	82.88124	.00000	46.38828	12
Std. predicted value	−1.553	1.569	.000	1.000	12
Std. residual	−1.527	1.524	.000	.853	12
[a]Dependent variable: CO_2_Emission.					

Source: Data processed through SPSS software.

This model considered the GFCF, FDI inflow, and GDP as independent variable and CO_2 emission as dependent variable. The regression model summary shows that the R-value is .991, which shows a strong correlation between independent and dependent variable. Again, adjusted R^2 of this model is .983, which explains that the dependent variable CO_2 emission is 98.3% dependent upon the GFCF, FDI inflow, and GDP. The adjusted R^2 and R^2 show slightly higher covariance. Furthermore, the Durbin–Watson test shows $d = 1.508$, which is between the critical value of $0 < d < 4$. Hence, it can assume that there exists a positive autocorrelation in this regression data, which is considered as normal. Again, the F-value is highly significant with 152.087 and P-value of .00, which rejects the null hypothesis and accepts the alternative hypothesis showing a significant impact of various economic indicators on CO_2 emission in India. The residual statistics shows that the standard residual (−1.527–1.524) is within the critical value of −3 and +3, which shows that the residuals are normally distributed. The multiple regression equation developed from this model is CO_2 emission = 267.23 + .563 × GFCF − 1.89 × FDI inflow + .07 × GDP.

Again, the data related to EU are analyzed for partial test of second hypothesis of this study. Here, the same variables of EU are considered for the test and depicted in Table 13.7.

TABLE 13.7 Multiple Regression Model Showing the Impact of Different Economic Indicators of European Union on CO_2 Emission.

Variables entered/removed[a]

Model	Variables entered	Variables removed	Method
1	GDP, FDI_Inflow, GFCF[b]		Enter

TABLE 13.7 *(Continued)*

[a]Dependent variable: CO_2_Emission.

[b]All requested variables entered.

Model summary[b]

Model	R	R square	Adjusted R square	Std. error of the estimate	Durbin–Watson
1	.981[a]	.961	.947	65.99330	2.817

[a]Predictors: (Constant), GDP, FDI_Inflow, GFCF.

[b]Dependent variable: CO_2_Emission.

ANOVA[a]

Model		Sum of squares	df	Mean square	F	Sig.
1	Regression	868,793.853	3	289,597.951	66.496	.000[b]
	Residual	34,840.923	8	4355.115		
	Total	903,634.777	11			

[a]Dependent variable: CO_2_Emission.

[b]Predictors: (Constant), GDP, FDI_Inflow, GFCF.

Coefficients[a]

Model		Unstandardized coefficients		Standardized coefficients	t	Sig.	95.0% Confidence interval for B	
		B	Std. error	Beta			Lower bound	Upper bound
1	(Constant)	5121.258	236.501		21.654	.000	4575.886	5666.630
	GFCF	.566	.164	.618	3.454	.009	.188	.944
	FDI_Inflow	.061	.144	.035	.426	.681	−.271	.393
	GDP	−.209	.025	−1.482	−8.329	.000	−.267	−.151

[a]Dependent variable: CO_2_Emission.

Residuals statistics[a]

	Minimum	Maximum	Mean	Std. deviation	N
Predicted value	3173.5649	3930.8250	3536.6167	281.03605	12
Residual	−123.83893	78.66637	.00000	56.27927	12
Std. predicted value	−1.292	1.403	.000	1.000	12
Std. residual	−1.877	1.192	.000	.853	12

[a]Dependent variable: CO_2_Emission.

Source: Data processed through SPSS software.

The model considered the GFCF, FDI inflow, and GDP as independent variable and CO_2 emission as dependent variable of EU. The model summary shows that the R-value is .981, which again shows a strong correlation between independent and dependent variable. The adjusted R^2 of this model is .961, which explains that the dependent variable CO_2 emission is 96.1% dependent upon the GFCF, FDI inflow, and GDP. The adjusted R^2 and R^2 show slightly higher covariance. Furthermore, the Durbin–Watson test shows $d = 2.817$, which is between the critical value of $0 < d < 4$ explains that there exists a negative autocorrelation in this regression data. Hence, it is found that the dependent and independent variable are negatively correlated. Again, the F-value is significant with 66.496 and P-value of .00, which rejects the null hypothesis and accepts the alternative hypothesis showing a significant impact of various economic indicators on CO_2 emission in EU. The residual statistics also shows that the standard residual (-1.877 to 1.192) is within the critical value of -3 and $+3$, which shows that the residuals are normally distributed. The multiple regression equation developed from this model is CO_2 emission $= 5121.26 + .566 \times$ GFCF $- .061 \times$ FDI inflow $- . 209 \times$ GDP.

Hence, it is concluded that both the hypotheses are rejected at .05% level of significance and the alternative hypotheses are accepted that there exists a significant difference between the economic indicators between India and EU, and there also exists a significant impact of various economic indicators on CO_2 emission in India and EU.

13.8 SUMMARY AND CONCLUSION

It is summarized from the above study that the trends of the trade and economic development of India and EU are showing increasing trend during the study period, whereas the economy of EU is larger than the Indian economy, but the economy of India grows much faster than the EU. All the economic indicators of EU, such as GFCF, FDI, and GDP are more than the Indian economy. From the analysis of the impact of various economic indicator on sustainable development, it is established that the growth rate of CO_2 emission of India shows a positive growth rate of 5.54 during the study period but it shows a negative growth rate of 2.13 in EU. It substantiate that EU has been using advanced technology in comparison to India for more sustainable development. However, the carbon footprint of India is too low from the EU countries. Thus, India needs additional technological support from EU to boost its economy.

The inference drawn from the test of first hypotheses established that there exists a significant difference between the economic indicators between India and EU as the null hypothesis set for this is rejected. The second hypothesis is also rejected and concluded that there exists a significant impact of various economic indicators on CO_2 emission in India and EU. Hence, both India and EU need more cooperation, which may boost the trade and economic development of India with sustainability.

Finally, it is concluded that India has been significantly shifting its economy from 2005 to 2017 in comparison to EU but it needs more FDI input for the growth of infrastructure for more sustainable development. Again, both should encourage to sign new FTA to boost their trade and economic development, and India also needs more advanced technology from EU for reducing the GHG emission. Although this study is based on limited economic indicators and confined to limited period, further studies may be undertaken for more comprehensive study.

KEYWORDS

- **GDP**
- **FDI**
- **CO_2 emission**
- **sustainable development**
- **environment**

REFERENCES

Abhyankar, R. M. India and the European Union. *India Q.* **2009,** *65* (4), 393–404.

Allen, D. The EU and India: Strategic Partners But Not a Strategic Partnership. In *The Palgrave Handbook of EU-Asia Relations*; Palgrave Macmillan: London, 2013.

Asteriou, D.; Spanos, K. The Relationship Between Financial Development and Economic Growth During the Recent Crisis: Evidence from the EU. *Finance Res. Lett.* **2019,** *28,* 238–245. .

Bajpai, S. R. *Social Survey and Research*; Kitab Ghar: Kanpur, 2007.

Bava, U. S. India-EU Relations: Building a Strategic Partnership. In *Europe-Asia Relations*; Palgrave Macmillan: London, 2008

Bava, U. S. India and the European Union: From Engagement to Strategic Partnership. *Int. Stud.* **2010,** *47* (2–4), 373–386.

Chanda, R. India-EU Relations in Health Services: Prospects and Challenges. *Globalization Health* **2011,** *7* (1), 1–14.

European Commission. *Countries and Regions;* European Commission, 2019. https://ec.europa.eu/trade/policy/countries-and-regions/countries/india/index_en.htm.

Eurostat. *India-EU—International Trade in Goods Statistics;* Eurostat, 2019. https://ec.europa.eu/eurostat/   statistics-explained/index.php?title=India-EU_%E2%80%93_international_ trade_in_goods_statistics.

Gupta, S.P. *Statistical Methods;* S. Chand & Son: New Delhi, 2010.

Hansen, P. European Integration, European Identity and the Colonial Connection. *Eur. J. Soc. Theory* **2002,** *5* (4), 483–498.

Hill, C.; Smith, M.; Vanhoonacker, S. *International Relations and the European Union;* Oxford University Press: Oxford, 2017.

Huang, L.; Zhao, X. Impact of Financial Development on Trade-Embodied Carbon Dioxide Emissions: Evidence from 30 Provinces in China. *J. Cleaner Prod.* **2018,** *198*, 721–736.

Jain, R. K. India, the European Union and Asian Regionalism. *Asia-Pac. J. EU* **2005,** *3* (12), 29–44.

Jain, R. K.; Pandey, S. The European Union in the Eyes of India. *Asia Eur. J.* **2010,** *8* (2), 193–209.

Jain, R. K.; Pandey, S. The Public Attitudes and Images of the European Union in India. *India Q.* **2012,** *68* (4), 331–343.

Kirchherr, J.; Piscicelli, L.; Bour, R.; Kostense-Smit, E.; Muller, J.; Huibrechtse-Truijens, A.; Hekkert, M. Barriers to the Circular Economy: Evidence From the European Union (EU). *Ecol. Econ.* **2018,** *150*, 264–272. https://doi.org/10.1016/J.ECOLECON.2018.04.028.

Lee, J. W. The Contribution of Foreign Direct Investment to Clean Energy Use, Carbon Emissions and Economic Growth. *Energy Policy* **2013,** *55*, 483–489.

Lévy, B. The Interface Between Globalization, Trade and Development: Theoretical Issues for International Business Studies. *Int. Bus Rev.* **2007,** *16* (5), 594–612.

Liu, Y.; Wang, F.; Jingyun, Z. Estimation of Greenhouse Gas Emissions from the EU, US, China, and India up to 2060 in Comparison with their Pledges under the Paris Agreement. 2017. Retrieved from https://www.mdpi.com/2071-1050/9/9/1587.

McLaren, L. Public Support for the European Union: Cost/Benefit Analysis or Perceived Cultural Threat? *J. Polit.* **2002,** *64* (2), 551–566.

Meunier, S.; Nicolaïdis, K. The European Union as a Conflicted Trade Power. *J. Eur. Public Policy* **2006,** *13* (6), 906–925.

Mohapatra, D. R. *Trade and Investment Flows Between India and the European Union: Issues and Challenges;* Romania. 2015. Retrieved from http://www.euacademic.org/BookUpload/12.pdf.

OECD. *Air and GHG Emissions (Indicator);* OECD, 2018. DOI: 10.1787/93d10cf7-en.

OECD. *Gross Domestic Product (GDP) (Indicator);* OECD, 2018. DOI: 10.1787/dc2f7aec-en.

OECD. *International Trade;* OECD, 2019. https://data.oecd.org/economy.htm#profile-International%20trade.

OECD. *Investment (GFCF) (Indicator);* OECD, 2018. DOI: 10.1787/b6793677-en.

Pao, H.; Tsai, C. Multivariate Granger Causality Between CO_2 Emissions, Energy Consumption, FDI (Foreign Direct Investment) and GDP (Gross Domestic Product): Evidence from a Panel of BRIC (Brazil, Russian Federation, India, and China) Countries. *Energy* **2011**, *36* (1), 685–693.

Pazienza, P. The Relationship Between CO_2 and Foreign Direct Investment in the Agriculture and Fishing Sector of OECD Countries: Evidence and Policy Considerations. *Intellec. Econ.* **2015**, *9* (1), 55–66.

Pirlogea, C.; Cicea, C. Econometric Perspective of the Energy Consumption and Economic Growth Relation in European Union. *Renew. Sustain. Energy Rev.* **2012**, *16* (8), 5718–5726.

Sachdeva, G. India and the European Union. *Int. Stud.* **2008**, *45* (4), 341–367.

Sachdeva, G. EU–India Economic Relations and FTA Negotiations. In *Challenges in Europe*; Springer Singapore: Singapore, 2019; pp 291–320. https://doi.org/10.1007/978-981-13-1636-4_15.

Saravanan, A. P.; Mathimani, T., Deviram, G., Rajendran, K., Pugazhendhi, A. Biofuel Policy in India: A Review of Policy Barriers in Sustainable Marketing of Biofuel. *J. Cleaner Prod.* **2018**, *193*, 734–747. https://doi.org/10.1016/J.JCLEPRO.2018.05.033.

Simionescu, M.; Albu, L.-L.; Raileanu Szeles, M.; Bilan, Y. The Impact of Biofuels Utilisation In Transport on the Sustainable Development in the European Union. *Technol. Econ. Dev. Econ.* **2017**, *23* (4), 667–686. https://doi.org/10.3846/20294913.2017.1323318.

Woolcock, S. *European Union Policy Towards Free Trade Agreements*; European Centre for International Political Economy (ECIPE); Brussels, 2007. https://www.econstor.eu/handle/10 419/174818.

Xiao, Y.; Norris, C. B.; Lenzen, M.; Norris, G.; Murray, J. How Social Footprints of Nations Can Assist in Achieving the Sustainable Development Goals. *Ecol. Econ.* **2017**, *135*, 55–65. https://doi.org/10.1016/J.ECOLECON.2016.12.003.

Zakarya, G. Y. et al. Factors Affecting CO_2 Emissions in the BRICS Countries: A Panel Data Analysis. *Proc. Econ. Finance* **2015**, *26*, 114–125.

Zhang, C.; Zhou, X. Does Foreign Direct Investment Lead to Lower CO_2 Emissions? Evidence from a Regional Analysis in China. *Renew. Sustain. Energy Rev.* **2016**, *58*, 943–951.

Zhu, H.; Duan, L.; Guo, Y.; Yu, K. The Effects of FDI, Economic Growth and Energy Consumption on Carbon Emissions in ASEAN-5: Evidence from Panel Quantile Regression. *Econ. Modell.* **2016**, *58*, 237–248. https://doi.org/10.1016/J.ECONMOD.2016.05.003.

CHAPTER 14

Media Coverage of Globalization and Sustainable Development in India

RAJ KISHORE PATRA*, AGNI KUMAR BEHERA, and NEHA PANDEY

Mass Communication and Media Technology, Khallikote University, Berhampur, Odisha, India

Corresponding author. E-mail: rkpatra_media@yahoo.co.in

ABSTRACT

A few buzzwords like globalization, sustainability, and development that keep engaging media houses/platforms in 21st century across the globe. On the other hand, media sets the tone by prioritizing the abovementioned words and literate the citizens. The current study is focused on the coverage of news stories, articles, and editorials related to globalization and sustainable development by the Indian media.

The aim of the study is to understand the prioritization of the content, placement, and presentation of the content in the leading daily English newspapers in India. The method of the research is based on content analysis of the news published in Times of India, Bhubaneswar edition for a period of 1 month (November–December, 2018). The findings of the study will contribute to the understanding of the media's orientation toward covering news related to globalization and sustainable development. That would imply the nation's interest and direction toward globalization and sustainable development.

14.1 INTRODUCTION

In contemporary sociopolitical space, the popular mass media provides the space and time to cover pressing themes on sustainability and sustainable development as well as social responsibility and corporate social responsibility (Barkemeyer et al., 2009). As per United Nations (1987), "sustainable development refers to economic, environmental, and social development that aspires to meet the needs of the present without compromising the ability of future generations to meet their own." However, guarding the natural environment and natural resources in consort with the social and economic wellbeing of the contemporary and future generations should be the fundamental priority of sustainable development concepts (Elliott, 2012). Sustainability is also prioritized as one of the ethical values for present-day civilization (Laws et al., 2004; Scholz, 2011). Therefore, social, financial, and environmental integration is the central focus (Hall and Vredenburg, 2012) and considered as three essential stakes of sustainability (Kajikawa, 2008; Schoolman et al., 2012).

Mass media is largely referred to as a mode of communication, occurred via various media technology platforms intending to reach a mass audience. The chronological order of mass media is as follows: starting from the 15th century, print media in reference to books, pamphlets, newspapers, magazines, etc.; the recording era emerged in the late 19th century with gramophone records, magnetic tapes, cassettes, cartridges, CDs, DVDs, etc.; cinema arrived in 1900, whereas radio in 1910 and television in 1930s followed by mobile phones in mid-1980s, and internet and social media in mid of 1990.

There is a constant rise in the global discourse on globalization, sustainability, and media. The significance of this study is to understand the media's approach toward globalization and sustainable development. And also it provides a substantial understanding of the media's orientation toward covering news related to globalization and sustainable development and how much the coverage is directed toward the nation's interest. Finally, the study evaluates the angles of perception and agendas of that coverage. The objectives of this chapter are to analyze the coverage of news stories, articles, and editorials related to globalization and sustainable development by the Indian media, to understand the prioritization of the content, and to assess the placement and presentation of the content.

14.2 CONCEPT OF GLOBALIZATION AND SUSTAINABILITY

In Tomlinson's (1999) words, globalization refers to the rapid development that included multifaceted exchanges between societies, cultures, institutions, and individuals worldwide. In this process, the world becomes a global village, where the demographic distance reduces and human beings come closer. As per the International Monetary Fund (IMF), globalization results in increasing economic interdependence of all the countries across the world by increasing capacity and diversity in transactions of goods and services across the borders, through the speedy and extensive dissemination of diffusion of technology as well as in terms of international money flows (IMF, in Wolf, 1997).

According to Blewitt (2014), a sustainable management strategy requires to manage the increasing interconnectedness between social, political, and economic scopes of world economies. Most of the thinkers define globalization from an economic point of view. Those who are in support of globalization credit it as an opportunity to enhance economic growth, whereas the opponents considered it as a threat to economic wealth, partisan sovereignty, and cultural integrity (Amavilah et al., 2014). Literature across the globe on globalization comprises several philosophical, conceptual, and ideological arguments, both in favor of and against (Glatzer, 2012).

It is like virtues of free-market (Glatzer, 2012; Baylis et al., 2013) versus cultural, political institutions fairness, economic, and environmental impact (Powell, 2015; Baylis et al., 2013). Friedman (2004) citing the enhancement in régime of the population worldwide, versus Klein (2007) claims the acceptance of the concept of globalization at the request of the World Bank as a prerequisite for fiscal aid has led to growing deficiency and rising disparity. However, it fails to get a clear definition of globalization, despite the follower's and foe's arguments (Jensen and Sandström, 2011; Rosenberg, 2004; Machida, 2012).

As a matter of fact, it is not necessary that globalization and media are always connected equally; however, both are related (Giddens, 1991; Castells, 1996). Rantanen (2005) referred to globalization as mediated globalization because it has spread worldwide through media communication.

Fiss and Hirsch's (2005) study on "The Discourse of Globalization" explains about the framing of message in three categories. The first frame is Positive Frame in which it portrays the possible advantages and aids of globalization. The second frame, that is, Neutral Frame, describes globalization as an evolutionary, original, and largely unavoidable development. Negative Frame, which is the third frame, indicates the growing probability for financial crisis, the risk to the livings of workforces, and the rising income disparity caused by globalization. A study done in 1986 claimed that approximately 90% of newspaper articles showed neutral framing. By 1998, because of the stock market downfall in the year 1987, the percentage of neutrally framed articles reduced to 25%. However, prior to 1995, positive articles were more common. By 1998, negative articles outperformed optimistic articles by two to one. However, in 2008, Greg Ip, stated that the number of articles published in newspapers showing negative framing rose from about 10% of the total in 1991 to 55% of the total in 1999.

14.3   MEDIA AGENDA VERSUS PUBLIC AGENDA

Media agenda is a "subject of perceived importance" (Dearing, 1989). Public agenda is "current topics and civil concerns linked to the national interest" (Shyles, 1983, page 335). Media agenda connects to the relative attention given to various sustainability challenges, such as environmental pollution, economic development, HIV/AIDS, or human rights violations. Studies on the public agendas revealed by media coverage first emerged in the first half of the 20th century (Dearing and Rogers, 1996; McCombs, 2004).

Media agenda usually goes hand in hand with public agenda in respect to particular issues, with perceived media prominence (e.g., Atwater et al., 1985). An individual's perception on the importance of an issue depends upon the amount of coverage it gets in the media. Therefore, the media agenda as well as the public agenda has the potential to influence public perception. The tonality and the shaping of message through media presentation (Carvalho, 2007; Carvalho and Burgess, 2005; Lewis, 2000; Sheafer, 2007) and particular features of the audiences (McCombs, 2004; McLeod et al., 1974) determine "the priming" effect of agenda setting (Sheafer and Weimann, 2005; Sheafer, 2007).

Print media have a greater agenda-setting impact over electronic media (McClure and Patterson, 1974; McCombs, 1977). The basic assumption is that there is a coherent relationship between the amount of media coverage a specific issue gets and the amount of public attention it draws (Beniger, 1978; Benton and Frazier, 1976; Carvalho, 2005; Dearing and Rogers, 1996; Mueller, 1973; Naisbitt, 1976). Most of the agenda setting research deals with examining media salience by the size or frequency of media exposure (Benton and Frazier, 1976; Funkhauser, 1973; Howlett, 1997). The media coverage on sustainability issues includes environmental norms (Bijsmans and Altides, 2007), climate change (Boykoff, 2007; Brossard et al., 2004), as well as news related to HIV/AIDS (Dearing, 1989).

A study by Barkemeyer et al. (2013) titled, "Sustainability-related media coverage and socioeconomic development: a regional and North-South perspective" reveals that significant differences exist in the national-level prioritizations of sustainability-related issues. Climate change is emerging as typical Northern issues, whereas issues pertaining to corruption and poverty show higher levels of coverage in the Global South. Overall, in 17 of 20 sustainability-related issues, a significant correlation between the level of socioeconomic development and levels of media coverage on a specific issue could be identified.

14.4   THEORETICAL MODEL

The social responsibility theory of the press defines that the mass media's aim must be cooperative and accomplishing social commitments (McQuail, 1987). Similarly, developmental media theory focuses on the belief that media and government should work mutually, for the development of the state. In addition to this, media should also essentially provide support to the government in delivering developmental programs to the beneficiaries. However, Cohen's (1963) agenda-setting hypothesis supported that the mass media all the time may not be successful in telling people what they should think, but they can be strikingly successful in telling its readers what to think about.

14.5   METHOD

The study employs qualitative method. The chapter adopts a descriptive analysis of the media coverage of globalization and sustainability related content in one leading English daily newspaper, The Times of India (Bhubaneswar edition). The method of the research is based on content analysis of the published news for a period of 1 month (November–December, 2018). Microsoft Excel code book and code sheet is used for coding the data and to analyze further. The study administered a standard content analysis procedure step by step (Weber, 1990; Krippendorff, 2004), proposed by Neuendorf (2002). The process of content analysis starts with the formulation of the research question, after which the universe of the study is decided. Then, finalization of unit of analysis after categorization of the content is done, which established a quantification process. Thereafter, coders code the content and analyzed the data. Finally, the conclusion is derived from the indicated patterns.

14.6 DATA ANALYSIS AND FINDINGS

The current research makes an attempt to understand the pattern of media coverage of news related to globalization and sustainable growth. For the same purpose, the study analyzes the collected data qualitatively by adopting content analysis and comes to major findings as follows:

A major chunk of the published news stories comprises themes on climate change, tourism, and sanitation. News related to climate change encompasses a wide range of stories such as global warming, sustainable growth, energy efficiency, biodiversity, and waste management. Since the 21st century is buzzed with global warming, stories based on climate change, sustainable development, and renewable energy sources get maximum news value. News stories based on climate change emphasize issues related to international conventions, bilateral treaties, and regional initiatives at both government and private level. Climate change also gets diverse attention in terms of news placement (regional, national, international, editorials, etc.) and news contributors (news agencies, correspondent reporters, and columnists). Most of the positive news coverage focus on global initiatives to tackle climate change, whereas negative coverages emphasize on dangers of global warming. However, a more in-depth analysis of these news contents reveals lack of broader prospective and grip of capitalism over the generation of the news contents.

The second most covered news stories about globalization and sustainable development are based on the theme of tourism. One of the major factors behind the higher coverage can be attributed to the interlinkage between tourism and climate change. News stories focusing on ecotourism, coastal area development, wildlife restoration, etc. attract highest media attention in comparison to tribal development or village tourism. So much focus on tourism may also be due to the scope of capital generation through sustainable development.

News stories based on the theme of sanitation such as toilets, waste treatment, cleanliness, and public hygiene also gather significant media attention due to the public discourse around "Swachha Bharat." Here media agenda also reflects the agenda of the government. Since quite a significant number of people avail the government subsidies to build toilets in home, news about sanitation gets media attention, which also refers to development media models. However, there is no significant coverage about the people who are engaged in manual scavenging.

Most of the articles are published on the themes such as climate change, tourism, and sanitation, and minimal coverage is given on the themes such as tribal development, migration, and violation of environmental laws (Fig. 14.1).

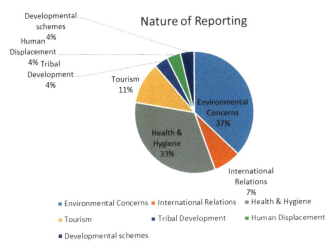

FIGURE 14.1 Nature of reporting.

Proximity carries maximum news value when it comes to coverage of sustainable growth. Regional issues get significantly more coverage in comparison with the international issues. Regional issues get more than 50% of the coverage, while global news gets 28% and national news get 21% of the total coverage (Fig. 14.2). Regional issues focus on diverse issues such as local government initiatives, ecosystem restoration, costal area development, and waste management while international issues focus on bilateral treaties and international NGOs. National news stories mostly carry negative stories about hazardous impacts of climate change.

Content Covering the Geographical Territory

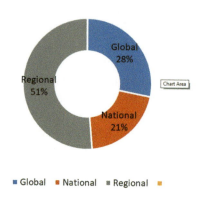

FIGURE 14.2   Content covering the geographical territory.

Most of the news stories on globalization and sustainable development are placed on regional or city pages, that is, page 2–3 (48%), while least number of stories are placed in editorial page (4%) and first page (7%). Times Global page (pages 9–10) accounts for 15% of international issues, and Times Nation page (pages 4–8) comprises 26% of the total national news (Fig. 14.3).

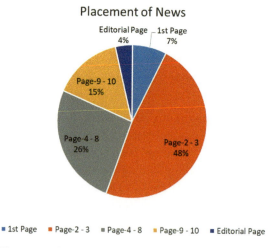

FIGURE 14.3   Placement of news.

A major share of the news stories are contributed by the local reporters and Times of India's own news network. Since most of the news are based on local issues and placed in regional pages, the local reporters contribute the most. The contributions by external arrangements such as news agencies and columnists have been scarce (4%) (Fig. 14.4).

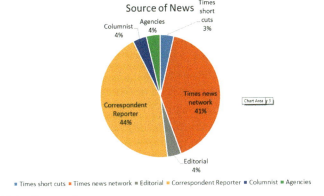

FIGURE 14.4   Source of news.

Most of the reporting slanted toward positive outline based on government initiatives, works done by international NGOs, bi-lateral treaties, etc., which is 63% of the total news published. On the other hand, the negative news coverage contributing to migration, public demand, environmental hazards, etc. is of 33%. However, only 4% of the news is neutral in nature (Fig. 14.5).

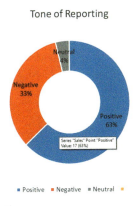

FIGURE 14.5   Tone of reporting.

14.7   CONCLUSION

In India, media's development agenda becomes very problematic due to its contradictory coverage of specific issues. The national media's least attention goes to themes such as tribal development, migration, and violation of environmental norms. The lack of media attention to these topics exclusiveness of neo-liberal economic policy of the national media organizations. When so much attention is given to environmental issues, still there is almost no coverage regarding big corporations who are involved in violation of environmental norms. The only news stories that focused on violation of environmental laws were about "Diwali" crackers. Similarly, news stories focusing on tourism development do not give emphasis to indigenous people of the locality. Tribal development gets the least media attention when they are known for their unique culture and default custodians of the forest ecosystem.

The average word count for news articles is 300, which indicates the lack of depth in analysis and broader perspective. The news stories also lack inclusiveness because they deprive the local community and indigenous people of their share in the development process. Only one editorial and one column show the lack of interest in academia to bring knowledge to the general public.

14.8   LIMITATIONS AND SOCIAL RELEVANCE

The major limitations of the study are taking one English daily instead of considering all newspapers and other platforms, as well as the duration of the study is less. The findings of the study will draw the attention of the media industry to ponder upon the issues of less coverage of news related to globalization and sustainable development. From a practical and social implication point of view, government and media organizations may take initiatives to evaluate and reframe the existing policies.

KEYWORDS

- **globalization**
- **sustainable development**
- **content analysis**
- **newspaper**
- **mass media**

REFERENCES

Amavilah, V. H. S.; Asongu, S. A.; Andrés, A. R. *Globalization, Peace & Stability, Governance, and Knowledge Economy*; African Governance and Development Institute WP/14/012, 2014.

Atwater, T.; Salwen, M. B.; Anderson, R. B. Media Agenda-Setting with Environmental Issues. *J. Q.* **1985**, *62*, 393–397.

Barkemeyer, R.; Figge, F.; Holt, D. Sustainability-Related Media Coverage and Socioeconomic Development: A Regional and North-South Perspective. *Environ. Plan. C: Gov. Policy* **2013**, *31*, 716–740.

Baylis, J.; Smith, S.; Owens, P., Eds. *The Globalization of World Politics: An Introduction to International Relations*; Oxford University Press: Oxford, 2013.

Beniger, J. R. Media Content as Social Indicators: The Greenfield Index of Agenda-Setting. *Commun. Res.* **1978**, *5*, 437–453.

Benton, M.; Frazier, P. The Agenda Setting Function of the Mass Media at Three Levels of "Information Holding". *Commun. Res.* **1976**, *3*, 261–274.

Blewitt, J. *Understanding Sustainable Development*; Routledge: London, 2014.

Boykoff, M. T. Flogging a Dead Norm? Newspaper Coverage of Anthropogenic Climate Change in the United States and United Kingdom from 2003 to 2006. *Area* **2007**, *39*, 470–481.

Brossard, D.; Shanahan, J.; McComas, K. Are Issue-Cycles Culturally Constructed? A Comparison of French and American Coverage of Global Climate Change. *Mass Commun. Soc.* **2004**, *7*, 359–377.

Carvaiho, A. Representing the Politics of the Greenhouse Effect: Discursive Strategies in the British media. *Crit. Discourse Stud.* **2005**, *1*, 1–29.

Carvaiho, A. Ideological Cultures and Media Discourses on Scientific Knowledge: Re-reading News on Climate Change. *Public Understanding Sci.* **2007**, *16*, 223–243.

Carvaiho, A.; Burgess, J. Cultural Circuits of Climate Change in UK Broadsheet Newspapers, 1985–2003. *Risk Anal.* **2005**, *25*, 1457–1469.

Cohen, B. C. *The Press and Foreign Policy*; Princeton University Press: Princeton, NJ, 1963.

Dearing, J. W. Setting the Polling Agenda for the Issue of AIDS. *Public Opin. Quart.* **1989**, *53*, 309–329.

Dearing, J. W.; Rogers, E. M. *Agenda Setting*; Sage: Thousand Oaks, CA, 1996.

Elliott, J. *An Introduction to Sustainable Development*; Routledge: New York, 2012.

Fiss, P.; Hirsch, P.. The Discourse of Globalization: Framing and Sense Making of an Emerging Concept. *Am. Sociol. Rev.* **2005**, *70* (1), 29–52.

Funkhauser, G. R. The Issues of the Sixties: An Exploratory Study in the Dynamics of Public Opinion. *Public Opin. Q.* **1973**, *37*, 62–75.

Giddens, A. *The Consequences of Modernity*; Polity Press: Cambridge, 1991; pp 70–78.

Glatzer, W. Cross-National Comparisons of Quality of Life in Developed Nations, Including the Impact of Globalization. In *Handbook of Social Indicators and Quality of Life Research*; Springer: The Netherlands, 2012; pp 381–398.

Greg, I. The Declining Value of Your College Degree. *Wall Street J.*, July 17, 2008.

Hafez, K. International news coverage and the problems of media globalization. In search of a 'new global-local nexus'. *Innovation* **2015**, *12* (1), 47–62. DOI: 10.1080/13511610.1999.9968587.

Hall, J.; Vredenburg, H. The Challenges of Innovating for Sustainable Development. *MIT Sloan Manage. Rev.* **2012**, *45* (1), 61.

Jensen, T.; Sandström, J. Stakeholder Theory and Globalization: The Challenges of Power and Responsibility. *Organi. Stud.* **2011**, *32* (4), 473–488.

Kerlinger, F. N. *Foundations of Behavioral Research*, 4th ed.; Holt, Rinehart & Winston: New York, 2000.

Kheeshadeh, M. Effects of Globalization on Mass Media in the World. *Int. J. Asian Soc. Sci.* **2012**, *2* (10), 1672–1693.

Klein, N. The Shock Doctrine: The Rise of Disaster Capitalism. Knopf: Canada, 2007.

Krippendorff, K. Reliability in Content Analysis. *Hum. Commun. Res.* **2004**, *30* (3), 411–443.

Machida, S. Does Globalization Render People More Ethnocentric? Globalization and People's Views on Cultures. *Am. J. Econ. Sociol.* **2012**, *71* (2), 436–469.

Makasi, A. Globalization and Sustainable Development: A Conceptual Model. *Mediterr. J. Soc. Sci.* 2015, *6* (4 S3), 341–349.

McClure, R. D.; Patterson, T. E. Television News and Political Advertising: The Impact of Exposure on Voter Beliefs. *Commun. Res.* **1974**, *1*, 3–31.

McCombs, M. E. *Setting the Agenda: The Mass Media and Public Opinion*; Polity Press: Cambridge, 2004.

McLeod, J. M.; Becker, L. B.; Bymes, J. E. Another Look at the Agenda-Setting Function of the Press. *Commun. Res.* **1974**, *1*, 131–165.

Mueller, J. E. *War, Presidents and Public Opinion*; John Wiley: New York, 1973.

Naisbitt, J. *The Trend Report: A Quarterly Forecast and Evaluation of Business and Social Development Center for Policy Process*; Washington, DC, 1976.

Neuendorf, K. *The Content Analysis Guide Book*; Sage: Thousand Oaks, CA, 2002.

Powell, J. L. Globalization and Scapes: A New Theory of Global Dynamics. *Int. J. Soc. Human. Sci* 2015, *8* (2), 168–175.

Sheafer, T. How To Evaluate It: The Role of Story-Evaluative Tone in Agenda Setting and Priming. *J. Commun.* **2007**, *57*, 21–39.

Sheafer, T.; Weimann, G. Agenda-Building, Agenda-Setting, Priming, Individual Voting Intentions and the Aggregate Results: An Analysis of Four Israeli Elections. *J. Commun.* **2005**, *55*, 347–365.

Shyles, L. C. Defining the Issues of a Presidential Election from Televised Political Spot Advertisements. *J. Broadcas. Electron. Media* **1983**, *27*, 333–343.

Tan, A. H. In *Text Mining: The State of the Art and the Challenges*, Paper Presented at the Pacific Asia Conference on Knowledge Discovery and Data Mining PAKDD'99 Workshop on Knowledge Discovery from Advanced Databases, 1999. http://www3.ntu.edu.sg/sce/labs/erlab/publications/papers/asahtan/tm_pakdd99.pdf.

Tomlinson, J. *Globalization and Culture*; Polity Press: Cambridge, 1999.

Index

F

Fixed costs, 106
Free trade agreement, 19, 22–23
Fuel accessibility
cooking, types of fuel used, 127
econometrics and data issues, 121–122
objectives, 121
past studies, review, 119–121
purification of drinking water, 126
results and findings
accessibility of fuels, 126–129
accessibility of water, 122–126
availability of electricity, 130–131
water and fuels, time spent on
collection, 129–130

G

GIST of the ANNA FM programs
diet and food regime for pregnant
women, 179–180
diet for women, 178–179
feeding your baby, 180–182
group discussions, findings, 184–185
interview, 178–179
parameters to analyze with, 182–183
Globalization and sustainable development
in India
media role
concept, 256–258
data analysis and findings, 260–263
geographical territory, 262
limitations and social relevancy, 264
media agenda *versus* public agenda,
258–259
method, 259–260
nature of reporting, 261
placement of news, 262
source of news, 263
theoretical model, 259
tone of reporting, 264

H

Hypothesis testing, 162–164

I

India–EU cooperation, 2–4
annual summits, 27–28
challenges
bilateral relations of India with,
19–20
China, 17–18
free trade agreement, 19
Indian Ocean, 18–19
cultural relations, 16–17
data source and methodology, 7
economy relations, 14–15
findings and analysis, 24–25
historical prospective, 8–9
in modern era, 9
political relations, 11–14
prospects
free trade agreement, 22–23
global challenges-climate change,
23–24
India is a young country, 21–22
Paris agreement, 23–24
sustainable development, 23–24
terrorism, 23–24
UN reform, 23–24
review of literatures, 4–7
social relations, 9–11
India's trade flows and balances, 243–244
Indira Gandhi Canal, 83
Indo-EU relation
data analysis and interpretation,
238–245
economic indicators of India, trends and
magnitudes, 238–239
emission of India and EU, 242
hypothesis, 237
test of, 245, 247–248, 250
independent *t*-Test of, 246
India's trade flows and balances,
243–244
material and methodology, 237–238
multiple regression model, 247–249
review of literature, 234–236
set forth for study, 236–237
Indoor mushroom cultivation, 94–95